The Political Economy of Investment Arbitration

INTERNATIONAL ECONOMIC LAW

Tania Voon is Professor at Melbourne Law School, the University of Melbourne.

The *International Economic Law* series, established by the late Professor John H. Jackson, addresses a range of issues in international economic law, which includes international trade law, international investment law, and the global financial order. The Series aims to encourage interest in the broad contours of international economic law, heightening awareness of its significance across the globe as well as its continuous interactions with other areas. The Series Editors encourage quality submissions from a wide range of perspectives, including doctrinal, theoretical, empirical, and interdisciplinary. Novel and cutting-edge research is particularly welcome, as are contributions from both emerging and established scholars from around the world.

ALSO PUBLISHED IN THIS SERIES

The Investment Treaty Regime and Public Interest Regulation in Africa
The Imperatives Theory
D. N. Dagbanja

International Adjudication on Trial
The Effectiveness of the WTO Dispute Settlement System
Sivan Shlomo Agon

China's International Investment Strategy
Bilateral, Regional, and Global Law and Policy
Edited by Julien Chaisse

Emissions Trading Schemes under International Economic Law
James Munro

The Trade Policy Review Mechanism
A Critical Analysis
Mathias Kende

Mega-Regional Trade Agreements: CETA, TTIP, and TiSA
New Orientations for EU External Economic Relations
Edited by Stefan Griller, Walter Obwexer, and Erich Vranes

Small and Medium-Sized Enterprises in International Economic Law
Edited by Thilo Rensmann

Domestic Law in International Investment Arbitration
Jarrod Hepburn

Treaty Shopping in International Investment Law
Jorun Baumgartner

The Political Economy of Investment Arbitration

ZOE PHILLIPS WILLIAMS

OXFORD
UNIVERSITY PRESS

OXFORD
UNIVERSITY PRESS

Great Clarendon Street, Oxford, OX2 6DP,
United Kingdom

Oxford University Press is a department of the University of Oxford.
It furthers the University's objective of excellence in research, scholarship,
and education by publishing worldwide. Oxford is a registered trade mark of
Oxford University Press in the UK and in certain other countries

First Edition published in 2022

Impression: 1

Published in the United States of America by Oxford University Press
198 Madison Avenue, New York, NY 10016, United States of America

British Library Cataloguing in Publication Data

Data available

Library of Congress Control Number: 2022935959

ISBN 978–0–19–886594–0

DOI: 10.1093/oso/9780198865940.001.0001

Printed and bound by
CPI Group (UK) Ltd, Croydon, CR0 4YY

Acknowledgements

Numerous people have contributed immensely to the successful completion of this book. First, I would like to thank all the interviewees who gave their time to this project and provided much insight into the political interests underlying investor-state disputes.

Jonathan Bonnitcha, Lauge Poulsen, and Taylor St John have at various times provided invaluable feedback. I also benefited greatly from both the academic insight and moral support of my colleagues in the Berlin Graduate School for Transnational Studies, particularly the members of our writing group, Maurits Meijers and Mathis Lohaus, who read much of the dissertation on which this book is based.

Finally, I would like to thank my parents, for their endless support of, and interest in, my projects, and Étienne Brown, without whom none of this would have happened.

Table of Contents

List of Abbreviations

ARENA	Allianza Republicana Nacionalista
ASEAN	Association of Southeast Asian Nations
BIT	bilateral investment treaty
CAFTA	Central American Free Trade Agreement
CAFTA-DR	Central American and Dominican Republic Free Trade Agreement
CEAA	Canadian Environmental Assessment Agency
CETA	EU–Canada Comprehensive Economic and Trade Agreement
CIEL	Center for International Environmental Law
CIS	Commonwealth of Independent States
CJEU	Court of Justice of the European Union
CUFTA	Canadian–US Free Trade Agreement
DFAIT	Department of Foreign Affairs and International Trade
DFO	Department of Fisheries and Oceans
DNR	Department of Natural Resources
EC	European Commission
ECT	Energy Charter Treaty
EIS	environmental impact statement
ERRA	Energy Regulators Regional Association
EU	European Union
FDI	foreign direct investment
FET	fair and equitable treatment
FIPA	foreign investment protection agreement
FMLN	Frente Farabundo Marti para la Liberacíon Nacional
FPIC	free, prior and informed consent
FTA	free trade agreement
GDP	gross domestic product
HCA	Hungarian Competition Authority
HEO	Hungarian Energy Office
ICA	Investment Canada Act
ICSID	International Centre for Settlement of Investment Disputes
IIA	international investment agreement
IIAPP	International Investment Arbitration and Public Policy
IMF	International Monetary Fund
IPE	international political economy
IR	international relations
ISA	investor–state arbitration
ISDS	investor–state dispute settlement
JRP	Joint Review Panel
MAI	multilateral agreement on investment

MARN	Ministerio de Medio Ambiente y Recursos Naturales
MFN	most favoured nation
MINEC	Ministerio de Economía
MLA	Member of the Legislative Assembly
MNC	multinational corporation
MNE	multinational enterprise
MP	Member of Parliament
MVM	Magyar Villamos Művek
NAFTA	North American Free Trade Agreement
NGO	non-governmental organization
NSEL	Nova Scotia Department of Environment and Labour
NT	national treatment
OECD	Organisation for Economic Co-operation and Development
PCA	Permanent Court of Arbitration
PDDH	Procuraduría para la Defensa de los Derechos Humanos
PITAD	PluriCourt Investment Treaty Arbitration Database
PPA	power purchase agreement
PROESA	Organismo Promotor de Exportaciones e Inversiones de El Salvador
TPP	Trans-Pacific Partnership
TTIP	Transatlantic Trade and Investment Partnership
UNCITRAL	United Nations Commission on International Trade Law
UNCTAD	United Nations Conference on Trade and Development
USMCA	United States–Mexico–Canada Agreement
WBGI	World Bank Governance Indicator
WTO	World Trade Organization
WWF	World Wildlife Fund
ZINB	zero-inflated negative binomial regression

1
The Political Economy of Investment Arbitration

In the midst of the heated 2009 presidential campaign, the incumbent president of the Republic of El Salvador announced the de facto suspension of all mining activity in the country. In 2006–07, the Hungarian government briefly reintroduced administrative pricing of electricity as part of its move towards a liberalized domestic energy market as required by the European Union (EU) and subsequently cancelled the long-term power purchase agreements (PPAs) it had signed in the mid-1990s with foreign-owned electricity generators. Also in 2006, both the federal government of Canada and the provincial government of Nova Scotia opted to heed the advice of an expert review panel and deny a permit to a US company which planned to construct and operate a gravel quarry in the Bay of Fundy. What do these three very different government decisions have in common? They, along with many others, were subsequently challenged by foreign investors via investor–state dispute settlement (ISDS) as alleged breaches of international investment agreements (IIAs) signed between these states and the home countries of the investors. These challenges take the form of legal proceedings before international arbitral tribunals.

A variety of different investment and trade agreements allow investors to sue the governments of the states in which they invest for monetary damages. These include the over 3,000 bilateral investment treaties (BITs)—agreements traditionally signed between a developed, capital-exporting (home) state and a developing, capital-importing (host) state. These agreements contain similar (although not identically worded) provisions on investment protection and allow investors access to ISDS. Regional trade agreements, such as the North American Free Trade Agreement (NAFTA)[1] and the Central American Free Trade Agreement (CAFTA), also contain ISDS provisions, as do the Energy Charter Treaty (ECT) and a number of other bilateral free trade agreements.

The inclusion of ISDS in IIAs was originally envisioned by World Bank officials in particular as a way to encourage the amicable settlement of disputes, avoid the involvement of the home state of the investor, and increase foreign direct investment (FDI) flows. The underlying assumption of the latter is that IIAs can solve the

[1] Now the United States–Mexico–Canada Agreement (USMCA), with significantly weaker ISDS provisions.

The Political Economy of Investment Arbitration. Zoe Phillips Williams, Oxford University Press. © Zoe Phillips Williams 2022.
DOI: 10.1093/oso/9780198865940.003.0001

time inconsistency problem that potentially plagues foreign investors. While states may extend favourable terms to investors in order to attract investment, once the investment is made, they need only treat the firm well enough to ensure it remains in the country, given the costs facing an investor if it chooses to disinvest.[2]

In theory, then, IIAs offer a way for host states to make a credible commitment to maintaining the conditions it has promised to investors upon entry by means of the enforcement mechanism of ISDS. This supranational dispute settlement mechanism is additionally appealing to foreign investors who may be less likely to be treated fairly by, or have more difficulty navigating, the host state's judicial system. IIAs should reassure investors who might otherwise be wary of investing in less stable developing states and lead to greater investment flows into these countries. In this way, IIAs are meant to benefit both capital-exporting states (by way of their investors) and capital-importing states. Indeed, although recent work casts doubt on whether IIA signings were the result of rational cost–benefit calculations on the part of capital-importing states, they were presented as important tools to attract investment by Western policymakers and international organizations.[3]

While remaining relatively obscure for decades, since the mid-2000s these agreements have come under increased scrutiny and criticism, particularly in light of the lack of evidence that IIAs do in fact increase investment flows to developing countries and ongoing discussions on the reform of the investment protection regime. Critics of IIAs claim that these agreements unduly limit domestic policy space and may lead to a situation of 'regulatory chill' in which host states are dissuaded from passing new regulation for fear that an investor may challenge the measure via ISDS.[4] While the idea of regulatory chill has gained significant traction among anti-IIA activists, an academic treatment of the concept is difficult as it requires proving a counterfactual: that in the absence of a treaty and the possibility of arbitration, a specific measure would have been taken. There is, nevertheless, significant anecdotal evidence to suggest that regulatory chill has been at work in specific cases.

However, while this book does not argue that regulatory chill never occurs as a result of IIAs and arbitration, it is not the only potential outcome. Instead, and often at the behest of 'public' interests, states evidently continue to take measures which are challenged by investors as potential violations of investment treaties, as evidenced by a growing number of claims against an expanding group of states. Indeed, a central claim of this book is that these disputes clearly highlight the

[2] Andrew T Guzman, 'Why LDCs Sign Treaties That Hurt Them: Explaining the Popularity of Bilateral Investment Treaties' (1997) 38 Virginia Journal of International Law 639.

[3] Lauge Poulsen, *Bounded Rationality and Economic Diplomacy. The Politics of Investment Treaties in Developing Countries* (Cambridge University Press 2015).

[4] Gus Van Harten, *Investment Treaty Arbitration and Public Law* (Oxford University Press 2007); Kyla Tienhaara, *The Expropriation of Environmental Governance: Protecting Foreign Investors at the Expense of Public Policy* (Cambridge University Press 2009); Nicole Yazbek, 'Bilateral Investment Treaties: The Foreclosure of Domestic Policy Space' (2010) 17 South African Journal of International Affairs 103.

tensions between commitments to economic liberalization and states' continued exercise of sovereignty and, more to the point, their responsiveness to democratic contestation or pressure. The international legal framework which supports economic globalization, of which IIAs and ISDS are an important part, can place significant demands on host states, which may come into conflict with the preferences of domestic actors. Exploring these tensions is the broad aim of this book.

The book examines how political institutions and actors in the host state of an investment contribute to investor–state disputes, combining insights from international relations and political economy. Specifically, it considers two opposing explanations for investor–state disputes: shifting state preferences towards FDI or the lack of state capacity to maintain an investment-friendly environment. This has important implications of our normative assessment of the regime and is highly relevant to current debates in both international law and international political economy about the relationship between investment treaties and domestic politics. This exploration concludes that democratic contestation in host states contributes to the emergence of investor–state disputes that culminate in arbitration. Nevertheless, issues of state capacity do play an important role, particularly as a factor shaping, and shifting, state preferences towards foreign investment.

1.1 Interactions between Domestic Policymaking and the Investment Protection Regime: A Critical View

In this book, investor–state disputes which culminate in ISDS highlight fundamental tensions that exist between domestic policies and politics and the exigencies of economic globalization. IIAs and ISDS face significant criticism on a number of fronts, from those related to fundamental aspects of the regime, such as its undue constraint of state sovereignty and anti-democratic elements, to more mutable features such as the inconsistency of arbitral awards. Perhaps the most important criticisms of the investment protection regime are those that relate to domestic policy space and regulatory chill—ultimately questions of democracy and state sovereignty—that come from the regime's fundamental blending of public and private interests. At its heart, the regime allows an international tribunal to rule on the legality of states' policy choices, based on standards which aim to create an environment conducive to the success of the private sector.[5] Considering that many IIAs do not require the exhaustion of local remedies, it can be argued that 'international investment law today is in charge of controlling the regulatory state'.[6]

[5] Santiago Montt, *State Liability in Investment Treaty Arbitration* (Hart Publishing 2009); Zachary Elkins, Andrew T Guzman, and Betha Simmons, 'Competing for Capital: The Diffusion of Bilateral Investment Treaties, 1960–2000' (2006) 60 International Organization 811.

[6] Montt (n 5) 19.

Thus, where these tensions manifest most dramatically is in constraints of host states' ability to respond to democratic contestation regarding investment-related issues and the related issue of the state's 'right to regulate'.

Many of the criticisms discussed in this section ultimately stem from international investment law's origins as part of a broader, 'ordo-liberal' project of international law.[7] As described by Slobodian in his intellectual history of neoliberalism, as well as other scholars writing in the law and political economy tradition,[8] throughout the twentieth century, the neoliberal intellectual project emerged to confront dual, emerging threats to private property—socialism and anti-colonialism—and aimed to constrain political contestation from interfering with the smooth operation of the market at the domestic, and ultimately the international, level. The intellectual fathers of this movement—economists like Mises and Hayek—saw increased political enfranchisement or mass democracy as a direct threat to economic activity. Thus, the neoliberal project is not first and foremost the rolling back of regulation, as it is commonly characterized, but instead the development of extensive rules and regulations, a 'set of institutional safeguards and legal constraints to prevent nation-states from transgressing their commitments to the world economic order'.[9] International investment law is an exemplary 'case of the political activism of neoliberals in their quest to encase the world economy'.[10]

With its intellectual origins in a tradition that is wary of 'too much' democracy in the realm of economics, it is unsurprising that today, IIAs and ISDS can clash with host state citizens' democratic demands—expressed both at the ballot box and via protest. All international agreements aim to constrain the sovereignty of contracting states to some degree; most tend to do so in the pursuit of (international) public goods—whether environmental or labour protection or standard setting of industrial activities.[11] What sets the investment protection regime apart is the manner in which it combines both public and private law and interests. Unlike commercial arbitration, which may involve the state as a private actor, investment arbitration allows private actors to challenge the state in its role as a public actor. Van Harten clarifies the distinction in the following way: 'the passage of legislation is a quintessentially sovereign act.... Alternatively, when the Government contracts with a company to tend the lawn in front of Parliament, the Government's conclusion of the contract is a commercial act of the State, one that a private party

[7] Quinn Slobodian, *The Globalists: The End of Empire and the Birth of Neoliberalism* (Harvard University Press 2018).

[8] Jedediah Britton-Purdy and others, 'Building a Law-and-Political-Economy Framework: Beyond the Twentieth-Century Synthesis' (2020) 129 Yale Law Journal 1600.

[9] Slobodian (n 7) 15.

[10] ibid 145.

[11] Attracting investment by offering greater protection to investors could be considered a public good. However, as is discussed in section 1.2, there is scant evidence that IIAs attract significant investment on their own.

could carry out.'[12] As we will see in Chapter 2, investors routinely challenge legislation and other policies that are, if not always in the 'public interest', then certainly acts which private parties could not carry out. Therefore, ISDS allows private, foreign actors to challenge policies and measures which may affect stakeholders far beyond the parties to the dispute.[13] Critics of the regime argue that this is normatively undesirable from a democratic perspective, given that investors are able to challenge legislation passed by elected officials. As mentioned earlier, the arbitral tribunal cannot force the state to overturn measures it has already taken if found to be in contravention of the IIA. However, respondent states suffer negative reputational effects, which may be accompanied by financial consequences in the form of declining investment inflows, solely by being involved in an arbitration, regardless of whether the tribunal rules that it has violated the IIA.[14] If a state loses the arbitration, it may be forced to pay a significant monetary award to investors. Therefore, while the state is not forced to repeal a democratically enacted policy, it may be punished for taking it. The ways in which democratic pressure or contestation contributes to the emergence of investor–state disputes is discussed at greater length in Chapter 4.[15]

Relatedly, IIAs and ISDS can function to constrain the host state's 'right' or ability to regulate in policy issues related to any given investment project and arguably place too high a premium on policy stability. The regime arguably protects private interests at the expense of public interests. For example, the regulatory goals of energy policy include 'assuring universal and affordable access … and aligning energy production and consumption with the objectives of sustainability and environmental protection'.[16] However, these priorities may conflict with the profit-maximization goals of investors in the energy sector, who may use ISDS as a tool to challenge policies. Public services more generally are also quite likely to be at the heart of conflicts between public and private interests when it comes to arbitration,

[12] Van Harten, *Investment Treaty Arbitration and Public Law* (n 4) 373.

[13] Stephan W Schill, 'Crafting the International Economic Order: The Public Function of Investment Treaty Arbitration and Its Significance for the Role of the Arbitrator' (2010) 23 Leiden Journal of International Law 401.

[14] Todd Allee and Clint Peinhardt, 'Contingent Credibility: The Reputational Effects of Investment Treaty Disputes on Foreign Direct Investment' (2011) 65 International Organization 401.

[15] Throughout the book, I use terms such as public pressure, or democratic pressure, to indicate instances of public interest group organizing to put pressure on state policymakers. This could take the form of electoral pressure, but may also include protests, demonstrations, and media campaigns, as these are all important ways in which the public can express preferences. The further assumption here is that the groups doing this pressurizing are not 'narrow' interest groups, such as industry associations or even individuals, but 'broad' interest groups advocating for policies or outcomes that they consider to be in the public interest (though not uncontroversial or free of trade-offs). This approach to democratic contestation and ISDS was earlier laid out in Jonathan Bonnitcha and Zoe Phillips Williams, 'State Liability for "Politically" Motivated Conduct in the Investment Treaty Regime' (2019) 33 Leiden Journal of International Law 77.

[16] Markus Krajewski, 'The Impact of International Investment Agreements on Energy Regulation' in Christoph Herrmann and Jörg Philipp Terhechte (eds), *European Yearbook of International Economic Law (EYIEL)* vol 3 (Springer-Verlag 2012) 3.

in particular as IIAs can 'lock in' policies that are in place at the time an investment is established. This makes it difficult for a state to update policies governing public services in the case of changing public preferences. For example, 'if regulatory frameworks are not developed or fully implemented before private companies begin supplying a particular service, it may become difficult to introduce regulations and activity controls once private actors have started on the market'.[17] More generally, the fact that IIAs constrain the ability of the host state to change policies may be particularly problematic for developing countries which liberalize certain sectors, such as public services or extractive industries, when regulatory standards are low and are subsequently unable to raise these standards for fear of provoking arbitration. Finally, at least under most IIAs today, the arbitral tribunal is not required to consider the goals of the state measures in question—most importantly to this discussion, whether or not a measure was taken in the 'public interest'. For example, a finding of indirect expropriation:

> depends predominantly on the degree of interference and the effects of the measure, but not on its purpose or intent. Hence, measures taken for regulatory purposes in public services can amount to indirect or regulatory expropriations if they adversely affect the investor's assets in such a way that it deprives the investor of the value of the investment.[18]

In this way, investors' rights are likely to be given priority over public interest goals if these are found to be in conflict by arbitrators.

This privileging of private over public interest may give rise to a situation of 'regulatory chill' if policymakers consider the possible costs imposed by ISDS and refrain from enacting new policies or legislation.[19] Sceptics of the regulatory chill hypothesis point to the lack of awareness among policymakers regarding IIAs, arguing that if government actors do not know about the regime, their policy choices necessarily cannot be inhibited by it.[20] However, as Tienhaara rightly argues, investors make states aware of the potential costs of certain policies by threatening to go to arbitration following the state taking a specific measure and thus ward off regulation which may adversely affect their interests.[21] Moreover, not just the threat of being found liable in arbitration but also the high costs of the arbitration process itself, no matter the outcome, has been cited by state actors as a factor

[17] Markus Krajewski, 'Investment Law and Public Services' (2013) 5 <SSRN:https://ssrn.com/abstract=2038514> accessed 24 April 2022.
[18] ibid 10.
[19] Tienhaara (n 4).
[20] Christine Côté, 'The Chilling Effect of Globalization: A Look at the Impact of International Investment Agreements on National Regulatory Autonomy in the Areas of Health, Safety and the Environment' (PhD thesis, London School of Economics and Political Science 2014) <http://etheses.lse.ac.uk/897/> accessed 9 April 2022.
[21] Tienhaara (n 4).

which may encourage states to negotiate with investors rather than defend their policies in arbitration.[22] As mentioned earlier in the section, while it is difficult to prove the regulatory chill hypothesis, it nonetheless is supported by anecdotal evidence and deserves consideration.

Other less fundamental, but still important criticisms are levelled at more specific aspects of the investment protection regime, which further complicate domestic regulatory processes. Connected to the regulatory chill hypothesis is the uncertainty facing states in the arbitration process due to a lack of consistency in arbitral awards—meaning that arbitral tribunals come to different conclusions in similar cases, an issue highlighted by international organizations and states in the ongoing UNCITRAL ISDS reform process.[23] One frequently cited inconsistency is the decisions reached by the panels in the *Metalclad v Mexico* and *Methanex v United States* NAFTA awards, both ruling on the issue of regulatory takings (indirect expropriation).[24] In the *Metalclad* case, a Mexican municipality revoked the licence to operate a waste disposal operation, and Mexico subsequently lost the case on the grounds that it had indirectly expropriated the development. In contrast, in the *Methanex* case, California banned a key chemical component of methanol and was challenged by a Canadian-owned methanol producer on the grounds that this measure was tantamount to expropriation.[25] However, in this case, the tribunal ruled that a non-discriminatory regulatory measure could not be deemed to violate NAFTA. As Mann concludes, 'Methanex and Metalclad are irreconcilable decisions. Yet both stand as binding awards, and both have adherents in the literature in other arbitral decisions.'[26] This was cited as a concern in a survey of governments conducted by the Organisation for Economic Co-operation and Development (OECD). A lack of consistency may detract from the 'legitimacy and perceived fairness' of ISDS, as well as reducing its cost effectiveness and ability of parties to avoid disputes.[27] This lack of consistency likely stems in part from the design of the regime (over 3,000 non-identical IIAs) as well as the *ad hoc* nature of the investment tribunals themselves.[28] Recognition of this uncertainty and lack of consistency in the arbitration process has spurred calls for reform of the system.

[22] David Gaukrodger and Kathryn Gordon, 'OECD Working Papers on International Improving the System of Investor–State Dispute Settlement' (2012).

[23] ibid; UNCITRAL Secretariat, 'Possible Reform of Investor–State Dispute Settlement (ISDS) Note by the Secretariat A/CN.9/WG.III/WP.142' <https://undocs.org/en/A/CN.9/WG.III/WP.142> accessed 22 February 2022.

[24] Howard Mann, 'Issues in International Investment Law and the Regulatory State: Can Exceptions Clauses Create a Safe Haven for Governments?' (2007) Issues in International Investment Law: Background Papers for the Developing Country Investment Negotiators' Forum, International Institute for Sustainable Development.

[25] Howard Mann, 'The Final Decision in Methanex v. United States: Some New Wine in Some New Bottles' (2005) International Institute for Sustainable Development <https://www.iisd.org/system/files/publications/commentary_methanex.pdf> accessed 6 April 2022.

[26] Mann, 'Issues in International Investment Law' (n 24) 5.

[27] Gaukrodger and Gordon (n 22) 16.

[28] Gaukrodger and Gordon (n 22); UNCITRAL Secretariat (n 23).

This section has not presented an exhaustive list of the criticisms levied at IIAs and ISDS. However, the problems highlighted here correspond to both areas of possible reform as well as to themes that recur throughout the book—changing preferences and the time inconsistency problem (inherently linked to the right to regulate), lack of capacity or understanding of the investment protection regime, and lack of consistency in arbitral awards and the resultant uncertainty for policymakers.

1.2 The Costs and Benefits of IIAs

The criticisms highlighted in section 1.1 take on greater saliency when we examine the relative costs and benefits of IIAs.

Unlike international trade, the governance of which is largely centralized in the World Trade Organization (WTO), investment flows are governed primarily by bilateral treaties. Indeed, as is underscored by the most recent debates over the inclusion of ISDS in the Transatlantic Trade and Investment Partnership (TTIP) and the Trans-Pacific Partnership (TPP), as well as the failure of the international community to agree on a multilateral agreement on investment (MAI), efforts to centralize international investment protection have long been controversial.[29] This is due in part to the very different, and at times conflicting, interests of participants in the regime of international investment protection; the preferences of capital-exporting and capital-importing states towards investment protection standards diverge significantly.

IIAs emerged in the second half of the twentieth century with the oft-cited BIT between Germany and Pakistan, signed in 1959, launching the first wave of BITs, although many of these early-era BITs contained only clauses for state-to-state, rather than investor–state, arbitration. However, many of the standards of investment protection with which we are familiar today were included in these early BITs, and many were signed between Western European nations and developing countries and quickly spread. Capital-exporting, or 'home' countries, such as the United States, Canada, and many European countries, have developed what are called 'Model BITs' (with some key differences between them), which are then generally presented to developing-country partners, thus ensuring that investors from one home country generally enjoy the same level of protection in whichever partner countries they invest.

IIAs were sold to developing states as a means to attract greater flows of investment by Western states and international organizations. However, the evidence for IIAs' success in attracting investment remains mixed at best.[30] Studies find that

[29] Elkins, Guzman, and Simmons (n 5).

[30] Jennifer Tobin and Susan Rose-Ackerman, 'When BITs Have Some Bite: The Political-Economic Environment for Bilateral Investment Treaties' (2011) 6 The Review of International Organizations 1.

BITs do attract foreign investment, but only in low- and middle-income countries with relatively attractive investment environments, thus acting as a complement to, not a substitute for, strong domestic institutions. Moreover, it is argued, as more countries sign these agreements, increased competition from similarly attractive countries decreases the marginal effect of signing a new BIT.[31] Kerner argues that BITs do increase FDI and further suggests that a signalling effect attracts investment from home countries beyond the parties to the treaty. On the other hand, Aisbett argues that these studies have not adequately accounted for the endogeneity problems inherent to much research on international institutions and FDI and trade flows.[32] Specifically, 'increased FDI flows in one year may cause a BIT to be signed in the next, or an improvement in the investment climate of the host [state] may cause a simultaneous increase in both FDI and BIT participation'.[33] Controlling for this endogeneity, it appears that BITs are generally signed when FDI flows are already increasing and that while there is correlation between BITs and FDI, a strong argument for causation in a specific direction cannot be made. She further finds no evidence of a signalling effect. The lack of consensus among these studies and others may be due in part to methodological differences and sample selection. However, it seems clear that while IIAs may go hand in hand with greater FDI flows, the causal direction is unclear, and they cannot be understood as the primary drivers of FDI.

While the benefits of signing an IIA in terms of increased FDI flows are unclear, the costs for host countries are much easier to identify. As Simmons succinctly argues, 'one consequence of ratifying bilateral investment treaties that contain dispute settlement provisions seems quite clear: they have led to a burst of (possibly unanticipated) litigation, especially since the late 1990s'.[34] She finds that the likelihood of investor–state arbitration increases for a state with each additional treaty signed, a finding that is replicated in this study (see Chapters 3–4). Similarly, Schultz and Dupont argue that investment arbitration was initially used by investors, as it was designed, to substitute for weak domestic courts.[35] However, they argue, investment arbitration is now used 'as a sword in the hands of economic interests of investors of rich countries against governments of poorer countries', and more recently against developed countries as well.[36] In other words, international

[31] Andrew Kerner, 'Why Should I Believe You? The Costs and Consequences of Bilateral Investment Treaties' (2009) 53 International Studies Quarterly 73.

[32] Emma Aisbett, 'Bilateral Investment Treaties and Foreign Direct Investment: Correlation versus Causation' (2007) CUDARE Working Papers 7188, University of California, Berkeley, Department of Agricultural and Resource Economics, 1032.

[33] ibid 3.

[34] Beth Simmons, 'Bargaining over BITs, Arbitrating Awards: The Regime for Protection and Promotion of International Investment' (2013) 66 World Politics 12, 28.

[35] Thomas Schultz and Cédric Dupont, 'Investment Arbitration: Promoting the Rule of Law or Over-Empowering Investors? A Quantitative Empirical Study' (2014) 25 European Journal of International Law 1.

[36] ibid 1150.

investment law is increasingly being used to set standards for investment protection in a way that privileges the interests of investors over those of states.[37]

1.3 The Puzzle: Changing Preferences or Lack of Capacity?

Why do host states find themselves in conflict with foreign investors, particularly given the costs posed by the investment arbitration regime? This book examines cases in which a policy is enacted and subsequently challenged by investors by initiating arbitration, in order to better understand when and where the preferences of domestic actors and foreign investors come into conflict; in other words, it examines instances in which the state chooses to side with domestic demands over those of international actors.

Within international political economy, there is an extensive body of work that examines the ways in which domestic institutional features (eg electoral institutions) and the preferences of domestic actors (both consumers and producers) determine trade policy, often with a focus on levels of protection of domestic producers. The literature on the interaction between levels of investment protection and domestic actors and institutions is comparatively underdeveloped beyond the widely accepted conclusion that democracies both attract more FDI and are less likely to expropriate.[38] Therefore, as discussed at greater length in Chapter 4, this book attempts to contribute to the development of theory on domestic preferences and foreign investment.

While investor–state disputes which culminate in arbitration are the result of domestic policy decisions, they also represent potential (depending on the ultimate ruling by the arbitral tribunal) instances of non-compliance with an international treaty. International relations literature on treaty compliance suggests a possible alternative to the hypothesis that domestic actor preferences contribute to investor–state disputes. Instead, these disputes may arise due to domestic institutional incapacity to fulfil obligations to foreign investors enshrined in investment treaties.[39]

[37] ibid.

[38] Nathan M Jensen, *Nation-States and the Multinational Corporation: A Political Economy of Foreign Direct Investment* (Princeton University Press 2008); Nathan M Jensen, 'Democratic Governance and Multinational Corporations: Political Regimes and Inflows of Foreign Direct Investment' (2003) 57 International Organization 587; Quan Li, 'Democracy, Autocracy, and Expropriation of Foreign Direct Investment', *International Studies Association Annual Meeting* (2005); Sonal S Pandya, 'Democratization and Foreign Direct Investment Liberalization, 1970–2000' (2014) 58 International Studies Quarterly 475.

[39] Abrams Chayes and Antonia Handler Chayes, *The New Sovereignty. Compliance with International Regulatory Agreements* (Harvard University Press 1995).

To capture both these possibilities, I ask the following question: '*What role do domestic actors and institutions play in investor–state disputes that culminate in arbitration?*'[40]

In order to assess the role of domestic actors and institutions in investor–state disputes which culminate in arbitration, this project poses a number of sub-questions, answered by the empirical chapters of this project. These include:

(1) Which domestic institutions are taking the measures that are subsequently challenged by investors? What is the content of these measures? Against investors in which industries are these measures taken?
(2) Under what economic and political conditions in the host state are investor–state arbitration cases most likely to occur?
(3) Are these policy changes towards investment better explained as the outcome of a shift in preferences on the part of state actors towards investment or are they instead the result of a lack of institutional capacity to uphold IIA obligations?

What is the relevance of an examination of which domestic actors, represented by which domestic institutions, come into conflict with investors? If we accept that, as is discussed earlier, ISDS has the potential to impose significant costs on states, it is important for proponents and opponents of the regime to understand for which policy measures, and at whose behest, states are incurring these costs. Trying to prove the counterfactual of the regulatory chill hypothesis beyond a few individual case studies is challenging, made more so by the reluctance of key actors to discuss the issue. Therefore, the primary research question and sub-questions take a different approach to the relationship between domestic policymaking and investment treaties, focusing on the underlying causes of investor–state disputes.

The first question is answered via an original dataset of investor–state arbitration cases. From this data, it is possible to identify patterns which can help guide further examination of the causes of these conflicts. This question focuses on broad patterns in investor–state disputes (the actors involved—both domestic institutions and investors—and the measures taken), which can go some way towards gaining an overview of which domestic interests are at the heart of these disputes.

The second question—'Under what political and economic conditions is investor–state arbitration likely to occur?'—encompasses a wide range of relevant variables by means of a statistical analysis. The hypotheses related to this analysis are drawn from the literature on political risk and the determinants of

[40] At the outset, I do not assume a causal direction for domestic actors and institutions on the outcome variable, and indeed, the variety of independent variables discussed here are not uniform in their relationship with the dependent variable. Thus, it may be that some institutional features make disputes more likely and others less.

expropriation. The variables include (relatively) time invariant factors such as the gross domestic product (GDP) per capita, corruption/governance effectiveness, and democracy levels of the states that have signed at least one IIA. This analysis further includes the effect that temporally delimited events, such as financial crises, may have on states' propensity to take measures which are challenged by investors in arbitration.

This analysis can again help us to determine which factors contribute to the likelihood of a dispute, which may hint at an answer to the final question—namely, whether investor–state disputes which culminate in arbitration are the outcome of cost–benefit decision-making on the part of state actors or instead the result of a lack of institutional capacity to comply with IIAs. This final question is addressed both by the large-N study and the case studies of specific disputes and has implications for our normative assessment of the regime. While all international cooperation requires some constraint of domestic behaviour, when the beneficiaries of this are foreign, private actors and those that bear the costs are domestic groups, criticisms of IIAs on the grounds that they overly constrain domestic policy space and harm domestic interests will be more convincing.

Of course, investor–state arbitration, while usually triggered by a state measure, will not occur unless an investor makes the choice to use this tool to settle the dispute and different investors may be more or less inclined to do so—they may not wish to jeopardize their relationship with the host state or outlay the significant financial resources required in the arbitration process. I do not attempt to include both the investor and the state 'sides of the equation' in the following analysis but instead focus on state decision-making in the face of competing pressures from domestic interests and foreign investors.

One final word is necessary on the choice of the dependent variable of the study as a whole—investor–state disputes that culminate in investment arbitration. While at first glance this may appear to be a fairly straightforward phenomenon, it is at once a very broad and very specific object of study. On the one hand, cases of investor–state arbitration are only a subset of investor–state disputes, many of which may be resolved (or not) through other means.[41] More generally, we can understand investor–state disputes as the incidence of an alleged breach by (an entity associated with) the host state of a contract, domestic investment law, or IIA, claimed by an investor. For various reasons, investor–state disputes may not end up before an arbitral tribunal and states may, as the regulatory chill hypothesis suggests, repeal the measure in question when threatened with arbitration by the investor or instead choose to settle with the investor out of arbitration. However, unlike studies that focus on one *type* of measure which leads to investor–state dispute, most often expropriation, this project seeks to explain disputes that are

[41] Rachel L Wellhausen, *The Shield of Nationality: When Governments Break Contracts with Foreign Firms* (Cambridge University Press 2015).

instead caused by a very wide range of policy measures. Therefore, the dependent variable of this study is ultimately a snapshot of the investment protection regime in action—comprising both the measures which investors see fit to challenge in arbitration and which policies states are willing to risk arbitration losses to defend—in other words, where domestic and international demands are most in tension.

1.4 Domestic Actors, Institutions, and 'Compliance' with IIAs

This book focuses on the role that domestic actors and institutions play in investor–state disputes, and I therefore adopt the assumptions that domestic actors are able to act collectively and influence national-level decision-making to the extent that the state may adopt as national preferences those of sub-state or non-state actors.[42] It is through domestic institutions that these interests are aggregated and policy is enacted.[43] In analysing this causal relationship, it is necessary to first identify the relevant actors and interests and, subsequently, how they are able to organize and impact state level preferences regarding policy towards foreign investors and the upholding of treaty commitments.

In addition, I employ concepts found in the international relations literature on compliance with international agreements. As I discuss in Chapters 3 and 4, the concept of compliance is potentially problematic when applied to investor–state disputes which culminate in arbitration, in part due to inconsistencies in arbitral findings, an issue highlighted previously in this chapter. Moreover, this book focuses on explaining the *emergence* of investor–state disputes under an IIA rather than the outcome of these disputes in terms of ultimate rulings of (non-)compliance by arbitrators. However, the two main approaches to compliance on which I draw—the enforcement approach and the managerial approach—suggest useful starting points to answer more general questions about why states may find themselves in conflict with foreign investors (and possibly in violation of an IIA).

Moreover, both of these approaches imply an important role for domestic actors in state compliance with international agreements. On the one hand, the enforcement approach to compliance argues that states only sign and subsequently comply with international agreements when it is in their interests to do so. Therefore, when faced with agreements which require substantial behavioural change, compliance can only be guaranteed if the agreement contains an enforcement mechanism

[42] Andrew Moravcsik, 'Taking Preferences Seriously: A Liberal Theory of International Politics' (1997) 51 International Organization 513; Andrew Moravcsik, 'Liberal Theories of International Law' in Jeffrey L Dunoff and Mark A Pollack (eds), *Interdisciplinary Perspectives on International Law and International Relations* (Cambridge University Press 2012).

[43] Jeffry Frieden and Lisa Martin, 'International Political Economy: Global and Domestic Interactions' in Ira Katznelson and Helen V Milner (eds), *Political Science: The State of the Discipline* (WW Norton 2003).

which can impose costs on the state for non-compliance which outweigh the benefits it may receive from not complying.[44] This suggests that state preferences are derived from cost–benefit calculations with the costs of non-compliance provided by the international regime and costs of compliance (or benefits of non-compliance) most likely supplied by domestic sub-state or non-state interest groups, thus highlighting the importance of domestic actors in international cooperation.

The managerial approach suggests very different sources of (non-)compliance, which nonetheless are to be found at least in part at the domestic level. As Chayes and Chayes argue, non-compliance with international agreements is due in large part to a lack of capacity of states to comply, whether because of unclear treaty obligations, lack of sufficient time to bring domestic regulatory processes and institutions into compliance, or, more generally, a lack of domestic capacity to act in a treaty-compliant manner.[45] Thus, while (non-)compliance is not the result of domestic preferences, it does depend on the strength of domestic institutions.

These two contrasting explanations for treaty compliance can be understood as possible broad 'causes' of investor–state disputes which culminate in arbitration at the domestic level, although, as will become clear, in the case of investor–state disputes, these are not mutually exclusive. However, as discussed, due to the primary role played by private actors (investors) in this regime, with their own motivations to enter into disputes with states, the 'causes' of arbitration cannot be found solely within the host state. Therefore, exposure to opportunities to be sued—in the form of the number of IIAs ratified, the amount of FDI hosted in the state, and the passage of time (which accounts for increased investor awareness of ISA)—must at the very least be controlled for, if not understood as an outright cause of these disputes.[46]

At the outset of this project, there was very little political science work on investor–state arbitration. Therefore, in Chapters 3 and 4, in which I develop the specific hypotheses related to the two broader explanations discussed earlier, I look at thematically adjacent literature, including the work on political risk and large-N studies of expropriation events. Expropriation—when the state forcibly divests an investor of its interest in an investment project—is the most obvious and dramatic manifestation of an investor–state dispute, and there is a significant body of work that looks at the conditions under which expropriations are most likely to occur. This literature comes to fairly clear conclusions about the role of domestic institutions in causing expropriations, in short, that democracies are less likely to expropriate, given their greater respect of rule of law, property rights, and higher

[44] George W Downs, David M Rocke, and Peter N Barsoom, 'Is the Good News about Compliance Good News about Cooperation?' (1996) 50 International Organization 379.

[45] Chayes and Chayes (n 39).

[46] For a discussion of the motivations that investors have to initiate legally weak claims against investors, see Schultz and Dupont (n 35) and Kristof J Pelc, 'What Explains the Low Success Rate of Investor–State Disputes?' (2017) 71 International Organization 559.

numbers of veto players, which increase policy stability.[47] However, as I show in Chapter 2, investor–state disputes which end up in arbitration are caused by a much wider range of measures than expropriation alone. Therefore, some of the earlier work on political risk which argues that a range of state measures and policies can contribute to political risk for investors also provides a useful starting point for the development of my hypotheses (see Chapter 4).[48] As will be discussed throughout the book, the issue then becomes one of policy stability, as much as democracy itself, and the importance of the causes of policy instability—changes in the preferences of domestic actors—in causing investor–state disputes.

The domestic interests and actors involved in investor–state disputes, as well as the broader causes of these conflicts, are particularly relevant at a time when the international investment community is considering various options for reform of the system as well as the development of domestic-level institutions to monitor investor–state relationships and avoid disputes.[49] If we conclude that investor–state disputes are caused by a lack of capacity of state bureaucracy to maintain investment-friendly regulatory environments or confusion over the significance of IIA provisions, then efforts to improve bureaucratic effectiveness and understanding of IIAs at the domestic level, and perhaps efforts to increase the consistency of arbitral awards to reduce uncertainty, should reduce the number investor–state disputes. On the other hand, if investor–state disputes are primarily caused by changes in preference towards investment or conflicts between regulatory goals and earlier commitments made to investors, then alternative dispute settlement mechanisms may help to avoid recourse to costly arbitration if investor and state positions are not completely irreconcilable. Finally, however, if domestic actors and investors are both consistently placing pressure on states to comply with irreconcilable demands, disputes will be difficult to avoid. In this case, the most beneficial reforms of the ISDS system, from the perspective of increasing the democratic legitimacy of the regime, will involve ensuring that ISDS does not systemically privilege the interests of one party over the other and, in particular, that arbitrators and investment lawyers do not face serious conflicts of interest that may render illegitimate or biased awards.

[47] Li (n 38); Benjamin AT Graham, Noel P Johnston, and Allison F Kingsley, 'How Sovereigns Steal: Political Constraints and the Choice Between Transfer and Expropriation Rents', *International Political Economy Society Annual Meeting* (2012); Facundo Albornoz, Sebastian Galiani, and Daniel Heymann, 'Foreign Investment and Expropriation under Oligarchy and Democracy' (2012) 24 Economics & Politics 24; Nathan M Jensen, Noel P Johnston, and Chia-yi Lee, 'Crisis and Contract Breach: The Domestic and International Determinants of Expropriation' (2020) 15 Review of International Organizations 869.

[48] Stephen J Kobrin, 'Political Risk: A Review and Reconsideration' (1979) 10 Journal of International Business Studies 67; Stephen Kobrin, 'Expropriation as an Attempt to Control Foreign Firms in LDCs: Trends from 1960 to 1979' (1984) 28 International Studies Quarterly 329.

[49] For example, Peru's Coordination and Response System for International Investment Disputes.

1.5 Overview of Main Arguments

The dependent variable in this study is in fact a quite heterogeneous collection of state policy measures which, according to investors, have a negative impact on investment projects. How can we understand these measures as a single phenomenon? What almost all investor–state arbitration cases have in common is a change in state behaviour towards (an) investment.[50] Therefore, policy stability is central to any explanation of the causes of investor–state disputes. While at one time the state committed itself to protecting foreign investment by means of an IIA and subsequently welcomed specific investment projects, a policy change occurs that the investor perceives to be disadvantageous.

As I explain at greater length later and in Chapter 4, the findings presented here about the role of political contestation and, in particular, 'audience costs' goes against the prevailing conclusions in much of the international political economy (IPE) literature on FDI, which, starting with the obsolescing bargain, makes several important assumptions. The first is that states 'take' from foreign investors largely in search of material gains to be extracted from the investment project. The second assumption is that, as FDI is generally beneficial, and specifically employment generating, democratic institutions provide a bulwark against anti-investor behaviour. Scholars working in this tradition build on these assumptions and often point to a relationship between the rise of democracy and the decline of expropriations to make the argument that democratic states tend to be better hosts of investment.

However, state actors may be moved to take measures that are detrimental to investors for reasons other than immediate material gain. Instead, ISDS-triggering measures may be taken at the behest of either narrow or broad interest groups, in other words, for distinctly political reasons. Moreover, as FDI does not necessarily have a uniformly positive impact on populations in the host state, domestic audiences cannot be depended upon to favour or enforce pro-FDI policies. Indeed, pressure from investment-affected populations has, in many cases, provoked measures later challenged by investors, in some cases with the matter rising to the level of an election issue. Thus, the relationship between democracy and the incidence of investment arbitration claims is not obviously negative.

As stated, I identify two potential explanations for this shift in policy towards foreign investment—a change in domestic preferences towards investment, as just discussed, and a lack of institutional capacity to maintain policy stability. Later, I discuss specific findings regarding the role that domestic preferences and institutions play in investor–state disputes, as they relate to the sub-questions stated earlier.

[50] Defining this shift as a purposive policy change towards investment does not adequately capture the possibility that a lack of capacity, for example to control the corruption of low-level officials, is driving investor–state disputes. In these cases, official policy towards an investment would remain the same, and only the actual fulfillment of this stated policy objective would be in question.

(1) *Which domestic institutions are taking the measures that are subsequently challenged by investors? What is the content of these measures? Against investors in which industries are these measures being taken?*

State measures can be classified by the branch of government which enacts them. Administrative measures have caused the majority of investor–state arbitration cases and two-thirds of all measures taken related to specific investors, rather than an industry or the private sector as a whole. Indeed, when taken together, the cancellation of, or refusal to grant, a licence or permit make up the largest category of state measures. The prominence of administrative decision-making in causing investor–state disputes may suggest that a lack of bureaucratic capacity contributes to investor–state disputes, and indeed, both control of corruption and government effectiveness are negatively correlated with the likelihood of a dispute (see Chapter 3).

On the other hand, the national legislature is the single institution most frequently implicated in these disputes (legislative measures have triggered one-third of all cases), and regulatory change is the fourth most frequent trigger of disputes. However, it is difficult, as an in-depth look at specific cases demonstrates, to infer much from the label of legislative or administrative measure; while we might assume that non-legislative measures are removed from direct public pressure, this ignores the reality that domestic interest groups may pressurize the state through non-electoral means and that administrative measures may be taken in reaction to that pressure. Moreover, while it might be tempting to assign a higher normative value to legislative rather than administrative measures, as the case studies demonstrate, administrative measures can be 'social regarding' in their aim, while legislative measures can advance the aims of quite narrow interest groups.

Disputes are concentrated in 'strategic' industries, such as oil, mining, and gas (extractive industries); energy utilities (electricity and heat); construction; and transportation. That it is investors from these industries that are most frequently involved in these disputes speaks to the degree to which investor–state arbitration has the potential to impact a wide range of stakeholders. For example, the regulation of energy utilities involves a variety of state-based institutions and has a significant effect on energy consumers—a fairly broad category. This underscores the public policy dimension of many investor–state disputes and suggests that the preferences of a wide range of non-state actors, such as energy consumers or communities in the vicinity of extractive projects, can have a role in state decision-making that leads to a dispute with an investor.

(2) *Under what economic and political conditions are investor–state arbitration cases most likely to occur?*

As mentioned, the original rationale for IIAs and ISDS was the protection of foreign investors in developing states with poorly functioning domestic institutions and leaders with a high propensity to expropriate (directly or indirectly). Given that most states acting as respondents in arbitration cases are middle-income, developing countries, this rationale seems to reflect the reality of investor–state disputes; although developed and developing states have signed a similar number of IIAs, it is primarily developing states that are sued by investors, which suggests that weak institutions are important drivers of these disputes. However, this likely has as much to do with the flow of investment that is covered by an IIA as with the development status of the state. Indeed, as the experience of the signatories to NAFTA clearly demonstrate, and the results of the statistical analysis reinforce, when highly developed liberal democracies act as hosts to investment that is covered by an IIA, they are frequently sued by investors. This partly undermines an explanation for investor–state disputes that depend on a lack of capacity of domestic institutions to maintain policy stability for investors. Moreover, the results of the statistical analysis suggest that a state's exposure to the IIA regime, and in particular, what appears to be growing awareness of ISDS on the part of investors (their lawyers), plays a significant role in increasing the numbers of investor–state disputes.

Nevertheless, the analysis presented in Chapter 3 shows that to some extent, capacity does matter; some indicators measuring government effectiveness and control of corruption are negatively correlated with the likelihood of a dispute. As we see in the case studies, developing and transition states may also be more likely to face challenges in their relationships with investors, both due to capacity issues and to a greater impetus for regulatory change, whether in the form of raising environmental standards or privatizing and liberalizing formerly state-owned enterprises. Indeed, the case studies on disputes between El Salvador and Pacific Rim, and Hungary and AES Summit and Electrabel highlight that investor–state disputes can be triggered by shifting domestic preferences towards specific industrial activity that is part of a much broader policy change. In addition, and more specifically, financial crises are associated with a greater likelihood of disputes. However, GDP per capita has no significant relationship with the number of disputes.

Indeed, as discussed at greater length in Chapter 4, there is much debate about the role of democratic institutions in state compliance with international agreements. However, the bulk of the literature on the relationship between democracy and expropriation concludes that democracy level is negatively correlated with the likelihood of expropriations. The results of the statistical analysis in this study show the positive correlations between democracy level and the likelihood of arbitration, suggesting that disputes may stem in part from governments responding to public pressure. As will be discussed at greater length in Chapter 4, this goes against expectations regarding the role of democracy in ensuring respect for international commitments and domestic property rights. Instead, it again underscores the public policy dimension, and wide reach, of investor–state disputes.

(3) *Are these changes in policy towards investment the outcome of a shift in preferences on the part of state actors toward investment, or are they instead the result of a lack of institutional capacity to respect IIAs?*

In the statistical analysis, several of the variables related to state capacity—particularly economic capacity, in terms GDP per capita and economic growth—has no relationship with the likelihood of a dispute. However, higher levels of government effectiveness and better control of corruption, which can serve as indicators of bureaucratic capacity, are negatively correlated with the likelihood of a dispute, suggesting that lack of capacity does contribute to instances of ISDS. The role of government capacity also emerged in the case studies, though in a more nuanced way. In the case of El Salvador, recognition that the government did not have the technical capacity or experience to regulate the extractive sector contributed to a change in preferences toward the mining industry (see Chapter 5). In Hungary, the demands of an emerging market economy in the early 1990s led to a push for agreements with investors that would later need to be re-evaluated to meet EU accession requirements (see Chapter 7). Finally, even in Canada, a country with significant ISDS experience, government experts were unable to predict whether a specific measure would both incite arbitration and lead to a negative ruling by the tribunal (see Chapter 6). Ultimately, this project concludes that domestic bureaucratic capacity issues do have a role to play in investor–state disputes.

On the other hand, domestic preferences towards investment also contribute to state decision-making which can lead to a dispute with an investor. The variables hypothesized to indicate both negative domestic preference towards investors and the receptiveness of domestic institutions to anti-investment/investor pressure consistently increase the likelihood of a dispute in the large-N study, including democracy level and the incidence of an election.

Moreover, in the three case studies, there are clear links between domestic actor preferences and subsequent changes in policy towards the investment in question. In the cases of Canada and El Salvador, the key non-state actors were broad interest groups—in both cases, local communities and environmental groups concerned about the impact of extractive projects—supported by key state agencies. In the case of Hungary, the most influential sub-state actor was the state-owned electricity company, although external pressure from the EU also had an impact on the state decision-making which led to the dispute. This case therefore exemplifies both the role that powerful special interests can play in investor–state disputes and the transnational dimension to the issue.

Therefore, a clear picture emerges regarding the role of changes in domestic preferences towards the investment in question in triggering investor–state disputes. It appears that many investor–state arbitration cases indicate instances in which the state has had to choose between the demands placed on it by domestic actors and its international commitments enshrined in treaties and agreements, and it sides with the former. As mentioned, this has normative implications for our assessment of the regime. If most investor–state disputes are caused by a lack of bureaucratic capacity or awareness of their obligations, IIAs cannot necessarily be said to impose too great a cost on using domestic policy space, as these disputes do not arise from the pursuit of specific policy goals of the host state but rather an inability to respect previously made commitments. This further implies that investor–state relationships can be relatively easily ameliorated with increased administrative or bureaucratic capacity. However, if investor–state disputes are instead caused by changes in state preferences towards investment, we may conclude that ISDS can impose costs on states for being responsive to domestic interests.

Policy instability or reversal can be attributed to weak domestic institutions. As the literature on veto players and political constraints suggests, higher numbers of independent institutions or individuals whose consent is needed to pass a policy measure increase the ability of states to make credible commitments to, for example, foreign investors.[51] However, the line between weak domestic institutions that encourage policy reversal and institutions that are responsive to changing domestic conditions can be difficult to identify. Because the reach of IIAs is so wide, and investors are incentivized to use the system to challenge measures they object to, maintaining policy stability for investors in order to avoid arbitration may come at the expense of responsive domestic institutions. As this book demonstrates, states are still choosing to defend their actions in investment arbitration at the behest of domestic interests, and thus the regulatory chill hypothesis does not hold across the board. However, ISDS does appear to put a cost on states responding to domestic pressure and, at a certain point, an assessment of the causes of investor–state disputes and the effect of the ISDS system becomes a normative rather than empirical question.

1.6 Outline

Following this introduction, Chapter 2 presents the broad patterns that result from a qualitative coding of all publicly available arbitral awards. Returning to theory, Chapters 3 and 4 address the two broad explanations for investor–state disputes already mentioned—lack of bureaucratic capacity and changing preferences towards

[51] Witold J Henisz and Edward D Mansfield, 'Votes and Vetoes: The Political Determinants of Commercial Openness' (2006) 50 International Studies Quarterly 189; Bennet A Henisz and Witold J Zelner, 'Political Risk Management: A Strategic Perspective' (2002). A Working Paper of the Reginald H. Jones Center; George Tsebelis, 'Veto Players and Institutional Analysis' (2000) 13 Governance 441.

an investment. In both chapters, theorizing is followed by the presentation of the results of a statistical analysis, based on an original dataset of cases of investment arbitration. Finally, the case studies presented in Chapters 5–7 look more closely at the relationships uncovered in the statistical analysis and focus on to what extent the state decisions to take certain policy measures, and subsequently defend them in arbitration, are the result of cost–benefit decision-making or a lack of state capacity to uphold standards of investment protection agreed upon in the relevant IIA. These chapters are based on fieldwork carried out in Canada, El Salvador, and Hungary, which included interviews carried out with government officials and others involved in the disputes which led to the investor–state arbitration cases that are the focus of the investigation.[52] Chapter 8 concludes with a discussion of the relevance of the preceding arguments to the ongoing efforts to reform the investment protection regime.

[52] A list of interviews can be found in the appendix under 'Chapters 5–7'.

2
Patterns in Investor–State Arbitration

Who are the key actors in investor–state disputes? Which states are getting sued most frequently and by which type of investors? On a sub-state level, which domestic institutions are enacting the measures that are subsequently being challenged by investors? This chapter paints an empirical picture of our dependent variable—investor–state disputes that go to arbitration—based an original dataset of known investor–state arbitration cases and includes information on the investor and its home state, the respondent state, the industry, the domestic institutions involved in the dispute, and the measure(s) taken which were challenged by the investor.

An overview of the domestic institutions involved and the policies which trigger investor–state disputes is necessary to understand the array of factors related to the host state, which contribute to the emergence of investor–state disputes as well as the impact of the investment protection regime on host states. As discussed in Chapter 1, critics of investor–state arbitration argue that these agreements contribute to regulatory chill and the shrinking of domestic policy space, for example, by punishing states for increasing regulatory standards. However, the bulk of research and reporting on the topic most often presents single case studies of high-profile, controversial disputes in order to advance claims about the negative impact of international investment agreements (IIAs). While these cases give us indications of the extent to which the regime can be used by investors in an attempt to impede the pursuit of legitimate policy goals, these studies leave many questions unanswered regarding broader patterns in investor–state dispute settlement. Therefore, the initial motivation for this data collection project was to provide an overview of broad patterns in the distribution of cases across industry and type of state, as well as the policy measures that are challenged by investors in arbitration.

The specific categories I have chosen to explore shed light on the causes of investor state–arbitration cases. For example, the concentration of arbitration cases in middle-income countries is in part a reflection of the pattern of bilateral foreign direct investment (FDI) flows which are covered by IIAs. Which industries are most frequently implicated in investor–state arbitration is also telling as not all economic activity has the same impact on the host state, and some types of economic activity may engender greater discontent among domestic actors than others. The institutions involved can also suggest which domestic interests are being taken into account when states choose to enter into conflict with an investor,

The Political Economy of Investment Arbitration. Zoe Phillips Williams, Oxford University Press. © Zoe Phillips Williams 2022.
DOI: 10.1093/oso/9780198865940.003.0002

despite the threat of losing the arbitration case. For example, legislation passed in a state parliament may be taken at the behest of different actors than the actions of a state-owned enterprise. Finally, looking at the policy measures themselves can give an indication of the degree to which a change in preference or lack of capacity contributed to the dispute.

Before presenting the results of this first empirical investigation, however, this chapter provides a brief overview of the history and functioning of investor–state arbitration, which I turn next.

2.1 History and Functioning of Investor–State Arbitration

2.1.1 History of the Investment Protection Regime

Unlike international trade, the governance of which is to some degree centralized by the World Trade Organization (WTO), investment flows are governed overwhelmingly bilaterally. Indeed, as is underscored by the recent debates over the inclusion of investor–state dispute settlement (ISDS) in the Transatlantic Trade and Investment Partnership (TTIP) and the Trans-Pacific Partnership (TPP), as well as the failure of the international community to agree on a multilateral agreement on investment (MAI), efforts to increase international investment protection has long been controversial. This is perhaps due in part to the very different, and at times contradictory, interests of participants in the regime of international investment protection; as will be discussed in greater detail in the following chapters, the preferences of capital-exporting and capital-importing state governments and populations towards investment protection standards may diverge significantly.

Early standards for the protection of foreign investors were based on customary international law. However, as Montt describes in detail, as early as the nineteenth century, developed and developing countries (in this case, the newly independent Latin American republics) ascribed to different standards of investment protection.[1] On the one hand, developing countries pushed for standards of national treatment, by which foreign investors are treated no worse than domestic investors, while, on the other, capital-exporting countries promoted international minimum standards of treatment, most famously enshrined in the Hull Rule, which meant to ensure 'prompt, adequate and effective compensation' in the event of an expropriation by a host state.[2]

IIAs emerged in the second half of the twentieth century—the oft-cited bilateral investment treaty (BIT) between Germany and Pakistan, signed in 1959, launched

[1] Santiago Montt, *State Liability in Investment Treaty Arbitration* (Hart Publishing 2009) 32.
[2] ibid 34.

this first wave of BITs, although many of these early-era BITs only contained clauses for state-to-state, not investor–state, arbitration. However, the standards of investment protection with which we are familiar today were included in the language of these early BITs, many of which were signed between Western European nations and developing countries. Capital-exporting, or 'home' countries such as the United States, Canada, and many European countries have developed so-called model BITs (with some key differences between them), which were then generally presented to developing country partners, thus ensuring that investors from one home country generally enjoy the same level of protection in whichever partner countries they invest.

During the late 1980s and through the 1990s, the speed at which these agreements were adopted increased substantially, with hundreds of new BITs signed. According to Poulsen, this burst of IIA signings accompanied a new focus on the attraction of FDI following the debt crises of the 1980s, and the agreements were seen as a complement to internal reforms.[3] This boom in new investment agreements was encouraged not just by capital exporting states but also by international economic institutions such as the United Nations Conference on Trade and Development (UNCTAD) and the Organisation for Economic Co-operation and Development (OECD), in the belief that IIAs contributed to the flow of investment to developing countries.[4] As recent work has shown, while capital-exporting nations and international organizations put some effort into the promotion of IIAs, the governments of host countries did not necessarily have a sufficient understanding of the content and consequences of these agreements.[5] Chapter 3 builds on this work to develop one broad argument for the emergence of investor–state disputes which culminate in arbitration.

ISDS provisions have also become common elements of free trade agreements, beginning with the North American Free Trade Agreement (NAFTA) in 1994, and followed by the Central American Free Trade Agreement (CAFTA), Association of Southeast Asian Nations (ASEAN), the Energy Charter Treaty, and the Peru–US Trade Promotion Agreement. Finally, as mentioned, mega-regional trade agreements between the European Union (EU) and the United States, the EU and Canada, and the United States and a number of Pacific Rim countries have in recent years been the subject of (in some cases unsuccessful) negotiations.

[3] Lauge Poulsen, *Bounded Rationality and Economic Diplomacy. The Politics of Investment Treaties in Developing Countries* (Cambridge University Press 2015).

[4] N Bernasconi-Osterwalder and others, 'Investment Treaties and Why They Matter to Sustainable Development: Questions and Answers' (2012) International Institute for Sustainable Development.

[5] Emma Aisbett and Lauge Poulsen, 'When the Claim Hits: Bilateral Investment Treaties and Bounded Rational Learning' (2013) 65 World Politics 1; Poulsen (n 3).

2.1.2 State Measures as the Causes of Investor–State Arbitration

Once an investment has been made in a IIA signatory host state, an investor enjoys protection from any state conduct that many fall foul of broadly defined treaty provisions. These include non-discrimination provisions—national treatment (NT) and most favoured nation (MFN) treatment. The former, NT, requires the host state to extend to the investor no worse treatment than it does to domestic investors. MFN, on the other hand, requires the host state to treat the investor no less favourably than it treats investors from any other country.[6] Although these are relative standards of treatment, most IIAs also include the absolute standard of fair and equitable treatment (FET). The FET standard has provoked much debate as most ratified IIAs do not define the term.[7] At the heart of the debate over the standard is whether FET should be interpreted as a requirement for treatment that conforms to international minimum standards set out in international law or whether it is a broader and more demanding standard of treatment that includes, for example, compensation in the face of financial loss not caused by expropriation.[8] According to some authors, the broad, ill-defined nature of the FET standard has also contributed to the steep increase in the number of claims faced by democratic states.[9] At the very least, it is one of the most frequently invoked standards and certainly captures a broad range of state measures that might not fit neatly into traditional conceptions of the causes of investor–state disputes such as expropriation.

Traditionally, expropriation or nationalization, in which the state seizes the property of the investor, has been a key concern for foreign investors.[10] Unsurprisingly, therefore, unlawful expropriation, in which the investor is not compensated adequately and the measure is not taken for a public purpose, is prohibited by BITs. However, beyond an outright seizure of property, IIAs tend also to prohibit measures 'tantamount to' or 'having an effect equivalent to' expropriation.[11] In this case, the definition of expropriation under a BIT expands

[6] UNCTAD (United Nations Conference on Trade and Development), 'Bilateral Investment Treaties 1995–2006: Trends in Investment Rulemaking' (2007).

[7] ibid.

[8] Graham Mayeda, 'Playing Fair: The Meaning of Fair and Equitable Treatment in Bilateral Investment Treaties' (2007) 41 Journal of World Trade 273 <http://papers.ssrn.com/sol3/papers.cfm?abstract_id=1427307> accessed 22 February 2022.

[9] Krzysztof J Pelc, 'What Explains the Low Success Rate of Investor–State Disputes?' (2017) 71 International Organization 559.

[10] Nevertheless, the Western state officials and investors active in the early years of the ICSID Convention and the push for IIAs and ISDS were also concerned about *indirect* expropriation, which today is a much more frequently breached IIA standard: see Taylor St John, *The Rise of Investor-State Arbitration: Politics, Law and Unintended Consequences* (Oxford University Press 2018).

[11] Benedict Kingsbury and Stephan Schill, 'Investor–State Arbitration as Governance: Fair and Equitable Treatment, Proportionality and the Emerging Global Administrative Law' (2011) 2 Transnational Dispute Management 9.

to include measures which 'negatively affect the property's substance or void the owner's control over it'.[12] This provision has therefore become controversial as IIAs do not establish criteria to determine whether or not a state measure has had this effect.[13]

Given the broad scope of these provisions, which measures are investors challenging as treaty breaches and arbitrators assessing in the course of an investment arbitration? Limited work exists in international political economy (IPE) or other fields that attempts to explain the drivers of investment arbitration itself (rather than the at once broader and narrower category of expropriation, for example, the literature on which is discussed at length in Chapter 4). In particular, while several authors have taken a quantitative approach (as I do in Chapters 3 and 4) and identify correlations between host-state-level variables and the incidence of an investment claim, only few studies have included a qualitative but nonetheless birds-eye view of the universe of known arbitration cases.

However, several exceptions to this general rule exist, in addition to the present chapter, which look at either the institutional sources of state measures at issue in investment arbitration cases or the target of these measures. For example, approaching the question in a similar way as I do here, Caddel and Jensen find that in their sample 264 International Centre for Settlement of Investment Disputes (ICSID) cases, most are triggered by action taken by the executive, while fewer disputes relate to legislative or judicial decisions. Based on this, they conclude that concerns about investment arbitration infringing on states' right to regulate are overstated.[14] Similarly, Stone Sweet and colleagues find that most are a reaction to 'targeted' measures—those aimed at a specific investor—rather than general regulatory measures. They conclude that investment arbitrators are not 'sitting in judgement' of states' legitimate regulatory measures.[15] While neither study makes this assumption entirely explicit, both seem to imply that if investors are only routinely challenging administrative measures or those aimed at an individual or small group of investors, we have no reason to be concerned that investment arbitration puts any limitations on democratic policymaking.

For its part, legal scholarship has focused primarily on arbitral reasoning and decisions rather than the politics underlying investment arbitration cases. However, Van Harten combines an analysis of arbitrators' approaches to judicial restraint with a similar coding project of the measures implicated in investor–state arbitration cases and comes to a similar conclusion on the distribution of executive,

[12] ibid 31.

[13] UNCTAD, 'Bilateral Investment Treaties 1995–2006' (n 6).

[14] Jeremy Caddel and Nathan M Jensen, 'Which Host Country Government Actors Are Most Involved in Disputes with Foreign Investors?' (2014) 120 Columbia FDI Perspectives 2.

[15] Alec Stone Sweet, Michael Yunsuck Chung, and Adam Saltzman, 'Arbitral Lawmaking and State Power: An Empirical Analysis of Investor–State Arbitration' (2017) Journal of International Dispute Settlement 1, 12>.

legislative, and judicial measures as I do here.[16] Moreover, his conclusions differ significantly from those analyses cited here as he finds that arbitrators are frequently called upon by investors to review 'decisions by legislatures and other elected actors as well as the discretionary conduct of governments that was authorized by a statute'.[17] Moreover, he finds that arbitrators routinely failed to show judicial restraint in light of the democratic accountability of state actors, the complexity of policy decisions, and the relative capacity of governments to make these decisions or the role of another adjudicative forum in the measure at hand. Particularly striking is the study's conclusion that, 'it appeared unexceptional for arbitrators to review democratically-accountable decisions taken on behalf of a population and to decide whether public compensation was warranted for an affected foreign asset owner'[18] and that, perhaps unsurprisingly, 'some arbitrators appeared to view electorally and politically-accountable processes with suspicion as opposed to the respect that courts often show. Where arbitrators referred to terms like elections and democracy, it was usually in the course of questioning decisions by other decision-makers.'[19] Often, however, despite their distrust of domestic political processes, arbitrators' rulings have clear political and distributional consequences for populations in the host state, especially, Van Harten notes, when investor–state disputes relate to extractive and energy- or public utility-related investment projects. Thus, Van Harten's findings underscore the importance of understanding the drivers of investor–state arbitration cases for normative assessments of the regime and largely echo the concerns raised in the present work.

2.2 Data Collection and Sources

In the second half of this chapter, I present the results of the qualitative coding of investor–state disputes, which was undertaken as the first stage of this research project.

The dataset includes 892 arbitration cases from 1990 to 2016 about which sufficient information could be found (at least the home and host state, investor and industry). The data collection began in 2012 and the dataset was updated at the beginning of 2019. Data were collected from a variety of sources. As mentioned in section 2.1, there were no comparable datasets at the beginning of this research. However, two databases of investment arbitration cases helped to give me an initial overview—the UNCTAD IIA database and the International Investment Arbitration and Public Policy (IIAPP) database created by Gus Van Harten at

16 Gus Van Harten, *Sovereign Choices, Sovereign Constraints: Judicial Restraint in Investment Treaty Arbitration* (Oxford University Press 2013). Notably, this study only looks at cases up to 2010.
17 ibid 4.
18 ibid 52.
19 ibid 72.

Osgoode Law School in Toronto.[20] Subsequently, *Investment Arbitration Reporter (IAReporter)*, a specialized legal news service focusing on investment arbitration, published its database of cases online, which greatly increased the number of cases I was able to include here. I was able to access most of the awards of the cases included from the ITALaw website,[21] the ICSID pending and concluded case lists, and *IAReporter*.

The information about the measures taken and actors and institutions involved in the cases was drawn primarily from two sources. The first source of information about an arbitration case is, of course, the arbitration award and any other documentation (eg the initial notice of arbitration) related to the arbitration proceeding. The number of these documents which are publicly available varies significantly from case to case—in some cases, nothing is published; in others, only the final award is made public, while in others, every procedural step of the arbitration, including submissions from respondents and claimants, is published online. The second source of information which was invaluable to the data collection undertaken here, especially in cases with little other public documentation, was reporting from *IAReporter*.[22] It generally provides articles on the background of the cases as well as analyses of the various rulings at different stages of the arbitration and the final award. In some cases, it was necessary to find further sources of information on the cases, usually from national news and business news websites.

2.3 Coding the Cases

The coding itself was undertaken in a series of steps. As mentioned in section 2.2, the entry for each arbitration case includes a number of different elements:

- the respondent state;
- the investor;
- the home state of the investor;
- the industry;
- the relevant IIA;
- the measure taken;
- the domestic institution involved, and more generally, the branch of government (administrative, legislative, judicial); and
- the 'target' of the measure.

[20] <http://www.iiapp.org> accessed 22 February 2022.
[21] <http://www.italaw.com> accessed 22 February 2022.
[22] <http://www.iareporter.com> accessed 22 February 2022.

The first five categories are, for the most part, unambiguous—most obviously, the respondent and investor are in the name of each arbitration case. The home state of the investor was considered to be the other signatory of the IIA, although this does not necessarily entail that the nationality of the investor, or ultimate parent company, belongs to that state. The industry was first coded inductively and then categorized more broadly according to the sector classification used by the World Bank.

The final four categories required substantially more investigation. Both the domestic institutions involved and the 'target' of the measure were coded based on a review of the arbitration proceeding documents and articles from the *IAReporter* website. The domestic institutions which were the sources of the triggering measure(s) were identified first. These institutions ranged from the office of the executive to the legislature to various ministries and state-owned enterprises. These were then further categorized as administrative if they were taken by a body made up of unelected officials or by executive decree; legislative if the measure in question was a law was passed by an elected body; or judicial if the measure was the decision of, or resulted from, the decision of a domestic court case. A measure was coded as general if it applied to an entire industry or the general population (eg the prohibition of a certain chemical substance) and specific if it applied to an individual investor or small group of investors within an industry (eg the refusal to grant an operating licence to a specific miner).

Coding the measure taken by the state which triggered arbitration was the most work-intensive part of the data collection and was done in two steps. I began by first inductively describing the measures after reviewing the relevant data sources. Subsequently, I created categories of measures and finally assigned each measure to a category. The first source of information was again the documents related to the arbitration proceeding. Specifically, most final awards contain a summary of the 'undisputed' facts of the case, which generally gives a timeline of events, and the specific actions of the state to which the investor objects. If this was ambiguous or unclear, I double-checked my interpretation of the measure using the *IAReporter* summaries and other secondary sources of information.[23] A description of each coding category can be found in Table 2.1. The next sections present the results of this data collection.

[23] Unfortunately, there was no opportunity to test for inter-coder reliability for this project. However, I attempted to control for intra-coder reliability, reviewing my entire database approximately eight months after it was first completed. A second review was undertaken in 2018. This exercise led to some changes, due also to the release of new information about some cases, but overall reinforced my initial coding scheme.

Table 2.1 Coding of measures

Measures	Definition
Legislative	A measure is coded as legislative if it is a law passed by an elected body—parliament, legislature, etc—at either the national or subnational level.
Administrative	A measure is coded as administrative if it is taken by the executive, ministries, or other government agencies (including SOEs), without the passing of a law. This includes contractual issues, permitting procedures, and other processes involved in the functioning of these bodies.
Judicial	A measure is coded as judicial if it is the conduct or decision of a domestic court.
Not applicable (NA)	A measure is coded as NA if the claimant identifies as lack of government action as being at issue —for example, a failure to protect an investment from terrorism.
Unknown	A measure is coded as UK if its source cannot be determined.
General	A measure is general if it applies to the entire population or entire industry.
Specific	A measure is specific if it applies to a specific investor or smaller group of investors.
Cancellation of licence/permit/ contract	This occurs where a state cancels an agreement with an investor.
Refusal to grant licence/permit/ contract	This is where a state refuses to grant permission for a project (this generally takes place after certain administrative steps have already been taken by the investor).
Unfulfilled contractual/ payment obligations	Here, the state allegedly fails to pay for services rendered or to fulfil other contractual requirements—for example, it changes tariffs related to a specific service provider.
Existing legislation	An investor challenges a law already in force rather than reacting to a change in law—examples include the Canada Health Act, and the Black Economic Empowerment provisions.
Failure to protect investment	The state fails to protect investment from third parties, including against terrorist attacks, protestors, squatters, etc.
Failure to enforce previous award/ settlement	The state fails to respect conditions of a previous award, either domestically or from a previous arbitral proceeding.
Trade controls	These are import and export duties, quotas, etc.

Table 2.1 Continued

Measures	Definition
Interference with investment	This is alleged harassment by government officials.
Expropriation/ nationalization	This is the nationalization/expropriation of investment (either legislative or administrative).
Domestic legal process	Individuals connected to the investment are subject to domestic criminal investigations or proceedings; domestic court cases connected to the investment; audit; bankruptcy proceedings.
Management of financial crisis	This can include a range of measures such as currency controls, devaluation, etc.
Regulation—general	This applies population or industry-wide; change to regulatory framework governing a specific industry. Examples include the ban of a specific activity or substance, the withdrawal of industry-wide subsidies, the imposition of plain packaging for cigarettes, change to minimum wage, and change to local content requirement rules for entire industry.
Regulation—tariffs/price controls	These include changes to tariffs or prices that affect the entire industry (utilities, telecom).
Regulation—tax	These include changes to taxation with broad effect.
Application of tax	This is the application of tax to a specific investor.
Tender process	This is the alleged problematic/discriminatory tender process.
Industry	Using ICSID and UNCTAD industry categories.

2.4 Results of Qualitative Coding

2.4.1 Home and Host States in Investment Arbitration

Most states have signed and ratified at least one investment treaty (with some notable exceptions, such as Brazil), and therefore a wide range of countries can, in theory, play the role of both home and host state for FDI. However, the reality looks somewhat different. Most BITs are in fact signed between developed, capital-exporting (home) countries and developing, capital-importing (host) countries. Therefore, in the event of an investor–state dispute covered by a BIT, it is generally the latter who is the respondent in arbitration, while the former is the home state of the claimant (the foreign investor). Large multilateral or regional investment agreements such as the Energy Charter Treaty (ECT) and NAFTA alter this

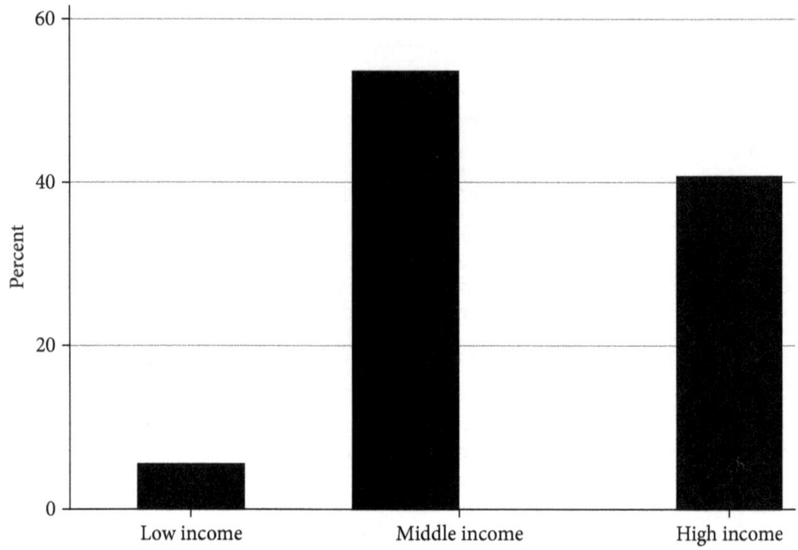

Figure 2.1 Income level of all IIA signatories

dynamic somewhat, although, at least with regard to the ECT, the respondents have generally been Eastern European and Commonwealth of Independent States (CIS) with investors coming from Western Europe.

Figure 2.1 shows the distribution of gross domestic product (GDP) per capita levels (as classified by the World Bank) for all signatories to at least one IIA.

Of course, not all states are equally likely to become respondents in an investment arbitration as they must, at minimum, be playing host to investment that is covered by a treaty. Developed countries, while still attracting more FDI than developing countries, have not historically signed IIAs among each other. Therefore, most investment that is covered by an IIA flows into developing or middle-income countries. On the whole, however, the world's least developed countries attract far less FDI, and therefore, most investor–state disputes take place in middle-income countries.

However, a slightly different pattern emerges when we look at the countries which have individually faced the greatest number of arbitration cases, as of the time of writing, shown in Figure 2.2. Interestingly, the top respondent countries are a mix of middle-income and high-income countries. Some of these states have experienced many cases that can be attributed to one or similar events or causes. For example, nearly all of Argentina's investment claims are related to measures it took during the financial crisis in the early 2000s. Under President Hugo Chavez, the Venezuelan government expropriated many foreign-owned industries, especially in the extractive sector, leading to an explosion of claims. Spain's decision to alter the regulatory framework governing its renewable energy sector also precipitated a great number of investment disputes. Many of the cases faced by Libya relate to the

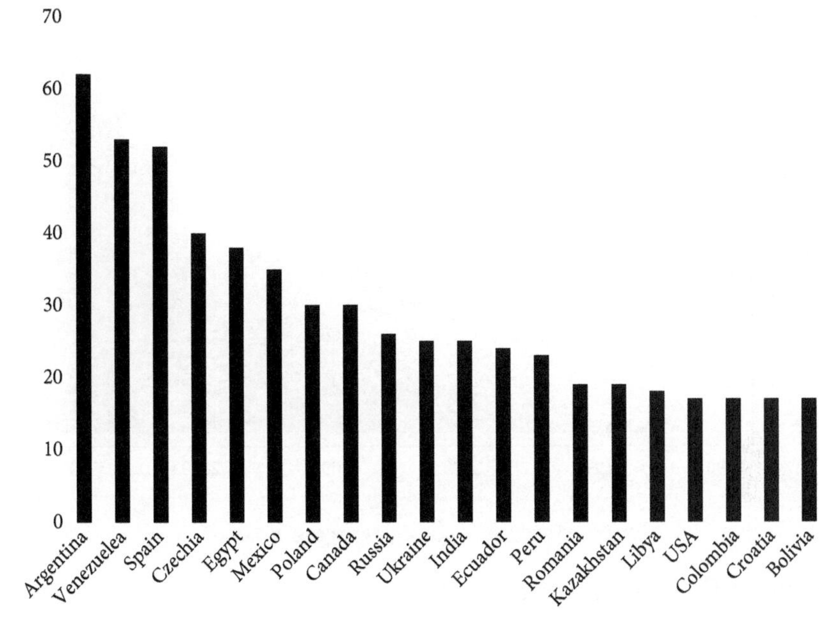

Figure 2.2 Frequent respondent states

civil war in that country. On the other hand, the cases in the remaining countries in this graph cannot be explained by any one cause.

Of note, in particular, is the inclusion of Canada, the United States, and Mexico—the signatories to NAFTA—among the most frequently respondent countries. Canada and the United States, both high-income countries, are not the first countries that come to mind as risky locations for investment. The expectation during the negotiation phase of NAFTA was that its investment protection chapter was for the benefit of US and Canadian investors in less-developed Mexico.[24] However, all three states have, in the end, faced a large number of cases. This rather equal distribution of cases under NAFTA suggests that the traditional rationale for ISDS as creating an additional layer of protection for investors in less stable, developing countries does not necessarily hold up when developed states sign IIAs among themselves. NAFTA cases suggest that either advanced and open democracies are just as likely to take measures which disadvantage investors as developing countries or that investors, once given the opportunity to use ISDS as a tool to pursue their aims, will do so in a much wider variety of situations than may have been predicted during NAFTA's design and negotiation phase.[25]

[24] Jennifer A Heindl, 'Toward a History of NAFTA's Chapter Eleven' (2006) 24 Berkeley Journal of International Law 672.

[25] Indeed, the NAFTA signatories have not been particularly happy with this state of affairs and, during the time this book was written, renegotiated the agreement to greatly restrict the use of ISDS.

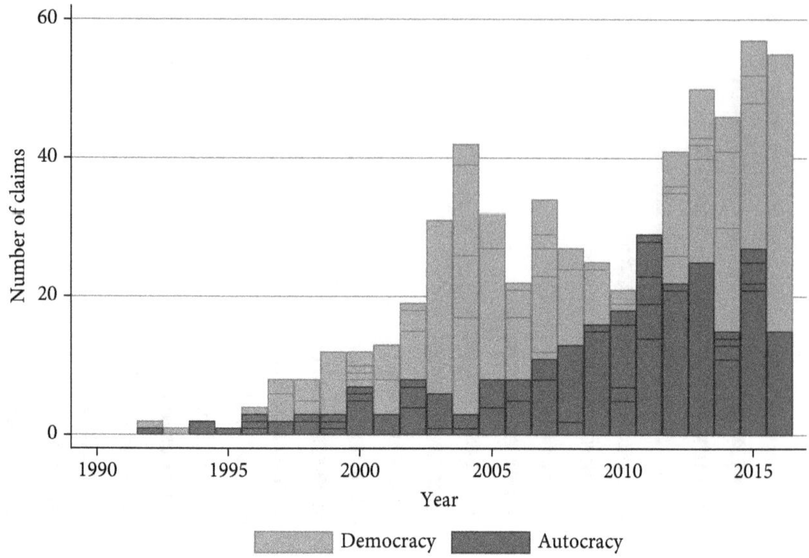

Figure 2.3 Claims by regime type

The distribution of democracies and non-democracies among IIA signatories is also of interest to this project, given the focus on the contribution of domestic-level politics and policymaking to investor–state disputes. As with GDP, the level of democracy is different when looking at all signatories of IIAs or the smaller group of states who have acted as a respondent in an arbitration case. In the general population of IIA signatories, the mean Polity score is 3.6 on a scale ranging from −10 (autocracy) to 10 (full democracy), placing it in the anocracy (neither fully autocratic nor democratic) category. However, in country-years with at least one arbitration case, the Polity score is slightly higher at 5.1. The distribution of claims by regime type can be seen in Figure 2.3. The relationship between democracy and investment arbitration will be discussed at greater length in Chapter 4.

Finally, transition, or formerly state-planned economies are very frequently implicated in investor–state arbitration cases. While they make up only 18 per cent of the country-years in the database, a transition economy is the respondent state in 32 per cent of the cases.

2.4.2 Industries in Investment Arbitration

While investors in a wide range of industries have made claims against states, disputes are highly concentrated in a few sectors, with the highest number of cases involving the extractive industries of oil, gas, and mining. The second largest category is comprised of disputes involving electricity and other energy, which includes the generation and distribution of hydro, coal, wind, solar, geothermal, and nuclear energy. The third largest category is construction, which often involves the building of large infrastructure projects such as highways and dams. Figure 2.4 shows the distribution of arbitration cases across other industries.

The top two industry categories—extractives and energy—present specific challenges to states, and it is unsurprising that they make up the majority of cases of investment arbitration. As will be discussed at greater length in Chapter 4, much has been written about the politics of extractive industries and the relationship between investors and states in this sector. Today, given the capital-intensive nature of mining and oil and gas extraction, these industries are dominated by foreign corporations in developing countries. However, as the extensive literature on the 'obsolescing bargain' and political risk makes clear, foreign investors in extractives are often seen to be especially vulnerable to policy reversal after an investment has been made, given the high sunk costs in any extractive project. Policy change or 'instability' is at the heart of many investor–state disputes, and policy measures such as the introduction of a windfall tax and the refusal to grant an exploitation permit following mining exploration activities have contributed to many investor–state disputes in the extractive sector.

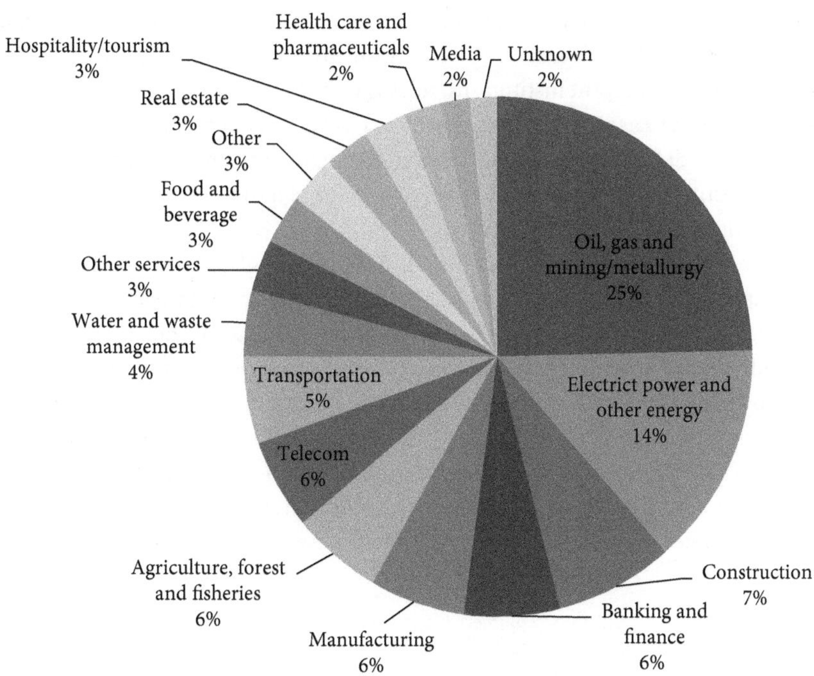

Figure 2.4 Industries in arbitration

On the other hand, energy generation, distribution, and consumption are important areas of national policy as both industrial and household consumers depend on stable and universally accessible sources of energy. In a liberalized energy market, governments must work with investors to achieve this, but the goals of energy companies and the demands imposed on governments by domestic constituents may not always be complementary, which may in turn contribute to investor–state disputes.[26] This dynamic will be discussed at greater length in Chapter 7, which focuses on disputes between Hungary and two foreign electricity generators.

Disputes are spread across other industries fairly equally. As stated earlier, I relied primarily on the categories of sectors used by the World Bank for classifying investor–state disputes by industry. In some cases, however, such as health care and pharmaceuticals, I have disaggregated categories (in this case, the World Bank categorizes pharmaceuticals as 'other industry') in order to highlight some industries that are particularly relevant to public policy.

2.4.3 Domestic Institutions and Types of Measures

The domestic institutions involved in an investor–state dispute are those that have formulated and/or enacted the policy measure(s) to which the investor objects. Therefore, we can derive from this an indication of the domestic interests at stake in these disputes. Not all cases involve only one institution, and therefore for each entry, I coded all relevant institutions, relying on the same data sources mentioned earlier. In some cases, there was significant ambiguity regarding the domestic actors involved; for example, many arbitration documents simply refer to 'regional' or 'local authorities', which makes coding difficult. Figure 2.5 displays the breakdown of domestic institutions.

While of all the domestic institutions listed here the legislature is the single institution most often involved, the majority are administrative or bureaucratic bodies. Indeed, 40 per cent (253) of cases were triggered by measures taken by national-level administrative bodies including the executive, 25 per cent (159) were triggered by legislative measures alone, and 14 per cent (86) were related to judicial decisions.[27] State-owned enterprises, regional/municipal authorities, and banks have also taken measures which have triggered cases, as can be seen in Figure 2.5. The remainder of cases for which enough information was available to code relate to instances in which the state failed to act—for example, failed to protect an

[26] Markus Krajewski, 'The Impact of International Investment Agreements on Energy Regulation' in Christoph Herrmann and Jörg Philipp Terhechte (eds), *European Yearbook of International Economic Law (EYIEL) vol 3* (Springer-Verlag Berlin Heidelberg 2012) 3.

[27] Unfortunately, sufficient information was available for only 636 of the total 892 cases to identify the relevant institutions and measures.

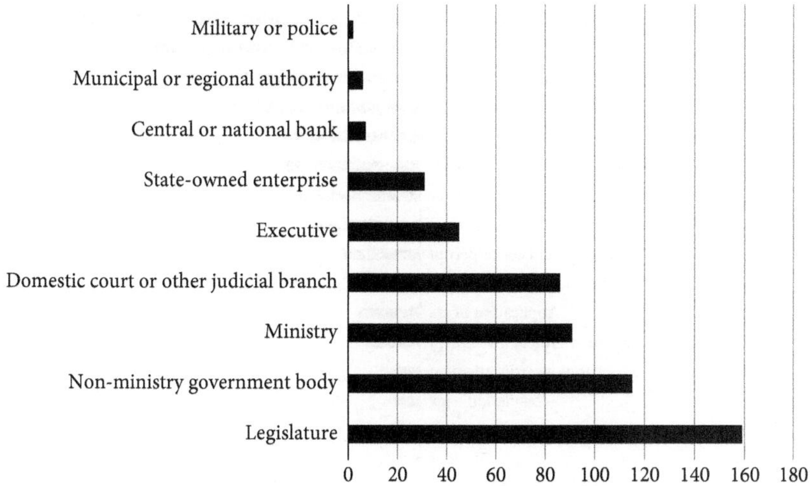

Figure 2.5 Domestic institutions involved in investor–state disputes

investment from physical harm—and therefore cannot be coded as legislative, administrative, or judicial measures *per se*.

A number of interesting patterns emerge when we look at the groupings of measures taken by institution, state, and industry. Slightly less than half of the cases in the legislative category involve Argentina, due to the 'pesofication' law passed by the country's parliament during the financial crisis in 2002. The other respondent countries in this category include Albania, Canada, the Czech Republic, Germany, Hungary, Mexico, Panama Slovak Republic, Spain, the United States, and Venezuela, the majority of which are high-income countries. Therefore, we can see that investors are most frequently challenging legislative measures in developed countries. On the other hand, investor–state disputes in which domestic courts were implicated included a much wider range of respondent states, with high-income countries such as Canada and the United States, but many more developing countries such as Egypt, Laos, India, Jordan, Indonesia, Kazakhstan, Pakistan, and Sri Lanka; judicial measures are more routinely challenged by investors in developing states. Unsurprisingly, cases involving state-owned enterprises were concentrated in disputes with extractive companies (oil, gas, and mining); public utilities (electricity and other energy and waste management); and telecommunications companies.

As stated, for the cases for which sufficient information was available, I further coded the type of measure taken by the state which was challenged by the investor, and the results are displayed in Figure 2.6. The clear majority of cases involve the cancellation of a project, agreement, or licence. Investor–state disputes triggered by this measure span different industries and levels of development but are generally administrative (although a few of these cases also involve judicial decisions).

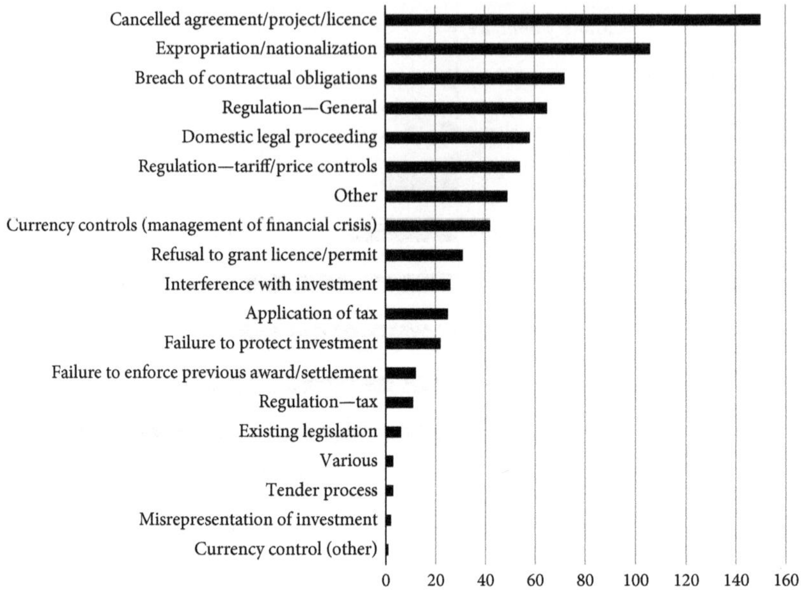

Figure 2.6 Measures

Expropriation of a foreign investment makes up the second largest category of measures taken, although it is important to keep in mind that Venezuelan Hugo Chavez's series of expropriations make up over 25 per cent of these cases. The third most frequent measure is the rather broad category of regulatory change. Included within this category are measures which ban specific industrial activities, ban certain substances (eg pesticides), or other changes to the regulatory framework of an entire industry. Unsurprisingly, the bulk of these are legislative measures, and, with the exception of Egypt's recent change to its minimum wage and Uruguay's imposition of plain packaging on tobacco products, all of the cases which see investors challenging regulatory measures have a developed country as the respondent. Additionally, half of these cases involve electricity or other energy companies, which underscores the public-policy dimension of these disputes.

As I note in the introduction, the measures taken can give a hint at the extent to which the underlying causes of investor–state disputes are related to lack of state capacity or, more simply, a change in preferences toward (a specific) investment. For example, the currency control category is made up primarily of investor–state disputes emerging from the Argentine financial crisis; these cases are therefore clearly connected to the state's inability to respect agreements made with investors previously. Similarly, the category of 'failure to protect investment' generally relates to the inability of the state to provide physical security to an investment, which is also likely connected to state capacity. Finally, the contractual/payment obligations category is more ambiguous, but as Wellhausen notes, at times governments 'have used breach of contracts with foreign firms as a means to supplement budgets in hard times .... Breach in the form of withholding payments can provide a third budgeting option apart from cutting spending or raising taxes from domestic actors.'[28] This suggests that at times contract breaches may be the result of difficult economic circumstances and an unwillingness to take other policy measures to deal with the crisis.

The final question, and what has only been hinted at, is whether most measures which are challenged by investors are aimed at individual investors or entire industries. Unsurprisingly, categories such as the cancellation of an agreement, contractual obligations, or the refusal to grant permits are associated with individual investors or projects, while regulatory changes or currency controls have a broader impact aiming to regulate behaviour universally or within a specific industry. Measures such as expropriations may target only individual investors or an entire industry. Indeed, the majority of measures that lead to arbitration (360 of the total number of cases for which sufficient information was available to code) are aimed at specific investors, while 157 were aimed at the general population or an entire industry. Again, the remaining two per cent of cases refer to those in which the state failed to act, for example, to provide an investor protection against terrorist attacks. Of course, 'specific' measures may nonetheless be associated with much broader policy changes—for example, the cancellation of a mining permit may be part of efforts by the government to put a halt to all mining activity in the country, as is exemplified by the case study of El Salvador presented in Chapter 5. It is therefore difficult, as in the case of the administrative measures, to infer too much from the fact that a measure was targeted at a specific investor.

2.5 Unknown Cases

One major challenge facing researchers of investment arbitration is the confidentiality surrounding many investor–state disputes. Indeed, cases only officially become public with the consent of both parties to the dispute, and even when the existence of a case is made public, the final award may not be published. Therefore, there are two types of unknown cases: the 'known unknowns' in which the incidence of a dispute is made public but the details of the dispute and final award are not; and the 'unknown unknowns'—that is, cases which exist but of which we are completely unaware.

Both types of unknown cases provide challenges for this research. This chapter presents the results of the coding of investor–state arbitration cases but is limited to cases about which a sufficient amount of information can be found; for example,

[28] Rachel L Wellhausen, *The Shield of Nationality: When Governments Break Contracts with Foreign Firms* (Cambridge University Press 2015) 18.

this database excluded cases for which information about the country of origin of the investor, and the type of investment, could not be identified. Therefore, this chapter does not present information about all investor–state disputes that have been made public. However, cases where at least the date of the initiation of arbitration and the respondent state are known do appear in the dataset I use for my statistical analysis in Chapters 3 and 4, as the dependent variable employed there is merely the incidence of arbitration in a given country-year. However, the spectre of 'unknown unknowns' is more troubling here. If there are statistically significant patterns of cases about which no information is made public (eg if certain states routinely do not disclose that they have been taken to arbitration), this may bias the results of the statistical study.

In an attempt to address this issue, I corresponded with a number of investment arbitration experts[29] about the issue of unknown cases and its potential impact on the validity of this study.

There was no clear consensus about the possible number of 'unknown unknowns'. One interviewee said he estimates that completely unknown cases make up about 10 per cent of the total, while another said it could be 'dozens and dozens'. On the other hand, Professor Salacuse countered that the number of completely unknown cases was likely not significant. There was a general agreement that the number of cases about which the existence is totally unknown is likely smaller than the cases for which only the final award remains confidential. This is likely because the existence of arbitration cases often becomes public over time. Indeed, all three agreed that the number of unknown cases is declining as more awards eventually are leaked to the public. In other cases, we are alerted to past arbitrations when either party attempts to enforce or set aside the final award in domestic courts.

In terms of the patterns of the 'unknown unknown' cases, it was suggested that Middle Eastern governments may be more secretive about their investment disputes than others and, more generally, that autocratic states might be more likely to keep awards confidential. However, there is at least one example of an advanced democratic state—the United Kingdom—refusing to release the award of an arbitration case in which it was the respondent.[30] In terms of industries, it was further suggested that cases related to defence/security interests would be more likely to be kept confidential.

Recent research which explains the variation in ICSID awards that are kept confidential or remain secret concludes that cases which involve an investment with

[29] These were: Jeswald Salacuse, investment arbitrator and professor of international law at Tufts University; Howard Mann, former NAFTA negotiator and defence lawyer for the Canadian government, currently legal advisor at the International Institute of Sustainable Development, which advises many developing countries in the negotiation of investment treaties; and Luke Peterson, editor of *IAReporter*, which systematically uncovers and researches investment arbitration cases. These interviews were carried out over e-mail in early 2015.

[30] *Sanchetti v United Kingdom* UNCITRAL.

a particularly long time horizon are more likely to remain secret due to strategic considerations of both parties.[31] It is suggested that investors in these industries may wish to avoid public knowledge of concessions made to host governments in an attempt to keep disadvantageous policies from being adopted by other states. These authors further argue that states that have already experienced numerous arbitration losses, as well as extremely litigious investors, may also be more likely to keep arbitration confidential. Their first claim is of most interest to this project, and the results reinforce their hypothesis—projects with long time horizons, such as infrastructure projects, mining, and oil investments, have the highest probability of being involved in a confidential arbitration. Given the focus on ICSID cases, this study does not immediately shed light on any patterns of 'unknown unknowns'; ICSID publishes the names of the claimant and respondent in all arbitration cases carried out under the auspices of the World Bank. However, it is feasible that the mechanism governing the choice to keep ICSID awards confidential may also be operating in cases under different arbitral rules in which there is no requirement to publicize the case at all; in other words, cases arbitrated under UNCITRAL rules may also be more likely to remain secret when the investment has a particularly long time-horizon. Given the already high number of known cases in the construction and extractive industries, this would suggest that—at least in terms of industry of the investor—the world of unknown cases is not significantly different than the known cases. Of course, this does not give us any clues as to the identity of the respondent states in these cases, which is of greater interest to this project, when it comes to the validity of the statistical results presented here.

2.6 Conclusion

The goal of this chapter was to provide an overview of the universe of known investment arbitration cases, with a focus on the industries and domestic institutions involved and the content and target of the measures taken which ultimately motivated the investor to pursue arbitration. A number of initial findings emerge from this first empirical analysis.

First, middle-income and, increasingly, high-income countries are the most frequent respondents in investment arbitration. This is due primarily to the development of the investment protection regime and global capital flows as most IIAs are signed between capital-importing and capital-exporting countries, and developed countries have not historically signed many IIAs together. Therefore, while overall more investment flows to developed countries, investment covered by an IIA flows primarily into developing—especially middle-income—countries, and these

[31] Emilie Hafner-Burton, Zachary Steinert-Threlkeld, and David Victor, 'Predictability v Flexibility: Transparency of Investor–State Arbitration' (2016) 68 World Politics 413.

countries face greater odds of being to be sued by investors. However, there are some exceptions to this rule—most apparently that of host states within NAFTA and some particularly frequent respondents such as Spain, Poland, and Czechia. While NAFTA's investment chapter was originally meant to protect American and Canadian investors in Mexico, all three signatories have faced a significant number of claims (in fact, all three countries are among the most frequent respondents overall). As was discussed in the introduction, IIAs were designed to protect investors in developing countries, and therefore the initial finding that these disputes are concentrated in developing countries is unsurprising. However, the fact that Canada and the United States are frequent respondents suggests that developed countries are not immune to investment arbitration but instead need only to play host to covered investment to be hit with claims. Moreover, it is at least in part the aforementioned development of the regime that has led to the concentration of disputes among developing countries and not the fact that high-income, liberal democracies do not take measures which investors find objectionable.

This chapter further examined the industries that are most often involved in investor–state disputes and found that it is investments with a significant public policy component—that is, those in extractive industries and electricity and other energy provision—which are among the most frequent claimants. As will be discussed in later chapters, these industries are quite heavily regulated and impact a wide range of stakeholders and interests, and this may contribute to the frequency with which investors in extractives and energy turn to arbitration.

A number of different domestic institutions are involved in these disputes. Legislative bodies—both national and subnational—are the single institution most frequently implicated in these disputes. However, they are outnumbered by a variety of administrative bodies—from national ministries to state-owned enterprises. Interestingly, it appears that disputes in developed countries more frequently involve legislative measures than those in developing countries, while investors are more often challenging judicial measures in developing countries. Administrative measures make up the greatest category and are frequent in all states. The fact that investors are more often challenging administrative rather than legislative measures may serve to weaken some of the arguments against ISDS. Critics of the regime worry that democratic processes are hindered by the existence of investment arbitration, particularly that investors are challenging legislation passed by democratically elected representatives. Proponents of the regime will point to the relatively few legislative measures that have been challenged as proof that the regime instead serves merely to keep in check discriminatory and arbitrary administrative measures. However, this line of argumentation may underestimate the 'legitimacy' of the goals of many administrative measures (while also perhaps overestimating that of legislation in some cases); as will be discussed at greater length in the case studies, it is not the case that administrative policymaking cannot have a significant 'public interest' component. Finally, given what is presumably the far higher rate of administrative than legislative decision-making and policy output generally, it is only logical that these administrative policies and institutions are most often implicated in investor–state disputes.

This chapter has presented broad patterns in the distribution of investor–state disputes in terms of states, industries, and domestic actors involved, and measures taken which are challenged by investors. However, while I have presented some possible explanations for these patterns, elaborating on the possible causal relationships that explains investor–state disputes is the work of the following chapters. The following chapters present two theoretical explanations for the drivers of investor–state arbitration cases and develop hypotheses that are tested using statistical analysis.

3
State Capacity and Investor–State Arbitration

As outlined in the introduction this book is structured around two broad explanations for the emergence of investor–state disputes that culminate in arbitration. The first is that a lack of state or bureaucratic capacity to maintain an investor-friendly environment (whether in general or with regards to a specific investor or investment) causes the emergence of a dispute, while the second is that these arbitral claims are the end result of political cost–benefit calculations made by government actors within the host state.

This chapter examines the argument that cases of investor–state arbitration are caused by a lack of capacity in host states, and in so doing, it draws on two bodies of work. The first is the managerial approach to international law compliance.[1] This approach suggests that states generally intend to uphold their treaty commitments and only violate treaties inadvertently. Violations occur when states face difficult conditions, such as financial crises, that impede compliance or when policymakers do not have sufficient knowledge of treaty obligations or basic bureaucratic capacity to uphold them. This work is not focused solely on states' attempts to comply with investment treaties, instead looking more broadly at the barriers that (primarily, though not exclusively, developing) states face in upholding their international legal commitments. There is, however, work that looks at the need for legal capacity-building in the areas of trade and investment which, as discussed later, supports the claims made by proponents of the managerial approach to compliance.

The second body of work on which this chapter draws is on the role of bounded rationality in the development of the investment treaty regime.[2] Poulsen's central claim is that developing country officials systematically overestimated the economic benefits and discounted the risks of investment treaties, and in some cases were unaware of them altogether, until hit with their first arbitral claim. While the book aims to explain why states signed investment treaties in the first place, Poulsen's work can, I argue, inform our understanding of the causes of arbitral claims as well.

[1] Abrams Chayes and Antonia Handler Chayes, *The New Sovereignty. Compliance with International Regulatory Agreements* (Harvard University Press 1995).
[2] Lauge Poulsen, *Bounded Rationality and Economic Diplomacy. The Politics of Investment Treaties in Developing Countries* (Cambridge University Press 2015).

The Political Economy of Investment Arbitration. Zoe Phillips Williams, Oxford University Press. © Zoe Phillips Williams 2022.
DOI: 10.1093/oso/9780198865940.003.0003

It is worth reiterating at this stage that while this and Chapter 4 draw on theories of compliance to help explain the emergence of investor–state disputes that lead to arbitration, I do not make the claim that the existence of a dispute itself amounts to a breach of an investment treaty. However, these theories of compliance centre domestic political processes and institutions, which clearly play a part in creating conditions that give rise to investor–state disputes, whether or not the actions of the state are found by the tribunal to ultimately constitute a breach.

This chapter subsequently develops specific hypotheses based on this theorizing. It then introduces the data set used here and in Chapter 4. Finally, using this data set, I test the hypotheses developed below.

3.1 The Managerial Approach to Compliance

One strand of literature which takes seriously the role bureaucratic capacity in international cooperation and (non-)compliance is the managerial approach to compliance. This work stands in opposition to the realist view, according to which compliance is only likely when it is in the material interest of treaty signatories. This view, according to proponents of the managerial approach, fails to account for the widespread normative commitment to, and empirical reality of, treaty compliance.[3] Instead of cost–benefit calculations, they suggest, non-compliance or treaty breach is generally inadvertent—due to a lack of bureaucratic capacity, the inflexibility of agreements to accommodate changes over time, and the vagueness of treaty provisions.[4]

Chayes and Chayes argue that lack of capacity to comply is a problem most acutely faced by developing countries, which are more likely to lack technical and bureaucratic resources.[5] Higher levels of administrative capacity require the education and training of personnel, access to sufficient information, and the requisite mandate or authority to implement compliant policies, without which 'rule-consistent behaviour may simply not be within a signatory's choice set'.[6] Moreover, a lack of political capacity may threaten compliance when a government is unable to ensure that the behaviour of domestic state and non-state actors (such as businesses) is compliant with international standards or its own legislation.[7]

More recent studies provide empirical evidence to support the importance of state capacity for the respect of international agreements in the areas of human

[3] Abrams Chayes and Antonia Chayes, 'On Compliance' (1993) 47 International Organization 175.

[4] Chayes and Chayes, *The New Sovereignty Compliance* (n 1); Chayes and Chayes, 'On Compliance' (n 3).

[5] Chayes and Chayes, *The New Sovereignty Compliance* (n 1).

[6] Beth Simmons, 'Compliance with International Agreements' (1998) 1 Annual Review of Political Science 75, 83.

[7] Jonas Tallberg, 'Paths to Compliance: Enforcement, Management, and the European Union' (2002) 56 International Organization 609.

rights treaties[8] and environmental protection standards drawing on the managerial approach.[9] Cao and Ward operationalize capacity as the ratio between predicted and actual tax extraction, with predicted levels as a function of gross domestic product (GDP) per capita.[10] On the other hand, Cole uses index measures of bureaucratic effectiveness, military involvement in the government, and control of corruption. Despite these differing measures, both studies find that higher levels of state capacity are positively correlated with states' compliance with international law.

3.2 State Capacity and Investment Law

Many treaties and other international agreements in areas such as environment, human rights, trade, and investment aim to regulate state behaviour at the sub-national level, thus limiting the set of policies a state can pursue while remaining compliant. This again underscores the role that domestic institutions play in the formulation and application of domestic policies as it is ultimately sub-national actors whose behaviour is circumscribed by these treaties. Here, I examine the possibility that cases of investor–state arbitration are caused primarily by a lack of capacity of these key domestic institutions, extending the concept of capacity to include host state awareness of the investment protection regime, and therefore discuss the implications of recent work on bounded rationality and bilateral investment treaty (BIT) diffusion.[11] This latter work contributes significantly to our understanding of the role of 'the capacities and limits of human decision-making' in policymaking.[12]

Indeed, the ability of an international regime to genuinely constrain domestic policy space is first and foremost dependent upon the relevant state actors' awareness and understanding of the regime in question and only subsequently its capacity to ensure that relevant state actors and institutions uphold these commitments. Work on legal capacity in the area of economic law highlights the importance of the individual policymakers' expertise and awareness of relevant information. In their discussion of legal capacity in the domain of World Trade Organization (WTO) law, Bohanes and Vidal-Leon define 'narrow capacity' as

[8] Wade M Cole, 'Mind the Gap: State Capacity and the Implementation of Human Rights Treaties' (2015) 69 International Organization 405.

[9] Xun Cao and Hugh Ward, 'Winning Coalition Size, State Capacity, and Time Horizons: An Application of Modified Selectorate Theory to Environmental Public Goods Provision' (2015) 59 International Studies Quarterly 264.

[10] ibid.

[11] Emma Aisbett and Lauge Poulsen, 'When the Claim Hits: Bilateral Investment Treaties and Bounded Rational Learning' (2013) 65 World Politics 1; Poulsen (n 2).

[12] Poulsen (n 2) 17.

'technical expertise' in a specific area of international law.[13] High levels of turnover in government bureaucracies and broader resource constraints make developing country governments less likely to have this expertise in house or to be able to retain outside counsel to defend their interests within the investment protection regime.[14]

The development of the investment protection regime, as well as the treaties themselves, may exacerbate any underlying weaknesses in a treaty signatory's bureaucracy when it comes to avoiding arbitral claims. First, investment treaties, while not overly complex, do contain vague standards allowing for very broad application. For example, the fair and equitable treatment (FET) provision, included in most international investment agreements (IIAs) is expressed in arguably 'abstract and subjective terms', and its exact meaning has been interpreted differently by various arbitral tribunals.[15] This makes anticipating which state decisions may breach broad treaty provisions like FET difficult. Moreover, despite not being overly complex treaties on an individual basis, the way in which IIAs have historically been negotiated has created a complex web of treaty obligations for developing states. Specifically, because developing states have tended to accept, with little negotiation, the model BITs of their developed country treaty partners, they are left with a 'a haphazard patchwork of investment obligations creating complex compliance challenges'.[16] Finally, as investment treaties give broad consent to arbitration for any covered investor, bureaucrats and policymakers in a wide range of sectors and agencies must be aware of their treaty obligations to avoid decisions or behaviour that may trigger arbitration.[17] Rather than assume that these individuals have access to all relevant information and can easily weigh the costs and benefits of any decision, a bounded-rationality framework suggests that policymakers are 'subject to cognitive constraints and often prone to mistakes'.[18] This may increase the difficulty of avoiding the emergence of investor–state disputes and subsequent arbitral claims.

Even if they are aware of their treaty obligations, the vagueness of treaty language, the complex and overlapping web of treaty obligations, and the treaties'

[13] Jan Bohanes and Christian Vidal-Leon, 'The ACWL's Contribution to Enhancing Legal Capacity of Developing Countries' in Joost Pauwelyn and Mengyi Wang (eds), *Building Legal Capacity for a More Inclusive Globalization: Barriers to and Best Practices for Integrating Developing Countries into Global Economic Regulation* (The Graduate Institute, Geneva 2019).

[14] Anna Joubin-Bret, 'Establishing an International Advisory Center on Investment Disputes' in Joost Pauwelyn and Mengyi Wang (eds), *Building Legal Capacity for a More Inclusive Globalization: Barriers to and Best Practices for Integrating Developing Countries into Global Economic Regulation* (The Graduate Institute, Geneva 2019).

[15] Jean Kalicki and Suzana Medeiros, 'Fair, Equitable and Ambiguous: What is Fair and Equitable Treatment in International Investment Law?' (2007) 22 ICSID Review 24.

[16] J Anthony Vanduzer, 'Can International Investment Agreements Be Instruments for Sustainable Development? Systemic Capacity Challenges for Sustainable Development' in Joost Pauwelyn and Mengyi Wang (eds), *Building Legal Capacity for a More Inclusive Globalization: Barriers to and Best Practices for Integrating Developing Countries into Global Economic Regulation* (The Graduate Institute, Geneva 2019) 32.

[17] Joubin-Bret (n 14).

[18] Poulsen (n 2) 17.

far reach into domestic policy space pose a challenge for policymakers. However, Poulsen suggests that bureaucratic awareness of the implications of signing IIAs has in fact historically been low, which could in turn further increase the likelihood of state behaviour that provokes an arbitral claim. Building on survey data of BIT negotiators and other relevant stakeholders, Aisbett and Poulsen find that:

> practically all officials noted that they were unaware of the far-reaching scope and implications of BITs during the 1990s, when the treaties proliferated ... few realized that the treaties had such a considerable reach and were enforceable not just in principle but also in fact.[19]

Indeed, it was not until states faced their first arbitration claims that policymakers understood the full extent of the costs of signing a BIT, which for most states did not occur until the turn of the twenty-first century, when BIT claims took off. Until that time, states that had never faced an arbitration claim underestimated the impact of the regime.

Although focused on explaining the reasons that states have continued to sign BITs despite the significant costs associated with arbitration, this argument complicates the straightforward explanation for the emergence of investor–state disputes based on cost–benefit calculations. In the context of specific disputes, work on bounded rationality suggests the possibility that states, or the sub-state agencies that took the offending measures, may not be making cost–benefit decisions regarding specific investment projects with a full understanding of the potential costs provided by IIA provisions and would thus take different measures regarding foreign investment if they were acting with full information. However, while this might explain earlier investor–state disputes, or the first disputes faced by an individual state, as time goes on and states face more claims, the assumption that states do not understand the consequences of these agreements may become less likely, barring a total lack of institutional memory. On the other hand, if bureaucracies are subject to high rates of staff turnover, institutional memory may be short enough that this lack of awareness continues to be a problem even after states are hit with an initial claim.

Ultimately, this focus on capacity and bounded rationality of decision-makers underscores the importance not just of electoral institutions and domestic interests in determining foreign policy choices, but also that of capable modern bureaucracies. Indeed,

> in complex, industrial societies, the technicality and complexity of many policy matters, the need for continuing control of matters, and legislators' lack of time and information have caused the delegation of much discretionary authority, which often includes extensive rule-making power, to administrative agencies.

[19] Aisbett and Poulsen (n 11) 11.

> Consequently, agencies make many decisions and issue many rules that have far-reaching political and policy consequences.[20]

While administrative agencies may have limited influence on broad policy direction, they do have significant input into the details of policy measures and how they are put into practice. When administrative decisions are made in a policy area that is additionally governed by an international regime, these agencies must consider both the policy goals set out by elected officials and the obligations of the state under the relevant agreement—a situation which may prove quite challenging, especially in developing states with weaker bureaucracies that lack personnel with specific issue-area expertise.[21] Therefore, it is not only pressure from domestic interest groups but also the capacity of the relevant institutions themselves that has an impact on policy outcomes; if administrative and regulatory bodies do not have the required information or capacity to integrate international rules into the formulation of policy, this will also affect a state's policymaking with regards to its international commitments.[22]

As was discussed in Chapter 2, bureaucratic or administrative state agencies are often implicated in investor–state disputes, and a focus on state capacity may also help to explain the concentration of investor–state arbitration cases in lower levels of GDP as these states face challenges related to corruption, political instability, and government capacity.[23] Adopting this line of argument, Freeman finds that investor–state disputes are caused primarily by a lack of capacity to control corruption and supply adequate private property protection to investors. He therefore concludes that his findings lend empirical support to the managerial school's understanding of compliance.[24]

Of course, the relevance of bureaucratic capacity extends beyond the protection of property rights when it comes to explaining the causes of investor–state disputes. As discussed in Chapter 2, investor–state disputes arise in a wide range of issue areas from environmental protection, to the granting of telecommunication licences, to financial regulation. Therefore, the state's lack of bureaucratic capacity may contribute to investor–state disputes not only due to its inability to secure the property rights of the investor or to maintain open investment policies but also due to its inability to effectively regulate the industry as a whole in which the investment takes place. The case study of the dispute between El Salvador and the

20 James E Anderson, *Public Policy Making: An Introduction* (Houghton Mifflin 2003) 53.

21 Poulsen (n 2).

22 Chayes and Chayes, *The New Sovereignty Compliance* (n 1).

23 Niels Keijzer, Florian Kraetke, and Jeske van Seters, 'Meeting in the Middle? Challenges and Opportunities for EU Cooperation with Middle-Income Countries' (2013) 140 European Center for Development Policy Management Discussion Paper.

24 Nathan W Freeman, 'Domestic Institutions, Capacity Limitations, and Compliance Costs: Host Country Determinants of Investment Treaty Arbitrations, 1987–2007' (2013) 39 International Interactions 54.

mining company Pacific Rim, presented in Chapter 5, underscores this point—in this case, the lack of bureaucratic capacity to effectively regulate the mining industry in El Salvador played a large part in the eventual decisions to take policy measures which triggered the dispute.

In addition, lack of bureaucratic capacity may be the result of temporal shocks, such as economic crises, which in turn may diminish or require the shift of state resources which can alter the conditions faced by investors and may trigger arbitral claims. Here, the anecdotal evidence is quite strong. Argentina's 2001 economic crisis famously provoked dozens of claims due to cancelled contracts and currency measures. Similarly, in the wake of the Eurozone crisis, Spain made changes to its renewable energy legislative framework that has led to at least forty investment claims, while bank bailouts in Cyprus and Greece have also triggered disputes. At the time of writing, some observers are calling for the investment community to take measures to reduce the risk that states are hit with claims due to measures taken to mitigate the COVID-19 pandemic.[25]

3.3 Hypotheses

As the managerial approach to explaining compliance with international agreements suggests, states may violate treaties because they do not have the capacity to comply. In the case of investment treaties, this implies not a deliberate change in policy due to a considered shift in state preferences towards an investor or investment project but instead policy change that either inadvertently provides investors with the basis of a claim due to a lack of understanding of treaty obligations or that is taken during a crisis. A state may also fail to live up to its commitment to protect investors through a lack of capacity to act rather than the enactment of a specific policy measure.[26] In this section, I develop hypotheses related to this explanation for the emergence of investor–state disputes that go to arbitration.

The first is simply that, all else being equal, developing countries, having fewer economic resources devoted to the ministries and agencies which are relevant to maintaining a stable and favourable climate for investors, are more likely to be involved in disputes with investors. Thus, I will test the hypothesis that:

- H_1: GDP per capita will be negatively correlated with the likelihood of an arbitral claim.

[25] Nathalie Bernasconi-Osterwalder, Sarah Brewin, and Nyaguthii Maina, 'Protecting against Investor–State Claims Amidst COVID-19: A Call to Action for Governments' (2020) International Institute for Sustainable Development <https://www.iisd.org/articles/policy-analysis/protecting-against-investor-state-claims-amidst-covid-19-call-action> accessed 9 April 2022.

[26] For instance, failure to provide an investment with full protection and security, in the case of *Ampal-American Israel Corporation v Arab Republic of Egypt*, ICSID Case No ARB/12/11.

More specifically, a strong bureaucracy and legal counsel should help governments take into account their commitments to international investors when developing new policies and thus avoid conflicts with investors.[27] Therefore,

- H_2: government effectiveness will be correlated with a lower likelihood of an arbitral claim.

Similarly, Freeman finds that a state's institutional capacity to protect investors' rights is a strong determinant of arbitral claims.[28] Specifically, he finds that measures which indicate a government's control of corruption and a strong rule of law are negatively correlated with the likelihood of an investor–state dispute. Therefore, I will also test the hypothesis that

- H_3: state capacity to control corruption will be negatively correlated with the likelihood of a dispute.

More generally, an institutional awareness of IIAs and state commitments to attract investors' rights may be linked to institutional capacity and have an impact on the likelihood of an investor–state dispute. As was discussed earlier, the purpose of IIAs is often assumed to be increasing the ability of states to make credible commitments to protect foreign investment.[29] However, the effectiveness of these agreements (or, from a more critical point of view, the likelihood that they create regulatory chill) depends on policymakers' awareness of the provisions of the agreement and the ability to incorporate this into the policymaking process. A survey of BIT negotiators and other relevant stakeholders casts some doubt on whether IIAs have an impact on domestic policymaking prior to the initiation of an arbitration by an investor as awareness of these agreements among relevant actors in host states was found to be very low.[30] Instead, their research suggests that IIAs were negotiated without full knowledge of the implications of the treaty on the part of the negotiators (generally officials from foreign affairs and trade offices), let alone the civil servants in the array of ministries and agencies which are often involved in investor–state disputes. In a similar study, it was found that Canadian policymakers in a variety of fields do not routinely consider IIA obligations when formulating new policies.[31] However, this may change over time; as states face more arbitration cases

[27] Some states are trying to combat policymaking patterns that lead to investor–state disputes by setting up dispute prevention institutions such as Peru's Coordination and Response System for International Investment Disputes.

[28] Freeman (n 24).

[29] Jonathan Bonnitcha, 'Investment Treaties and Transition from Authoritarian Rule' (2014) 15 The Journal of World Investment & Trade 965>.

[30] Aisbett and Poulsen (n 11).

[31] Christine Côté, 'The Chilling Effect of Globalization: A Look at the Impact of International Investment Agreements on National Regulatory Autonomy in the Areas of Health, Safety and the

and become more familiar with the implications of the agreements, they should be able to make more calculated decisions in the face of competing domestic and investor demands. On the other hand, states that have faced few or no arbitral claims (and/or have very weak administrative capacity) may unknowingly take measures which have the potential to trigger investor–state disputes.[32] Of course, this assertion requires the caveat that it will always be difficult for state actors to predict whether taking a policy measure will result in an investor making a claim. It is likely quite challenging for states to predict when an investor will choose to send a notice of intent to arbitrate and then follow through with the arbitration process as a number of factors on the 'investor side of the equation' may have an impact on their choice to do so. However, it is possible that past arbitration experience may enable a state to better predict what measures will be negatively viewed by investors:

- H_4: states' previous experience with arbitral claims, an indicator of awareness of the regime, may decrease the likelihood of an investor–state dispute, as procedures are put into place to ensure that new policies comply with provisions in IIAs.

Finally, as discussed, temporal shocks such as economic crises may have an impact on foreign investors. The notable number of investor–state disputes that arose from the Argentine financial crisis clearly demonstrates that investors' interests can be threatened by deterioration of a host country's economic condition. On the other hand, economic crises may lessen the likelihood of an expropriation event and increase market-friendly policies in general.[33] This is due in part to greater host sensitivity regarding reputational damage during a crisis. Furthermore, economic crises make the host state more vulnerable to measures such as the suspension of bilateral or multilateral foreign aid, which could result from a turn towards less market-friendly practices. In this case, political actors external to the state act as a constraint on domestic policy towards foreign investors.[34] Therefore, while there is no clear consensus at this stage, I will test the hypothesis that

- H_5: incidence of financial crises will be positively correlated with arbitral claims.

Environment' (PhD thesis, London School of Economics and Political Science 2014) <http://etheses.lse.ac.uk/897/> accessed 9 April 2022.

[32] This pattern can be seen on a more macro level as some states that have faced a large number of arbitration claims withdraw from ICSID and terminate their BITs. On the other hand, institutional learning may be hampered with high bureaucratic turnover, a problem in many developing countries: Poulsen (n 2).

[33] Nathan M Jensen, Noel P Johnston, and Chia-yi Lee, 'Crisis and Contract Breach: The Domestic and International Determinants of Expropriation' (2020) 15 Review of International Organizations 869.

[34] Of course, expropriation is only one of many types of measures that may be detrimental to an investor, and other types of measures, such as currency controls, may be more likely in times of crisis.

3.4 Empirical Analysis

Here, I present the results of a regression analysis focusing on the relationship between a number of variables related to state capacity, identified in the hypotheses presented, and the incidence of an arbitral claim in a given country-year.

This analysis is based on an original data set of treaty-based and domestic law-based investor–state arbitration claims, including International Centre for Settlement of Investment Disputes (ICSID) cases which take place at the World Bank's dispute settlement centre and United Nations Commission on International Trade Law (UNCITRAL) and other arbitral rule cases which take place at a range of arbitral institutions such as the Permanent Court of Arbitration, the International Chamber of Commerce, the Stockholm Chamber of Commerce, and the Moscow Chamber of Commerce. These disputes were collected from numerous sources, including ICSID and the United Nations Conference on Trade and Development's (UNCTAD's) online databases of investor–state arbitration cases and *Investment Arbitration Reporter*, an online news outlet dedicated to covering investor–state disputes. Finally, the data set was checked against the recently released PluriCourt Investment Treaty Arbitration Database (PITAD) of investment claims. The country-year panel data contains data for 139 countries from 1990 to 2016 and contains 837 disputes. Included in the data set are the states which have signed and ratified at least one IIA, making them potential respondent states. Figure 3.1 shows the total number of cases per year by income level.

3.4.1 Estimation Strategy and Variables

The dependent variable is a count variable, representing the number of investment arbitration claims initiated in a given country-year. As can be seen in Figure 3.2 in the appendix, the variable is over-dispersed and characterized by a high number of zeros; most country-years do not see a claim. This has dictated the estimation strategy. Rather than using a standard count model such as a negative binomial regression or a Poisson, I have elected to use a zero-inflated negative binomial regression (ZINB). ZINB models are useful when more than one underlying process may be generating zeros, with the first process modelled by a logistic regression and the second by a count model.[35] Substantively, in the present case, we have two groups of states. In the first group are states that face no real risk of being hit with an arbitral claim; these are traditional home states of investment in treaty dyads. In the second group are states that face a non-zero risk of facing a claim; host states in treaty dyads, which traditionally have been developing countries.

[35] J Scott Long and Jeremy Freese, 'Predicted Probabilities for Count Models' (2001) 1 The Stata Journal 51.

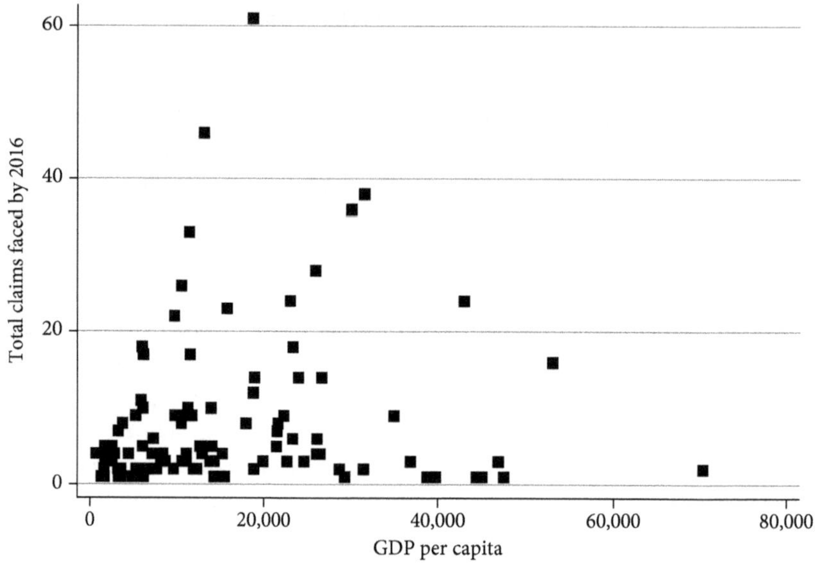

Figure 3.1 Number of cases by income level

The control variables (see Tables 3.2 and 3.3 in the appendix) are used to model the logistic regression stage of the ZINB model.[36] What variables might allocate a state into the zero-risk group? The minimum conditions to be at risk of facing a claim are, of course, ratifying an investment treaty and playing host to investment from a treaty partner state. Unfortunately, dyadic foreign direct investment (FDI) data is not available for enough country-years to construct a 'treaty-protected FDI' variable. Instead, I have created a dummy variable which indicates whether a state has ratified an investment treaty signed with another state which falls into the category of the top ten most frequent home states of investor claimants.[37] This variable, I argue, is a useful proxy for modelling the home state/host state distinction because while these home states sign a large number of investment treaties, they do not, with the exception of the North American Free Trade Agreement/United States–Mexico–Canada (NAFTA/USMCA) signatories, sign investment treaties with each other. Furthermore, while they may in fact host significant levels of foreign investment, this is not investment that to date has been covered by an investment treaty. For example, the Netherlands, one of the most frequent home states of investors, has signed over a hundred investment treaties, mostly with developing or transition economies. As these countries have not historically exported capital to the Netherlands,

[36] Descriptive statistics and correlations can be found in Tables 3.2 and 3.3 in the appendix.

[37] The United States, Netherlands, United Kingdom, Germany, Spain, France, Canada, Luxembourg Italy, and Turkey

signing these treaties has not meaningfully increased the Netherlands' risk, to date, of being hit with a claim. The same can be said for other frequent home states, such as Switzerland, Germany, and the United Kingdom. At the same time, this variable does allow for NAFTA/USMCA signatories Canada and the United States to be possible host states in our model, which a variable based on development level might not capture.

In the count model, I also include variables which represent the minimum condition for an investment claim to occur: FDI stock and the number of IIAs in force. As discussed earlier, the first two variables represent the minimum conditions necessary for a state to face an investment claim at all, and the more treaties ratified, and greater amount of FDI hosted, the more potential claims a state could face. I also control for the year, as investor awareness and thus use of investor–state dispute settlement (ISDS) has increased over time.

The explanatory variables included relate to levels of state capacity and awareness of the regime. First, GDP per capita[38] provides an indication of the administrative capacity of the host state. I then include two indicators of the economic 'health' of the host state: GDP growth[39] and a dummy variable indicating whether a state was experiencing a banking, sovereign debt, or currency crisis in a given year.[40] I lag this variable one and two years to account for the time for any measures taken during the crisis to (a) affect an investor; and (b) then the investor to subsequently turn to arbitration. I also include several 'good governance' indicators. The first of these is the Rule of Law index from the Varieties of Democracy project, which measures 'To what extent are laws transparently, independently, predictably, impartially, and equally enforced, and to what extent do the actions of government officials comply with the law?' on a 0–1 scale, with higher numbers indicating greater rule of law.[41] In addition to the V-Dem indicator, I use the World Bank Governance Indicators (WBGI) for control of corruption and government effectiveness as secondary indicators of state capacity.[42] Finally, to account for state awareness of the regime, I use a cumulative count of claims faced by each state. I also include this variable squared to account for a possible non-linear relationship between the number of claims faced and the likelihood of a claim.

[38] Michael Coppedge and others, 'V-DEM 10 Codebook—March 2020' (2020) <https://www.v-dem.net/en/data/data-version-10> accessed 22 February 2022.

[39] ibid.

[40] Data file to accompany paper 'Systemic Banking Crises Database II' (Laeven & Valencia 2020) <https://www.imf.org/en/Publications/WP/Issues/2018/09/14/Systemic-Banking-Crises-Revisited-46232> accessed 9 April 2022.

[41] Coppedge and others (n 38).

[42] Daniel Kaufmann and Aart Kraay, 'Worldwide Governance Indicators' <http://info.worldbank.org/governance/wgi/> accessed 9 April 2022.

Table 3.1 Factor change in expected number of claims

	Factor change	*p* Value	SD
Treaties	1.027	0.000	24.5
Year	1.70	0.000	7.218
(Log) GDP per capita	0.0	1.000	1.18
Two-lag fin crisis	1.95	0.001	0.27
Control of corruption	−1.37	0.023	1.04
Govt effectiveness	−1.33	0.043	0.98

3.4.2 Results

This section presents the results of the regression analysis, the full output of which can be found in Table 3.4 in the appendix.

Model 1 includes only the control variables and GDP per capita. The control variables themselves merit discussion. First, both the year and the number of treaties ratified by the state have a positive, statistically significant relationship with the dependent variable, the count of claims faced by a state in a given year. As Table 3.1 shows, a one-unit increase in the number of treaties ratified increases the number of expected claims by a factor of 1.027 (or 2.7 per cent).

For its part, however, a one-unit increase of logged GDP per capita has no impact on the number of expected claims. As can be seen in Table 3.4 in the appendix, GDP growth similarly has no impact on the dependent variable. Neither the existence of a financial crisis in the same year nor with a lag of one year has a statistically significant relationship with the number of claims. However, the financial crisis dummy, lagged two years, increases the number of expected claims by a factor of 1.95. As discussed earlier, this lag reasonably may account for the time for a measure in response to a crisis to be taken and for the investor to respond.

Two of the three of the governance indicators also have a statistically significant relationship with the dependent variable when controlling for GDP per capita. While the V-Dem Rule of Law index does not significantly decrease the number of expected claims, as Table 3.1 shows, both the WBGI Control of Corruption and Government Effectiveness decrease the number of expected claims by 1.37 and 1.33, respectively.[43]

Finally, there does appear to be a non-linear relationship between number of previous claims faced by a state and the expected count of claims in a given

[43] These variables are, unsurprisingly, highly correlated. Moreover, these indicators have many more years for which data is missing than the V-Dem indicators and thus may be a less reliable measure.

country-year. However, as can be seen in Table 3.4 in the appendix, the magnitude of the effect is quite small—almost none for the quadratic term—suggesting that this is not a clear indication of state learning leading to an increase in 'capacity' to prevent investment claims.

3.5 Conclusion

This chapter began with a discussion of broad arguments about the impact of capacity on states' ability to uphold their international commitments, drawing on the managerial approach to compliance. While this is not a study of compliance in a strict sense, the managerial approach provides a useful starting place for understanding why a state might take measures which can reasonably be construed by a foreign investor as being a possible breach of an investment treaty. Subsequently, the chapter narrows its focus to the ways in which state capacity (or lack thereof) may condition a state's propensity for being involved in disputes with foreign investors, looking at both work on bounded rationality—which argues that lack of understanding of investment treaties and arbitration led states to sign investment treaties—and more policy-orientated research on state capacity in the areas of trade and investment law. Drawing on this theorizing, I develop hypotheses that are subsequently tested using regression analysis.

This empirical analysis indicates that the 'state capacity' explanation for the emergence of investment claims has some merit. Both of the selected World Bank's indicators of governance quality are negatively correlated with the number of expected claims, with states enjoying higher governance quality being hit with fewer claims (although it is notable that V-Dem's Rule of Law index, which both covers more years than the WBGIs and seems particularly well calibrated to capture governance issues related to investor–state disputes, does not have a statistically significant relationship with the number of expected claims).[44] The temporal shock of a financial crisis also, unsurprisingly given the anecdotal evidence discussed here, increases the number of expected claims.

At the same time, previous experience with investment arbitration does not appear to have a measurable effect on the number of expected claims, at least if measured by a running total of previous claims. There are several potential explanations for this. The first is that this may simply not be a good measure of state 'awareness' that is actionable, in terms of improving relations with investors or better understanding their legal obligations to investors. On the other hand, experience with past claims may not increase awareness of treaty obligations or increase a state's ability to prevent disputes if there is high turnover within state agencies, leading to

[44] These indicators additionally differ on the source of data, which is surveys for the WBGI and expert assessment for the V-Dem indicators.

little institutional memory and capacity-building. Finally, it may be that awareness does nothing to prevent arbitral claims if investor–state disputes are frequently arising from measures taken as a result of political cost–benefit calculations that ultimately favour some domestic group over the foreign investor. I expand on this idea in Chapter 4. Finally, each additional treaty signed by a state increases the likelihood of an arbitration, pointing to the importance of the 'investor side of the equation' when trying to explain the emergence of investor–state disputes.

However, it is arguably unrealistic to expect that disputes will arise solely because of lack of capacity on the one hand, or political considerations on the other. Indeed, as the case studies in Chapters 5–7 demonstrate, a lack of capacity—for example, at the moment of entry of an investment—can condition or determine political decisions taken later which may provoke an investment claim.

4

Domestic Politics and Investor–State Arbitration

This chapter examines the contribution of domestic interest groups and political institutions to the emergence of investor–state disputes. Building on the empirical findings presented in Chapter 2 (eg that investor–state arbitrations are clustered in highly politicized industries such as extractives and utilities), this chapter puts forth an argument about the linkages between the domestic politics of the host state and the emergence of investor–state disputes which culminate in arbitration. As in Chapter 3, it subsequently develops specific hypotheses based on this theorizing and provides a statistical analysis based on an original data set of cases of investment arbitration. This chapter finds significant evidence that links domestic political contestation—for example, elections or protest movements that revolve around investment-related issues—with the likelihood of an investment arbitration. In other words, democratic institutions—particularly the ability of domestic audiences to hold elected officials accountable for decisions which negatively impact them—can lead to the emergence of these types of disputes.

Very little work in international political economy (IPE) looks specifically at the underlying drivers of cases of investor–state arbitration. Therefore, this chapter discusses a number of strands of literature which examine investor–state relations more generally, including literature on the determinants of foreign direct investment inflows; factors contributing to political risk and the obsolescing bargain; and finally, work in political economy which explains incidences of expropriation and/or makes a link between foreign direct investment (FDI) inflows and regime type. Going beyond a focus on formal institutions, I also discuss the role of domestic non-state actors' (eg citizens, social movements, communities) preferences towards FDI in investor–state disputes—a relationship that is often determined at least in part by the impact of investment on these groups. Therefore, I present a number of reasons why different domestic groups might oppose investment projects, drawing in part on the patterns presented in Chapter 2.

4.1 Creating an Investment-Friendly Climate

Host state institutions matter to foreign investors. As discussed in Chapter 3, states with weak institutional capacity may have difficulty upholding

The Political Economy of Investment Arbitration. Zoe Phillips Williams, Oxford University Press.
DOI: 10.1093/oso/9780198865940.003.0004

treaty commitments, which can subsequently trigger investor–state arbitration cases. However, arguments about host state capacity and international law tend to rest on the assumption that breaches of commitments are inadvertent, which may not be the case. Here, I focus more broadly on the ways in which host state institutions may contribute to (un)favourable conditions for foreign investors, while subsequent sections develop arguments about why states may purposively take measures which have detrimental effects on investors, even if harming the investor is not the specific goal.

While features of a host state, such as the presence of specific natural resources or large domestic markets, may be of most importance to investors, a set of policies must be in place to ensure that investors are able to take advantage of them. One way of indicating to foreign investors that investment protection is a domestic priority is to sign international agreements to that effect—bilateral investment treaties (BITs) and other international investment agreements (IIAs) are, in theory, designed to help states make credible commitments regarding the protection of investors' rights. This commitment—that states will ensure an investment-friendly environment after an investor has sunk significant resources into their territory (see discussion of obsolescing bargain in section 4.2)—should theoretically help to attract investment. However, the body of work on the effectiveness of BITs in increasing FDI inflows is characterized primarily by a lack of consensus; the empirical evidence, including, as discussed later, surveys of investors, that IIAs do in fact increase inward FDI flows remains inconclusive at best.[1] Indeed, given the widespread adoption of BITs and other IIAs, creating, at least on paper, similarly investment-friendly environments, it is unsurprising that country-specific economic attributes and domestic policies remain of central importance to investors.[2]

But beyond the impact of specific policies on FDI, policy *stability* is of central importance to investors; as 'physical investment is partly irreversible, rational behaviour by the private sector calls for withholding investment until much of the residual uncertainty regarding the success of the reforms is eliminated'.[3] When significant resources have been sunk into an investment project and policies relevant to the investment are changed, investors can lose considerable sums. Domestic political institutions, therefore, also play a role in attracting and protecting FDI by making it easier for foreign firms to reap locational benefits, and perhaps most importantly, by ensuring policy stability.

[1] For a comprehensive overview, see Jonathan Bonnitcha, Lauge Poulsen, and Michael Waibel, *The Political Economy of the Investment Treaty Regime* (Oxford University Press 2017).

[2] Matthias Busse and Carsten Hefeker, 'Political Risk, Institutions and Foreign Direct Investment' (2005) 23 European Journal of Political Economy 397.

[3] Dani Rodrik, 'Policy Uncertainty and Private Investment in Developing Countries' (1991) 36 Journal of Development Economics 229, 231.

4.2 Understanding Political Risk

While investments may become unprofitable due to changes in the economic conditions, FDI is also vulnerable to changes in policy preferences or broader political climate. This is the essence of the obsolescing bargain theory of company–state relations, which assumes that the balance of power between firms and states evolves over time.[4] Prior to the entry of a multinational enterprise (MNE) to a host country, the government is in a weaker bargaining position as it attempts to attract FDI, presumably at the expense of other competing countries, by offering investment incentives. However, once the investment has been made and is costly to withdraw, the balance of power supposedly shifts in favour of the state, which can then alter the policy framework in which the investment was made.[5] This vulnerability to changing political winds can be understood as 'political risk'.

According to Kobrin, political risk concerns 'the impact of events which are political in the sense that they arise from power or authority relationships and which affect (or have the potential to affect) the firm's operations'.[6] Risk may be categorized in a number of ways. For example, the impact of political events may be on a macro scale, where all FDI in a country is negatively affected, regardless of home country or sector. Alternatively, political processes may create 'micro risk', where only particular firms or sectors experience an adverse impact from a political decision.[7] Additionally, political events may impact either the firm's ownership or its operations. In the case of the former, assets may be forcibly expropriated, while in the latter case, measures are taken which constrain profitability without destroying the enterprise, for example, through the levying of higher taxes.[8]

Expropriation, the forced divestment of equity ownership, has typically been the most highly visible manifestation of political risk and has attracted the most scholarly attention.[9] Expropriation was relatively common in the 1960s and early 1970s, as post-colonial states took control of foreign-owned businesses, especially in strategic industries such as oil, gas, and mining, due in part to a political emphasis on independence. Expropriation became rarer in the 1980s, as the number of projects left available for expropriation declined and managerial and administrative ability improved, allowing governments to exert influence over foreign investors

[4] Lorraine Eden, 'Bringing the Firm Back In: Multinationals in International Political Economy' (1991) 20 Millennium—Journal of International Studies 197.

[5] ibid.

[6] Stephen J Kobrin, 'Political Risk: A Review and Reconsideration' (1979) 10 Journal of International Business Studies 67.

[7] Stephen J Kobrin, 'Political Risk: A Review and Reconsideration' (1979) 10 Journal of International Business Studies 67; Stephen Kobrin, 'Expropriation as an Attempt to Control Foreign Firms in LDCs: Trends from 1960 to 1979' (1984) 28 International Studies Quarterly 329; Imad A Moosa, *Foreign Direct Investment. Theory, Evidence and Practice* (Palgrave 2002).

[8] Kobrin, 'Expropriation as an Attempt to Control Foreign Firms in LDCs' (n 7).

[9] Quan Li, 'Democracy, Autocracy, and Expropriation of Foreign Direct Investment', *International Studies Association Annual Meeting* (2005).

by less direct means and as developing countries became more dependent on FDI.[10] The number of expropriations increased slightly in the 2000s, again primarily in the extractive industry, particularly in socialist-leaning Bolivia, Ecuador, and Venezuela. However, most expropriations today can be defined, at least in the context of investor–state disputes, as indirect, or 'creeping expropriations', where governments 'use selective enforcement of laws to expropriate the assets or income streams of firms'.[11]

Of course, while expropriation is likely the worst-case scenario for foreign investors, firms can experience adverse effects from a wide range of government actions and policies. For example, recent surveys of investors conducted by the World Bank find that adverse regulatory changes, breach of contract, and transfer and convertibility restrictions are the most common sources of conflict with governments.[12] These findings echo Kobrin's prescient argument that political risk would come primarily in the form of threats to operations rather than ownership.[13]

Kobrin and Krasner further argue that the oft-cited problems of political instability and violence are not what pose the biggest threats to FDI. While sudden regime changes may cause upheaval, they do not necessarily entail the adoption of anti-FDI attitudes. In fact, they argue that policies negatively affecting investors are likely 'to result from the regular functioning of the political process owing to losses or gains in the regime's power or to changes in the character and power of the opposition or of interest groups'.[14] If this observation holds, political risk is not only a feature of authoritarian or unstable states with unrestrained executives but may also routinely affect investors in relatively well-functioning, politically stable, democratic host states. However, as will be discussed in section 4.3, this is not the conclusion drawn in the bulk of the IPE literature on regime type and FDI.

4.3 The Domestic Politics of Investment

IPE scholars have paid considerable attention to the relationship between regime type and levels of risk for foreign investors, as well as FDI openness. Much of this

[10] Kobrin, 'Expropriation as an Attempt to Control Foreign Firms in LDCs' (n 7); Sonal S Pandya, 'Democratization and Foreign Direct Investment Liberalization, 1970–2000' (2014) 58 International Studies Quarterly 475; Roberto Echandi, Ivan Nimac, and Dongwook Chun, 'Retention and Expansion of Foreign Direct Investment: Political Risk and Policy Responses' (2019) <http://documents1.worldbank.org/curated/en/387801576142339003/pdf/Political-Risk-and-Policy-Responses.pdf> accessed 23 February 2022.

[11] Nathan M Jensen, Noel P Johnston, and Chia-yi Lee, 'Crisis and Contract Breach: The Domestic and International Determinants of Expropriation' (2020) 15 Review of International Organizations 869.

[12] Echandi, Nimic, and Chun (n 10).

[13] Kobrin, 'Expropriation as an Attempt to Control Foreign Firms in LDCs' (n 7).

[14] Stephen J Kobrin and Stephen Krasner, *Managing Political Risk Assessment: Strategic Response to Environmental Change* (University of California Press 1982) 39.

work concludes that democracy and FDI friendliness go hand in hand.[15] However, while this literature provides a useful starting point for the present investigation, it makes significant assumptions, both when it comes to the benefits of FDI for the host state and the reasons states might have to take measures which are detrimental to foreign investors, which obscure the ways in which democratic political contestation may contribute to investor–state disputes.

Commonly identified features of democracy—transparency, the rule of law (particularly regarding property protection), and relatively predictable policymaking—are found to both attract and protect FDI.[16] As discussed in section 4.2, beginning with the obsolescing bargain, much of the IPE work on domestic institutions and investment has focused on nationalization or expropriation as its dependent variable.[17] This work concludes that in the absence of democratic checks, or veto players, state actors are freer to breach contracts made with investors and expropriate, capturing revenue beyond what the state could hope to gain through taxation.[18] Indeed, the existence of higher numbers of 'veto players' is often employed to explain democratic regimes' respect for property rights.[19] Veto players are individuals or groups in a political system whose consent is necessary for a change to the status quo, and 'as the number of veto players in a political system increases, policy stability increases'.[20] In democracies, institutions such as the legislature and independent judiciaries serve to limit the ability of the executive to engage in opportunistic policymaking, thereby 'making the government's commitment to private property credible, reducing expropriation risks for foreign investors, and attracting more FDI'.[21] Effective veto players thus contribute to policy stability and the ability of governments to make credible commitments. This in turn has been linked to economic growth,[22] currency

[15] Nathan M Jensen, *Nation-States and the Multinational Corporation: A Political Economy of Foreign Direct Investment* (Princeton University Press 2008); Carl Knutsen, 'Democracy, Dictatorship and Protection of Property Rights' (2011) 47 Journal of Development Studies 164; Li (n 9); Pandya, 'Democratization and Foreign Direct Investment Liberalization' (n 10).

[16] Busse and Hefeker (n 2); Jensen, *Nation-States and the Multinational Corporation* (n 15); Knutsen (n 15); Li (n 9); Pandya, 'Democratization and Foreign Direct Investment Liberalization' (n 10).

[17] Raymond Vernon, *Sovereignty at Bay: The Multinational Spread of US Enterprises* (Routledge 1971).

[18] Jo Jakobsen, 'Does Democracy Moderate the Obsolescing Bargain Mechanism?' (2006) 15 Transnational Corporations 67; Jensen, *Nation-States and the Multinational Corporation* (n 15); Li (n 9); Vernon (n 17).

[19] Witold J Henisz and Edward D Mansfield, 'Votes and Vetoes: The Political Determinants of Commercial Openness' (2006) 50 International Studies Quarterly 189; Douglass C North and Barry R Weingast, 'Constitutions and Commitment: The Evolution of Institutions Governing Public Choice in Seventeenth-Century England' (1989) XLIX Journal of Economic History 803; Stephen Weymouth, 'Political Institutions and Property Rights: Veto Players and Foreign Exchange Commitments in 127 Countries' (2010) 44 Comparative Political Studies 211 <http://cps.sagepub.com/cgi/doi/10.1177/0010414010382629> accessed 23 February 2022.

[20] George Tsebelis, 'Veto Players and Institutional Analysis' (2000) 13 Governance 441, 446.

[21] Li (n 9) 3.

[22] Antonio Fatás and Ilian Mihov, 'Policy Volatility, Institutions, and Economic Growth' (2013) 95 The Review of Economics and Statistics 362.

stability,[23] and commercial openness,[24] as well as increased FDI flows. However, as Graham, Johnston, and Kingsley argue, this relationship does not hold if we look at a broader set of policies rather than just expropriation.[25] Specifically, they find that governments facing significant constraints by veto players are able to engage in taking from foreign investors via transfer restrictions. The low political salience of such a policy, they argue, allows governments, which would face sanction from domestic actors if they engaged in expropriation, to place restrictions on foreign investors without consequence. This suggests that domestic constituents also play a role in investor protection.

Indeed, 'domestic audiences' are also thought to act as an enforcement mechanism for investors' rights; for example, with their preferences for property rights protection, voters may act as a constraint on the executive, decreasing the political gains to be had from expropriation.[26] Jensen in particular focuses on the so-called 'audience costs' of investment-unfriendly policies, arguing that, as with international treaties, if governments 'make agreements with multinational firms, and renege on contracts after the investment has been made, democratic leaders may suffer electoral costs'.[27] Firms will withdraw their investment in the face of unfavourable government action, and it is assumed that domestic audiences in favour of FDI will punish elected officials accordingly. Therefore, 'leadership turnover in democratic systems (or the potential for leadership turnover) can be associated with more market-friendly policies for multinationals'.[28]

However, like the literature on expropriation, this work focuses solely on rent-seeking behaviour and does not engage with the possibility that the role of audience costs may also be moderated by the underlying goal of the policy measure. In this way, it echoes the suspicion of public pressure in the area of economic policymaking held by the post-war ordoliberals described by Slobodian.[29] This distinction is important when trying to explain the relationship between domestic political institutions and investor–state arbitration. The occurrence of an arbitral claim indicates that an investor perceives a policy measure taken by the state to be detrimental to its interests but does not necessarily indicate rent-seeking behaviour on the part of the state.

Indeed, as Aisbett and Bonnitcha argue, investment treaties seek to regulate two distinct dynamics of investor–state relations—the time-inconsistency problem (ie the obsolescing bargain) and the problem of 'undervaluing' investors' interests

[23] Weymouth (n 19).
[24] Henisz and Mansfield (n 19).
[25] Benjamin AT Graham, Noel P Johnston and Allison F Kingsley, 'How Sovereigns Steal: Political Constraints and the Choice Between Transfer and Expropriation Rents', *International Political Economy Society Annual Meeting* (2012).
[26] Knutsen (n 15).
[27] Jensen, *Nation-States and the Multinational Corporation* (n 15) 31.
[28] ibid.
[29] Quinn Slobodian, *The Globalists: The End of Empire and the Birth of Neoliberalism* (Harvard University Press 2018).

when responding to new information.[30] The first, reneging on commitments a state has made to investors, is well documented by the literature on the obsolescing bargain. However, the second problem is more complex; as the authors understand it, new information

> encompasses a diverse range of changing circumstances, including new knowledge about an investment's impacts, changes in commodity prices and underlying shifts in citizens' political preferences. All these events may encourage a state to change the way it regulates foreign investment, to the detriment of an investor.[31]

When responding to this new information, a state might be motivated to take actions that harm investors' interests for gains which are not rent-seeking per se but rather have political, or even social, welfare aims.[32] In this case, domestic political institutions, and as I argue later, democratic audiences in particular, will play a different role in moderating states' relationship with foreign investors.

Of course, domestic audiences may mobilize for pro-FDI policies (and thus push state actors to treat investors more favourably) if they believe they will benefit from investment projects. This is the underlying assumption of much of the work on FDI and democracy and is not an unreasonable one—FDI has the potential to contribute to the development of the host state in a variety of ways, including an increase in employment, technology transfer, and greater government revenues.[33] In particular, the resulting increase in demand for employment is considered an important link between democracy and FDI-friendly policies as democratic politicians, who are particularly incentivized to make policies which benefit a large selectorate, will welcome foreign investors in an attempt to boost employment.[34] Relying on similar findings regarding FDI and employment generation, Pinto argues that left-wing governments are more open to FDI as they depend on the support of labour, rather than domestic capital, to maintain power.[35] Thus, it would appear that because democratic governments depend on mass support, they will pass pro-FDI policies in an attempt to curry the favour of labour rather than the much smaller group of local business elites competing with inward FDI. The inverse also appears to be true, with governments enjoying the support of right-wing,

[30] Emma Aisbett and Jonathan Bonnitcha, 'Compensation under Investment Treaties—as if Host State Interests Mattered' (2018) UNSW Law Research Series 18 <http://www5.austlii.edu.au/au/journals/UNSWLRS/2018/80.pdf> accessed 20 April 2022.

[31] ibid 3.

[32] While largely ignored in the IPE literature on foreign investment, this understanding of state action is widely held by investment lawyers and arbitrators. Treaty provisions such as 'fair and equitable treatment' cast a wide net to encompass precisely this type of state action.

[33] Jensen, *Nation-States and the Multinational Corporation* (n 15).

[34] Sonal S Pandya, 'Political Economy of Foreign Direct Investment: Globalized Production in the Twenty-First Century.' (2016) 19 Annual Review of Political Science 455.

[35] Pablo M Pinto, *Partisan Investment in the Global Economy* (Cambridge University Press 2013).

conservative, or nationalist electoral bases favouring domestic businesses and engaging in anti-FDI policies.[36]

However, many of these studies focus on manufacturing FDI, which tends to have employment-generating effects.[37] They ignore the more ambiguous impact on host state populations of other types of FDI such as resource-seeking investment and the privatization of formerly state-owned utilities.[38] FDI into some sectors has a greater potential to generate negative externalities for host state populations, and unsurprisingly, it is investors in these sectors that are most frequently involved in investment arbitration. Indeed, along with the results of the qualitative coding presented in Chapter 2, recent work on the investment treaty regime finds that, in fact, investors are challenging a wide array of host state policy measures, many of which can be categorized, as mentioned earlier, as regulatory responses to new information.[39] Investors have challenged broad environmental, health, and labour policies as well as more targeted measures such as the restriction of specific investment activities posing harm to environmental and human health.[40] Moreover, as Pelc argues, investors may use arbitration strategically to ward off regulation in both the immediate context and in other states considering similar policy measures.[41] Taken together, these findings suggest that investors are not just using arbitration to protect themselves from rent-seeking behaviour from states, and thus domestic institutions may not always constrain states from behaviour which cause investors to turn to arbitration. If claimants are indeed challenging state measures taken in pursuit of popular policy goals, domestic actors may instead push states into conflict with these investors.

4.3.1 The Impact of the FDI on Domestic Interest Groups and Investment Arbitration

Given that investment arbitration cases are not triggered only by outright expropriation or other attempts at rent-seeking by the state, what is the relationship

36 Jo Jakobsen and Tor G Jakobsen, 'Economic Nationalism and FDI: The Impact of Public Opinion on Foreign Direct Investment in Emerging Markets, 1990–2005' (2011) 6 Society and Business Review 61.

37 Pandya, 'Democratization and Foreign Direct Investment Liberalization' (n 10); Pandya, 'Political Economy of Foreign Direct Investment' (n 34).

38 Sarah Bauerle Danzman, 'Contracting with Whom? The Differential Effects of Investment Treaties on FDI' (2016) 42 International Interactions 452; Alison E Post, *Foreign and Domestic Investment in Argentina* (Cambridge University Press 2014).

39 Aisbett and Bonnitcha (n 30).

40 Kyla Tienhaara, *The Expropriation of Environmental Governance: Protecting Foreign Investors at the Expense of Public Policy* (Cambridge University Press 2009); Beth Simmons, 'Bargaining over BITs, Arbitrating Awards: The Regime for Protection and Promotion of International Investment' (2013) 66 World Politics 12, 28; Mavluda Sattorova, *The Impact of Investment Treaty Law on Host States* (Hart Publishing 2018); Aisbett and Bonnitcha (n 30).

41 Krzysztof J Pelc, 'What Explains the Low Success Rate of Investor–State Disputes?' (2017) 71 International Organization 559.

between democratic 'audiences' and arbitration? Arguably, democratic audiences in the signatory states of IIAs cannot be relied upon to hold government actors accountable for investment-friendly behaviour. Instead, domestic audiences may provide an incentive for policymakers to take measures which are subsequently challenged by investors before arbitral tribunals.

Much of the literature on domestic institutions and treaty compliance, which provides a useful starting point for this analysis (despite our focus not being on strict treaty compliance *per se*), finds that democratic audiences act as an enforcement mechanism, holding governments accountable to their international commitments.[42] While the incidence of an arbitration does not in itself indicate that an investment treaty was breached, domestic audiences may nonetheless pressurize states to minimize behaviour that *may* result in the finding of a breach, due to a preference for treaty compliance rather than any specific sentiment toward FDI, and thus reduce the likelihood of the emergence of an investor–state dispute.

Others argue that for domestic audiences to be able enforce their government's treaty commitments, they must both be aware of, and feel they benefit from, the commitments their government has made.[43] However, as Poulsen thoroughly documents in his work on developing countries and IIAs, the signing and ratification of the majority of IIAs were relatively 'under-the-radar', low-salience events to the extent that many host state government officials were unaware of their treaty commitments until the first time that an investor initiated arbitration proceedings against them.[44] Moreover, there is little evidence that these treaties were signed because of a domestic demand for greater commitments to investment protection; rather, the pressure generally came from 'above'—from home state governments, international organizations such as the United Nations Conference on Trade and Development (UNCTAD), or specific actors within host state bureaucracies.[45] Thus, it is unlikely that domestic audiences in host states would act as a force which generally favours investment treaty compliant behaviour based on their knowledge of, and support for, the treaties themselves and a general desire to hold their governments accountable to commitments made.

[42] Kurt T Gaubatz, 'Democratic States and Commitment in International Relations' (1996) 50 International Organization 109; Edward D Mansfield, Helen V. Milner, and B Peter Rosendorff, 'Why Democracies Cooperate More: Electoral Control and International Trade Agreements' (2002) 56 International Organization 477; James D Fearon, 'Domestic Politics, Foreign Policy, and Theories of International Relations' (1998) 1 Annual Review of Political Science 289; Beth Simmons, 'Treaty Compliance and Violation' (2010) 13 Annual Review of Political Science 273.

[43] Stephen Chaudoin, 'Audience Features and the Strategic Timing of Trade Disputes' (2014) 68 International Organization 877; Michael Tomz, 'Democratic Default: Domestic Audiences and Compliance with International Agreements', *Annual Meeting of the American Political Science Association* (2002); Stephanie J Rickard, 'A Non-Tariff Protectionist Bias in Majoritarian Politics: Government Subsidies and Electoral Institutions' (2012) 56 International Studies Quarterly 777.

[44] Lauge Poulsen, *Bounded Rationality and Economic Diplomacy. The Politics of Investment Treaties in Developing Countries* (Cambridge University Press 2015).

[45] ibid.

Of course, voters may not be aware of their government's treaty commitments but still prefer that the state treat (foreign) investors well. As discussed earlier, this is often attributed to FDI's employment-generating effects as well as to a general preference for respect for property rights. However, these studies assume that FDI is consistently employment-generating and does not create externalities which cause domestic audiences to evaluate the presence of foreign investors more negatively.[46] Thinking more broadly about the impact of different types of investment on populations in the host state, however, suggests that the relationship between democracy and investment protection may not be so straightforward. In short, domestic audiences may not act as a bulwark protecting the rights of foreign investors if they do not believe the investment itself benefits them.

Instead, the issue of investment protection often becomes quite salient for domestic audiences but in ways which may increase the likelihood of the emergence rather than avoidance of a dispute with a foreign investor. As we saw in Chapter 2, investor–state arbitration is concentrated in a handful of industries—namely extractives (oil, gas, and mining) and electricity and other energy generation and distribution. Water, waste management, and telecommunications investors are also frequent claimants.[47] These are often considered 'strategic' industries, which in many countries were at one time state-owned and which still include higher levels of state participation. Thus, while domestic business in these sectors may be affected by the entrance of foreign firms, there may also be numerous government actors with an interest in these investments. The most powerful stakeholders involved in these disputes may be domestic competitors or government officials with an interest in extracting rents from foreign investors.

Additionally, these industries are often highly salient for broader interest groups and citizens in general, and foreign investment in both the extractive and utilities sectors can be politically contentious. In particular, investment projects which generate negative externalities for local populations are likely to provoke anti-FDI sentiment. The most obvious example of this is investment in the extractive industries (oil, gas, and mining). Extractive industry investments have a direct environmental impact on those living in the vicinity of the project; open-pit mining routinely leaches chemicals such as arsenic and cyanide into groundwater, while drilling can cause oil spills such as those which have had devastating impacts on communities in the Amazon basin, the Gulf of Mexico, and the Niger Delta.[48] Mining and oil investments also contribute to higher levels of social conflict and the destruction of traditional livelihoods such as subsistence farming in surrounding areas.[49]

46 Pandya, 'Democratization and Foreign Direct Investment Liberalizaton' (n 10); Pinto (n 35).

47 UNCTAD, 'Investment Policy Hub' <http://investmentpolicyhub.unctad.org/ISDS/FilterByCountry> accessed 23 February 2022.

48 Anne-Emanuelle Birn, Leah Shipton, and Ted Schrecker, 'Canadian Mining and Ill Health in Latin America: A Call to Action' [2018] Canadian Journal of Public Health 18.

49 Rachel Davis and Daniel Franks, 'Costs of Company–Community Conflict in the Extractive Sector' (2014) Shift Project, Corporate Responsibility Initiative, Harvard Kennedy School ; Paul Haslam

In the face of these impacts, domestic groups often put pressure on governments to take measures which are subsequently challenged by investors. For example, in Mongolia, a public debate about the role of mining for national development led the government to the passage of legislation which implemented a windfall tax, which subsequently provoked a mining investor to turn to arbitration.[50] In both Italy and Canada, popular opposition has led to the passage of legislation which bans gas extraction in specific regions, policy decisions which were later challenged by investors.[51] In Peru, Colombia, and El Salvador, mass anti-mining protests driven by concerns over environmental degradation led to a reversal of government support for mining and the cancellation of specific projects. The investors behind these projects subsequently turned to arbitration.[52]

In addition to extractive industry activity, foreign investment in infrastructure projects and utilities—water and waste management, household energy and telecommunications—is frequently politically contentious, particularly when the privatization of public services leads to foreign acquisitions of water, gas, and electricity utilities.[53] When the status quo is changed, voters may punish incumbents, and governments fear being saddled with the blame for removing a programme that benefits voters. If privatization leads to higher utilities prices or reduced access, domestic actors may pressurize governments to take compensatory measures which shift the burden onto investors or push for re-nationalization of key services.[54] Here again, there are numerous examples of pressure from domestic audiences contributing to the formation of policies that are later challenged by investors. In Hungary, debate in both parliament and the media about end-user energy prices contributed to the cancellation of long-term power purchase agreements, a decision which provoked at least two arbitration cases.[55] More recently in Colombia, government actions following the complaints of energy consumers regarding levels of service led a Spanish investor to pursue arbitration.[56] Famously,

and Nasser Ary Tanimoune, 'The Determinants of Social Conflict in the Latin American Mining Sector: New Evidence with Quantitative Data' (2016) 78 World Development 401.

50 *Sergei Paushok, CJSC Golden East Company and CJSC Vostokneftegaz Company v The Government of Mongolia*, UNCITRAL.

51 *Rockhopper Italia S.p.A., Rockhopper Mediterranean Ltd, and Rockhopper Exploration plc v. Italian Republic*, ICSID Case No ARB/17/14; *Lone Pine Resources Inc v The Government of Canada*, ICSID Case No UNCT/15/2.

52 *Bear Creek Mining Corporation v Republic of Peru*, ICSID Case No ARB/14/21; *Pac Rim Cayman LLC v Republic of El Salvador*, ICSID Case No ARB/09/12; *Gran Colombia Gold Corp v Republic of Colombia*, ICSID Case No ARB/18/23; *Cosigo Resources, Ltd, Cosigo Resources Sucursal Colombia, Tobie Mining and Energy, Inc v Republic of Colombia*, UNCITRAL.

53 *Bear Creek Mining Corporation v Republic of Peru*, ICSID Case No ARB/14/21; *Pac Rim Cayman LLC v Republic of El Salvador*, ICSID Case N

54 Bauerle Danzman (n 38).

55 *AES Summit Generation Limited and AES-Tisza Erömü Kft v The Republic of Hungary*, ICSID Case No ARB/07/22; *Electrabel SA v Republic of Hungary*, ICSID Case No ARB/07/19.

56 *Gas Natural Fenosa Electricidad Colombia SL and Gas Natural SDG SA v Republic of Colombia*, ICSID Case No UNCT/18/1.

the privatization of the water delivery system in Cochabamba, Bolivia led to mass protests known as the 'water wars'. In reaction, Bechtel, the multinational behind the project, turned to arbitration against the state.[57]

Aside from the specific industry of the investment, the historical context of a state may contribute to its relations with foreign investors, shaping the preferences of the population towards FDI and making these types of investor–state disputes, which are at their core distributional conflicts, more likely. The early scholarly focus on expropriation was due in large part to the effect of colonialism and subsequent independence on the propensity of a state to expropriate.[58] Similar dynamics reappeared in the early 2000s in some Latin American countries, with the widespread nationalization of key industries.

However, other historical experiences may have an impact on investor–state relations as well. Transition economies—that is, formerly state-planned economies—are very frequently the respondents in arbitration cases, which may be explained in part by the higher levels of corruption in a number of these countries.[59] However, they may also be more often faced with competing international and domestic pressures. For example, policies which have privatized formerly public services such as water, gas, and electricity have been met with resistance from populations who had previously enjoyed universal access.[60] As Salacuse notes, the economic liberalization that was undertaken by most countries in the 1980s privileged investors' rights, which 'may have led foreign investors to undertake their investment with high and perhaps unrealistic expectations about their importance to the country and their status in it'.[61] The subsequent disappointment of these expectations (eg when privatization efforts meet domestic resistance to higher prices) may lead to more frequent investor–state disputes. Moreover, as Muchlinksi notes with regard to the Czech Republic (and which can be said of a number of transition economies, at least in Europe), 'a complex series of hitherto distinct regulatory fields—foreign investment, privatisation and competition—and the distinct levels of Czech national and European supranational laws, are coming together into an integrated web of standards'.[62] This alone may create a situation in which investors are disadvantaged by regulatory confusion. A number of cases in which the respondent

[57] *Aguas del Tunari v Bolivia*, ICSID Case No ARB/02/3.

[58] Kobrin, 'Expropriation as an Attempt to Control Foreign Firms in LDCs' (n 7).

[59] The mean control of corruption score for countries in my dataset is −0.347 for transition economies and 0.086 for non-transition economies, with lower scores indicating higher levels of corruption.

[60] Markus Krajewski, 'The Impact of International Investment Agreements on Energy Regulation' in Christoph Herrmann and Jörg Philipp Terhechte (eds), *European Yearbook of International Economic Law (EYIEL) vol 3* (Springer-Verlag Berlin Heidelberg 2012) 3.

[61] Jeswald W Salacuse, 'Explanations for the Increased Recourse to Treaty-Based Investment Dispute Settlement: Resolving the Struggle of Life against Form?' in Karl P Sauvant (ed), *Appeals Mechanism in International Investment Dispute* (Oxford University Press 2008) 23.

[62] Peter T Muchlinski, 'A Case of Czech Beer: Competition and in the Transitional Economies Competitiveness' (1996) 59 Modern Law Review 658, 659.

states argue that regulatory changes were made in order to comply with European Union (EU) law suggest this possibility.[63]

More recently, nationalist or 'new right' governments in former Soviet states, such as Hungary and Poland, have reacted to anti-foreign investment sentiment of their citizens, engaging in policies restricting FDI and promoting local business.[64] This fits with earlier finds that right-leaning populations tend to support anti-FDI, economic nationalist policies.[65]

Therefore, investment protection may become highly salient for domestic audiences, leading to pressure on government actors to take measures detrimental to the interests of foreign investors. The diffuse benefits of FDI for domestic populations through a larger tax base, increased demand for employment, and technological spill over are unlikely to be associated with a specific investment project (save by the direct employees). However, if a project negatively impacts groups in the host state, particularly when this impact relates to livelihood issues such as the ability to continue to engage in traditional economic activities or access to essential services, these are likely to be more immediately salient and thus increase the likelihood of mobilization against specific investment projects.

As these examples of investor–state disputes indicate, this 'democratic pressure' may take a number of forms, lending empirical support to Cotula's argument that investment law can intersect with both 'rules-based' and 'action-based' conceptions of democracy.[66] With regard to the former, elected representatives may react to concerns raised by constituents about a specific investment activity and pass legislation that addresses the issue. Particularly in the context of elections, officials may take measures, or commit to taking measures, which are detrimental to foreign investors at the behest of potential voters. These may be legislative acts but, as the case study later indicates, administrative measures may also be taken in response to voter mobilization. Finally, referenda may also be used by citizens to demand policies that are detrimental to investors.[67] However, as Cotula argues, action-based theories of democracy which emphasize grassroots contestation and mobilization, based on civic rights to freedom of expression and assembly, are also relevant when trying to understand the relationship between investment law and democracy.[68] Indeed, as the examples cited and the case studies discussed in

[63] *Eastern Sugar B.V. (Netherlands) v Czech Republic UNCITRAL SC No. 088/2004*; *Electrabel SA v Republic of Hungary* ICSID Case No. ARB/07/19 (n 56); *Ioan Micula, Viorel Micula v Romania*, ICSID Case No ARB/05/20.

[64] Roger Schoenman, 'What Happens When the Party is Over? The Impact of New Right Parties in Government on FDI Regulation' 1.

[65] Jakobsen and Jakobsen (n 36).

[66] Lorenzo Cotula, 'Democracy and International Investment Law' (2017) 30 Leiden Journal of International Law 351.

[67] Indeed, recent referenda in Colombia and Italy have triggered arbitration claims brought by mining and oil companies.

[68] Cotula (n 67).

the next chapters indicate, civil society groups, non-governmental organizations (NGOs) and unions are also frequently involved in mobilizing against investors, and government representatives may react to this type of popular pressure by taking measures which are subsequently challenged by investors.

Therefore, while an initial bargain between a state and a foreign investor can be said to have 'obsolesced', this is not necessarily because the state is motivated to expropriate or otherwise 'take' from the investor. Instead, states may be facing new information about the impact of an investment—particularly a negative impact on domestic actors—and may adjust their policies accordingly, thus triggering the first stage in the process leading to investment arbitration described earlier.

What about the state's choice to attempt a negotiated settlement or proceed with arbitration? My primary goal here is to identify the political dynamics underlying the measures challenged by investors, and an in-depth investigation of this third stage is beyond the scope of this chapter. However, we may be able to infer that democratic audience costs play a crucial role at this final stage. Indeed, in her work on the domestic politics of World Trade Organization (WTO) disputes,[69] Davis makes a similar argument, finding that states undertake this highly visible action to assure important domestic constituencies that they are working to defend their interests in the international trading system. It may be that similar mechanisms are at work in investor–state arbitration. Given the formal steps that lead to arbitration, we can infer that relevant policymakers are ultimately making cost–benefit calculations regarding the choice to go through the arbitration process or offer a negotiated settlement once they have been formally notified of a claim. Indeed, if an issue related to foreign investment is sufficiently salient for domestic audiences to agitate for a specific measure, this audience may additionally pressurize the state not to 'back down' in the face of the threat of arbitration.

In summary, I argue that democratic institutions—particularly the ability of domestic audiences to hold elected officials accountable for decisions which negatively impact them—can, under certain conditions, put pressure on policymakers to take actions which harm investors' interests, and which in turn may trigger an investment arbitration. This relationship is most likely to hold when a specific investment project becomes salient to domestic constituencies due to the negative externalities of that investment. This in turn is most likely to be the case for investment projects that, while creating no increase in demand for labour, do engender negative impacts on the livelihood of domestic constituents.

Of course, given the heterogeneity of state conduct that triggers investor–state disputes which culminate in arbitration, I do not argue that democratic contestation

[69] Christina Davis, Why Adjudicate? Enforcing Trade Rules in the WTO (Princeton University Press 2013).

is the sole cause of the phenomenon. Both rent-seeking and policymaking in the face of new information are behaviours that investment treaties aim to constrain and both can be understood as broadly stated causes of disputes.[70] Indeed, lack of bureaucratic capacity, non-transparent decision-making, and corruption and rent-seeking behaviour can all contribute to the emergence of investor–state disputes, as discussed in Chapter 3. Nevertheless, democratic contestation causes an empirically and theoretically important subset of these disputes.[71]

4.4 Hypotheses

This chapter has, until now, explored arguments about the relationship between domestic political institutions and actors and the emergence of investor–state disputes which culminate in arbitration. The point of departure has been IPE work on investor–state relations and FDI attraction and protection. However, as I have argued, much of this literature is limited in its focus on FDI in manufacturing on the one hand, and a focus on expropriation or other rent-seeking behaviour on the part of states on the other. I contend that as FDI does not have a uniformly positive impact on domestic populations and investors challenge a wide array of state measures, the political economy of investment arbitration may need to rest on a different understanding of the relationship between domestic politics and adverse outcomes for investors, particularly when it comes to the role of 'domestic audiences'. In this section, I develop hypotheses related to the foregoing arguments, to be tested in section 4.5.

The first of these hypotheses relates to regime type. Democracy and FDI friendliness are generally thought to go hand in hand in IPE investigations into the relationship. However, as I have argued, while democratic institutions may deter governments from engaging in expropriation, the dynamics of investor–state disputes that go to arbitration are significantly different; expropriations represent one important subset of the causes of investor–state arbitration, but many disputes are caused by vastly different government measures, including democratically enacted legislation. Moreover, investor–state disputes that go to arbitration are concentrated in politically salient industries, such as oil, gas and mining, energy, and other public utilities. Investment in these sectors cannot be assumed to have a consistently positive impact on domestic populations and thus governments may

[70] Aisbett and Bonnitcha (n 30).

[71] Moreover, these causes are not always mutually exclusive. Capacity issues may shape how state actors respond to competing pressures from investors and domestic groups, and citing irrational, non-technical policymaking is a frequently employed argument by investors when challenging politically popular policies detrimental to their interests: Jonathan Bonnitcha and Zoe Phillips Williams, 'State Liability for "Politically" Motivated Conduct in the Investment Treaty Regime' (2019) 33 Leiden Journal of International Law 77. As discussed in the case study on El Salvador, states may also take measures in good faith that are nevertheless, because of capacity issues, an obstacle for investors.

be pushed by constituents to take measures which are detrimental to investors' interests.

The first hypothesis is of primary interest for this chapter. The following six add detail regarding possible channels through which political contestation contributes to the emergence of investor–state disputes. Thus, I test the hypothesis that

- H_1: electoral democracy levels will be positively correlated with the incidence of an investor–state arbitration.

On the other hand, as discussed in section 4.3, veto players are assumed to constrain unilateral actions from one branch of government and may limit the responsiveness to special or broad interest groups advocating for policies detrimental to investors. Therefore, I will test the hypothesis that

- H_2: the presence of greater numbers of veto players will be correlated with a decreased number of expected investment arbitration cases.

Similarly, if groups in the host state are particularly opposed to a certain investment project or a problem caused by an investment becomes particularly salient, investment projects may be 'at issue' in host state elections, with governments pressurized to take measures which are detrimental to investors, either in the run-up to an election or shortly afterwards, to fulfil campaign promises. Thus, I test the hypothesis that

- H_3: elections will be positively correlated with the incidence of an investor–state arbitration.

I test this hypothesis with several lags to capture the different possible timings of a dispute pre-, during, or post-election.

As mentioned briefly, the ideology of the ruling party may have an impact on policy affecting foreign investors, playing some role in determining the responsiveness of the government to foreign investors compared to domestic interest groups—whether these are workers, community groups, or domestic industry competitors. While recent waves of expropriation in the early 2000s were carried out by leftist leaders in South America, IPE work on the topic finds that leftist leaders are more FDI-friendly in general. On the other hand, nationalist, often right-leaning governments may engage in restrictive FDI policies and favour local business actors. Thus, I test the hypotheses that

- H_4: left-leaning governments are less likely to be involved in investment arbitration, while

- H_5: nationalist governments are more likely to be involved in investment arbitration.

Relatedly, I test the hypothesis that

- H_6: post-communist states are more likely to be involved in investment arbitration.

Finally, given the political salience of extractive industry investments, I test the hypothesis that

- H_7: the percentage of gross domestic product (GDP) which is comprised of resource exports will be positively correlated with the likelihood of a dispute.[72]

Section 4.5 presents the results of the empirical analysis.

4.5 Empirical Analysis

In this section, I present the results of a regression analysis focusing on the relationship between a number of variables related to (shifting) political preferences related to FDI or specific investment projects, identified in the hypotheses in section 4.4, and the incidence of an arbitral claim in a given country-year.

The analysis is carried out using the same dataset described in Chapter 3, with investment arbitration cases in 139 countries, covering the years 1990–2016. Figure 4.1 shows the number of claims by democracy level. There is a fairly even distribution of claims across democracy levels, although notably, the states that have faced the highest number of claims, including most of those above forty, are those with higher levels of electoral democracy.

4.5.1 Estimation Strategy and Variables

As in Chapter 3, the dependent variable is a count of the number of arbitral claims lodged against a state in a given year, and the same estimation strategy—a zero-inflated binomial model—is used, with the same inflator variable (see discussion in Chapter 3 for more details).

[72] Unfortunately, I have not been able to find sufficient data on utilities privatization to include this in my regressions.

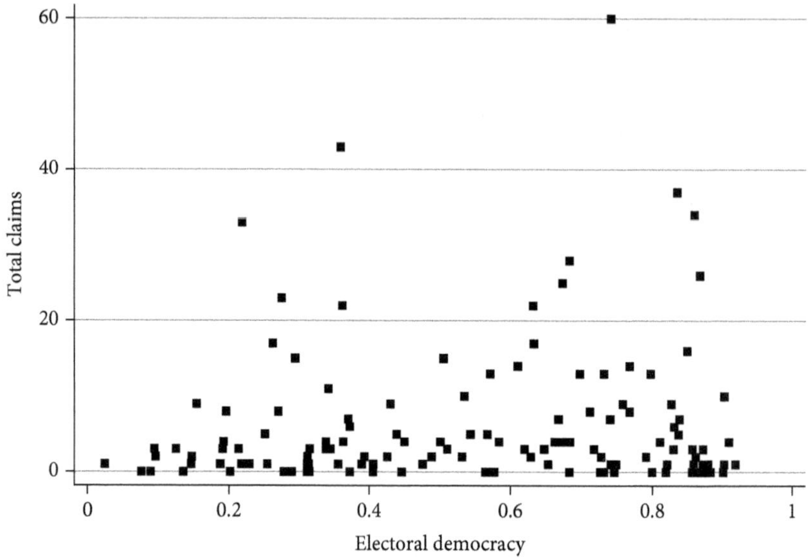

Figure 4.1 Number of claims by electoral democracy index

Several control variables are included in the following models.[73] The first are GDP per capita and the amount of FDI stock hosted by the state, as in Chapter 3. These are important, given that the states with the higher democracy levels tend to be more developed states and play host to more FDI. The year and number of treaties ratified by the host state are also included in all models, given that both are positively correlated with the number of claims faced by a state. I have also included a dummy variable for formerly communist-bloc, transition economies. Many of these countries have subsequently become democracies with fairly high levels of democracy, but, as discussed earlier, may be uniquely prone to investor–state disputes due to their frequently changing regulatory environment as they transition to liberalized market economies.[74] Additionally, as mentioned in section 4.3, privatization and liberalization of certain key services may create opposition amongst the domestic populations or competing firms in these states (and indeed, many of the disputes related to formerly public utilities are in this transition). The list of countries that are included in this category are all East and Central European countries, Central Asia, and Mongolia. This variable was obtained from the Varieties of Democracy (V-Dem) data set. Finally, in one model I have a dummy variable for North American Free Trade Agreement

[73] Descriptive statistics and correlations can be found in the appendix in Tables 4.2 and 4.3.

[74] Muchlinski (n 63). For example, the removal of subsidies or the cancellation of power purchase agreements to comply with EU directives on state aid have resulted in arbitration claims against transition economies.

(NAFTA) signatories, which for the time period relevant to this analysis included investor–state arbitration (ISA) provisions. NAFTA countries are very frequent respondent states and are also high-democracy countries. While many NAFTA claims do in fact fit the model of politicized, public-interest-driven cases discussed earlier, there may also be a particular dynamic to the legal culture in these countries which makes arbitration more likely, and thus it is worth including as a control variable.

The electoral democracy index is taken from the V-Dem project's data set. It is an index comprising measures for freedom of association, clean elections, freedom of association, freedom of expression and suffrage and is, according to the V-Dem Codebook, the core democracy measure, reflecting the responsiveness of the government to its citizens.

The veto players indicator is represented by the political constraints index (POLCONV) created by Henisz.[75] This indicator measures 'the number of independent veto points over policy outcomes and the distribution of preferences of the actors that inhabit them'.[76] These veto points include the upper and lower houses of the legislature, sub-federal units, and the judiciary.

The measures of government ideology are also from the V-Dem project, specifically the project's measure of the ideological character of the government's legitimation strategy. This measure is based on the extent to which an incumbent government justifies its place based on a specific ideology or social model. This measure takes into account the chief executive as well as ministries and agencies, which is an attractive feature, given the plethora of government bodies which may be implicated in investor–state disputes. The measure includes options for nationalist, socialist/communist, conservative, separatist, and religious. I have included the results for the first two categories here as they strike me as the most relevant for relations with foreign investors.

Additionally, I include a dummy variable indicating whether a legislative or executive branch election has taken place in a given year, also obtained from the V-Dem data set. I have included both branches to take into account that both legislators and executives may be responsible for the measures which trigger investor–state disputes.

Finally, I include a measure of the percentage that oil, gas, and mining revenues contribute to a state's GDP. This is taken from the V-Dem data set.

[75] Witold Jerzy Henisz, 'POLCON_2005 Codebook' (2005) <https://mgmt.wharton.upenn.edu/wp-content/uploads/2016/12/CODEBOOK_2005.pdf> accessed 20 April 2022.
[76] ibid 13.

4.5.2 Results

This section discusses the results of the regression analysis testing the hypotheses discussed here, employing the variables related to political interests and institutions in the host state of investment. The full output of the regression analysis can be found in the appendix in Table 4.4; Table 4.1 shows only factor change or how much a one-unit increase in a variable increases or decreases the likelihood of claims.

Model 1 in Table 4.4 contains the same control variables as used in Chapter 3 (number of treaties ratified, year, FDI stock and GDP per capita), as well as the dummy variable for post-communist states and the indicator for electoral democracy. As can be seen in Table 4.4 as in the results discussed in Chapter 3, both an additional year and an additional ratified treaty increase the expected number of investment claims against the host state. Additionally, as can be seen in the appendix and in Table 4.1, a one-unit increase in the electoral democracy index for a host state increases the expected number of claims by a factor of more than three. The positively, statistically significant relationship between democracy and the dependent variable is consistent across the models. As can be seen in Table 4.5 in the appendix, this relationship holds even with the addition of a dummy variable for NAFTA signatories, suggesting that the relationship is not driven by the high number of claims, unusual for wealthy democracies, faced by Canada and the United States. On the other hand, the post-communist dummy variable does not have a statistically significant effect on the number of claims.

The second model includes the measure for political constraints or veto players. While the coefficient has a negative relationship with the dependent variable, as expected, this is not statistically significant.

The third model includes the dummy variable for a nationalist government, which, as indicated in Table 4.1, increases the number of expected claims by a factor of more than two. On the other hand, Model 3 in Table 4.4 tests the relationship between a socialist or communist government and the dependent variable, finding that these governments decrease the expected number of claims by a factor of 0.5.

Models 5–7 in Table 4.4 include dummy variables for an election, an election with a one-year lag, and an election with a two-year lag. As can be seen in Table 4.1, an election increases the number of expected claims in the same year by a factor of 1.27. As can be seen in Table 4.4 in the appendix, an election with a one-year lag has no effect on the dependent variable, while an election with a two-year lag increases the number of expected claims by a factor of 1.34.

Finally, as shown in Model 8, the percentage of a country's GDP made up of resource rents is weakly significant and increases the number of expected claims by a factor of 1.018.

4.6 Conclusion

This chapter began with a discussion of the work, largely in the IPE camp, which examines the relationship between FDI friendliness and regime type. Much of this work, starting with the obsolescing bargain, makes several important assumptions. The first is that, as the obsolescing bargain literature makes clear, states 'take' from foreign investors largely in search of material gains to be extracted from the investment project. The second assumption is that, as FDI is generally beneficial, and specifically employment- generating, democratic institutions provide a bulwark against anti-investor behaviour. Scholars working in this tradition build on these assumptions and often point to a relationship between the rise of democracy and the decline of expropriations to make the argument that democratic states tend to be better hosts of investment.

However, as I argue in this chapter, state actors may be moved to take measures that are detrimental to investors for reasons other than immediate material gain. Instead, arbitral claim-triggering measures may be taken at the behest of either narrow or broad interest groups, in other words, for distinctly political reasons. Moreover, as FDI does not necessarily have a uniformly positive impact on populations in the host state, domestic audiences cannot be depended upon to favour or enforce pro-FDI policies. Indeed, pressure from investment-affected populations has, in many cases, provoked measures later challenged by investors, in some cases with the matter rising to the level of an election issue. Thus, the relationship between democracy and the incidence of investment arbitration claims is not obviously negative.

The empirical analysis lends some support to these arguments. Specifically, the electoral democracy index discussed earlier has a consistently positive, statistically significant relationship with the number of claims in a given country-year, suggesting that democracies can expect more claims, controlling for GDP and the amount of investment hosted. At the very least, this suggests that it is plausible that democratic contestation can lead states to take measures that trigger investment arbitration.

The positive relationship between the dependent variable and the nationalist governments lends further evidence to the political nature of these disputes, while the negative relationship between leftist governments and the number of claims is in line with the predictions in the literature. Finally, the relationship between elections and investment claims also suggests a link between these disputes and domestic political demands. The fact that both an election in the same year as a claim and two years prior has a statistically significant, positive relationship with the number of expected claims suggests that the timing may play out in several ways, when we take into consideration the time it takes to register a claim. Specifically, a claim in an election year suggests that the measure was taken in the lead-up to the election, while the positive relationship with the lagged variable suggests that measures may be taken to fulfil campaign promises.

Of course, not all investor–state disputes which go to arbitration are the result of democratic contestation; however, a subset of these is, which arguably accounts for some of the pushback against the regime and should determine the avenues for reform that are pursued. The case studies presented in Chapters 5–7 explore in more detail the connections between democratic contestation, including elections, and investor–state disputes.

5
Pacific Rim Cayman v El Salvador

This chapter examines the investor–state arbitration case between the Republic of El Salvador and the Canadian gold mining company Pacific Rim. The company began exploration activities in El Salvador in the early 2000s but after significant delays was ultimately unable to obtain exploitation licences or the necessary environmental permit to carry out the project. The state measure at the heart of the dispute is the president of El Salvador's declaration of a de facto ban on mining, which resulted in a decision to suspend the release of exploitation permits for a number of mining companies with exploration permits in the country. This measure was taken in the context of growing public opposition to mining in the lead-up to a highly contested election, as well as a realization on the part of the Ministry of Environment that it did not have the technical capacity to assess and monitor the effects of mining on the country.

While El Salvador has been very open to foreign investment and made efforts to attract foreign direct investment (FDI) in the mining sector, this case suggests that, under certain conditions, public—and particularly electoral—pressure will induce an investment-friendly state to take anti-investor measures. However, it also underscores the relationship between state capacity and investor–state disputes. While it was not necessarily a lack of awareness on the part of relevant policymakers of their obligations under international investment agreements (IIAs) that contributed to the dispute, the lack of technical capacity in the policy area in which the investment took place appears to have contributed to the decision to suspend mining permits in the country. Therefore, to some extent this case is exemplary of both the broad 'causes' of investor–state arbitration cases discussed in Chapters 3 and 4.

The dispute between Pacific Rim and El Salvador is in many ways a typical case. As a middle-income country, El Salvador is certainly represented in the categories of most frequent respondent states. Moreover, as the dispute involves an extractive industry claimant, this case also highlights why mining, oil, and gas companies are so often embroiled in investor–state disputes—namely, the threat that the industry is perceived to pose to both the environment and traditional livelihoods by local communities.

Beyond the actors in the dispute, the case exemplifies the convergence of factors that may contribute to the concentration of these disputes in middle-income countries. On the one hand, the lack of bureaucratic capacity in the Ministry of Environment led first to a long series of delays for the investor and, allegedly, to

The Political Economy of Investment Arbitration. Zoe Phillips Williams, Oxford University Press. © Zoe Phillips Williams 2022.
DOI: 10.1093/oso/9780198865940.003.0005

the government's decision to suspend mining permits. However, this case also suggests that countries which are in the process of defining their development priorities, as El Salvador was regarding the place of mining in its development strategy, may be particularly constrained by IIAs—a problem that may face middle-income countries most acutely. Additionally, this case elucidates the connection, first presented in Chapter 4's statistical analysis, between election cycles and investor–state arbitration. As discussed in Chapter 4, elections are positively correlated with the incidence of an investor–state arbitration, and the investor–state dispute presented here was clearly affected by the electoral interests of key decision-makers.

Finally, the case, while not a clear-cut example of regulatory chill, does suggest that investment arbitration can impact domestic policymaking. The domestic anti-mining groups' goal was the passage of legislation banning mining in the country. Presidents Saca's and Funes' responses, to announce and then uphold a de facto ban on mining, fell short of this goal. There is evidence to suggest that passing legislation banning mining was considered but not attempted while the arbitration was ongoing.[1] However, once El Salvador prevailed in the arbitration, an anti-mining law was passed by the Salvadoran legislature in 2017.

5.1 Investment and Mining in El Salvador

El Salvador is Central America's smallest and most densely populated country and, as a lower middle-income country, suffers from high levels of poverty and inequality as well as water shortages and environmental degradation.

Following the 1989–92 civil war, which pitted the conservative central government against left-wing guerrillas, El Salvador made significant efforts to liberalize its economy and attract foreign investment. These initiatives, spearheaded by the conservative *Allianza Republicana Nacionalista* (ARENA) party which ruled from 1989 to 2008, included the writing of a new domestic Investment Law in 1999, which contains a provision for investment arbitration; the creation of the investment promotion agency, PROESA, in 2000; and the 2000 dollarization of the economy. Successive ARENA governments have signed twenty-four IIAs with developed and developing country partners, as well as joining the Central American and Dominican Republic Free Trade Agreement (CAFTA-DR) in 2004. Both the Investment Law and the Central American Free Trade Agreement's (CAFTA's) Chapter 10 provide significant investment protection, committing the government to extend the same rights to foreign investors that domestic investors enjoy, prohibiting expropriation without compensation, and providing recourse to international arbitration at the International Centre for Settlement of Investment

[1] I discuss the dynamics of this in a 2016 article: Zoe Phillips Williams, 'Investor–State Arbitration in Domestic Mining Conflicts' (2016) 16 Global Environmental Politics 32.

Disputes (ICSID). These efforts have been recognized by international audiences. For example, in 2006 (during the time period of interest for this study), the World Bank's *Doing Business* report ranked El Salvador 76 out of 155 for ease of doing business—notably, ahead of its regional competitors Costa Rica, Guatemala, Honduras, and the Dominican Republic.[2] In 2007, the same publication noted that El Salvador was leading on pro-business reforms in Latin America.[3] However, despite these efforts to create a climate that was friendly to investment and a generally stable macroeconomic environment, El Salvador has failed to attract significant FDI compared to its Central American neighbours.[4]

In a survey of investor perceptions of El Salvador, 49 per cent of investors cited the high crime rates and related gang activity as the biggest impediment to investment,[5] with fears of corruption and lack of policy stability following.[6] These sentiments were echoed in interviews I carried out with government officials in El Salvador, who recognize that the country has trouble 'selling itself' internationally (interview with anonymous official, PROESA, 7 August 2014). This is due in part to its violent image and lack of policy stability; 'almost always, when we are close to an election, policy uncertainty is the first [concern for investors], and when the government has already been in power one or two years, insecurity and crime take first place'.[7] However, despite this policy instability, prior to the case discussed here, El Salvador had only faced one publicly known investment claim, over which the tribunal declined jurisdiction.

ARENA was in power for the majority of the post-civil war era, a time in which 'pro-market elite coalitions were forceful, enjoying a broad electoral base'.[8] The *Frente Farabundo Marti para la Liberacíon Nacional* (FMLN) became the primary opposition party in 2004, when it first participated in presidential elections. The FMLN's origins date back to the civil war, during which it brought together a number of left-wing guerrilla organizations to fight the central government. With the signing of the ceasefire in 1992, the guerrillas demobilized and the organization was transformed into a political party. The FMLN has been the dominant party in the poorer provinces of Cabañas and Chalatenango, which bore the brunt of government repression during the civil war.[9] However, in the 2009 presidential

[2] World Bank, 'Doing Business in 2006' in *Doing Business* (World Bank 2006).

[3] World Bank, 'Doing Business in 2007' in *Doing Business* (World Bank 2007).

[4] Luis Felipe Zegarra, Martha Rodriguez, and Carlos Acevedo, 'Competitiveness and Growth in Latin America. Country Case: El Salvador' (2007) Inter-American Development Bank <https://kipdf.com/country-case-el-salvador_5adeb9fc7f8b9af55f8b4604.html> accessed 9 May 2022.

[5] A well-founded fear, as El Salvador has consistently had the first or second highest homicide rate in the region, currently hovering around 70 homicides for every 100,000 persons.

[6] Zegarra, Rodriguez, and Acevedo (n 4).

[7] Interview with Marjorie Trigueros, FUSADES, 22 July 2014.

[8] Rose J Spalding, 'Transnational Activism and National Action: El Salvador's Anti-Mining Movement' (2011) Paper presented at workshop on the Domestic Effects of Transnational Activism, 11–12 April 2011 2.

[9] Elizabeth Wood, *Insurgent Collective Action and Civil War in El Salvador* (Cambridge University Press 2003).

election, the FMLN's centre-left candidate Mauricio Funes (the first party leader without guerrilla credentials) won with 51.3 per cent of the votes.[10] Funes' election marked a shift to the left of the Salvadoran electorate, a country that has traditionally been ideologically to the right of many countries in Latin America. Votes for ARENA candidates have typically been motivated by concerns regarding security and crime and the country's relationship with the United States. However voter self-placement shifted leftwards in the mid-2000s, with voters placing economic and welfare concerns ahead of security.[11] Nonetheless, Funes was not a leftist leader in the style of Hugo Chávez or Evo Morales—according to interviewees, both the Funes government and his FMLN successor President Salvador Sánchez Cerén continued to enact free market reforms, including promoting a public–private partnership law which faced significant civil society criticism.[12]

One issue which rose to prominence along with this leftward shift was the role that mining should play in the country's development. Although mining has had a historical presence in El Salvador, it never contributed substantially to the economy, and the few foreign mining companies operating in El Salvador pulled out during the civil war.[13] However, mining became part of the ARENA government's efforts to attract FDI in the 1990s, and in 1996 the government rewrote the Mining Law to lower royalties and streamline the process of applying for permits. By 2006, eight foreign gold mining companies were operating in some capacity in the country, primarily conducting exploration in the provinces of Cabañas and Chalatenango.

The presence of these companies was a cause of concern for local communities and organizations, which eventually came together under the banner of the Mesa Nacional Frente a la Minería Metálica (National Round Table against Metals Mining) in 2005. Their resistance campaign—later joined by the Catholic Church, international and national non-governmental organizations (NGOs), and Salvadoran universities—proved quite successful. In 2007, a public opinion poll taken by the Universidad Centroamericana in San Salvador found that 62.5 per cent of the population believed that mining was inappropriate for El Salvador.[14] As will be discussed in greater detail in the following sections, the national anti-mining mood had a clear impact on the prospects of mining companies in the country as political actors at the highest levels turned against mining. In 2008 and 2009, two foreign mining companies, Pacific Rim Cayman and Commerce Group Ltd, sent Notices of Intent, the first step in arbitration proceedings, to the government of El Salvador.

[10] Dinorah Azpuru, 'The Salience of Ideology: Fifteen Years of Presidential Elections in El Salvador' (2010) 52 Latin American Politics and Society 103.

[11] ibid.

[12] Interview with Edgardo Mira, CEICOM, 29 July 2014.

[13] Spalding (n 8).

[14] Juan Carlos Durán, 'Estudio Sobre Conocimientos y Percepciones Hacia La Mineria' (2007) 63 Estudios Centroamericanos 59.

5.2 The Dispute between Pacific Rim Cayman and El Salvador

Pacific Rim Mining Corporation, originally headquartered in Vancouver, Canada, began exploration activities in the province of Cabañas in 2002, impressed by the country's pro-foreign investment and mining legal framework.[15] During 2004–05, the company began the process of obtaining an exploitation licence from the Ministry of Economy's Bureau of Hydrocarbons and Mines. This process required the submission of proof of legal ownership of the land of the concession site, a feasibility study for the project, and an environmental approval from the Ministry of the Environment and Natural Resources (MARN for its initials in Spanish). In order to obtain the environmental permit, a company was required to submit an environmental impact statement (EIS) detailing the potential environmental impacts of the projects and the steps that will be taken to remediate them. The final decision on the granting of the permit was made by the Minister of Economy (MINEC), who was required to make their decision based on 'national interest, the financial and technical capacity of the applicant, and the characteristics of the proposed mining operation'.[16]

The process to obtain all required environmental permits and exploitation licences took Pac Rim several years, with the company encountering many delays, which it attributed to the lack of expertise of the MARN and MINEC, given their limited experience with mining operations.[17] In particular, one aspect of the process—proving that the company held an ownership title to the land it planned to exploit—was fraught with a lack of clarity. Specifically, it was unclear whether the company was required to purchase the land from local communities or merely obtain the licence from the state to exploit the subsoil. In correspondence between MINEC and the Secretary for Legislative and Legal Affairs in the Office of the President, the Minister of Economy wrote that Pacific Rim argued, 'they will be mining the subsoil and the subsoil belongs to the State; if they request permission from the landowners it would amount to saying that the owners of the surface land are owners of the subsoil'.[18] Pac Rim noted that various relevant government bodies did not hold a common view on the matter and actively suggested changes of the Mining Law to the government, arguing that the requirement to seek landowners' permission to mine the subsoil was not consistent with the norms of ownership in the Salvadoran legal system (Memorial on the merits).[19] Throughout 2005, this issue remained unresolved.

[15] Notice of Arbitration, *Pac Rim Cayman LLC v Republic of El Salvador*, ICSID Case No ARB/09/12.
[16] MINEC (Minister of Economy), 'The Republic of El Salvador's Preliminary Objections under Articles 10.20.4 and 10.20.5 of the Dominican Republic–Central America–United States Free Trade Agreement (CAFTA), ICSID Case No ARB/09/12' (2010) 17.
[17] 'Claimant Pac Rim Cayman LLC's Memorial on the Merits and Quantum, ICSID Case No. ARB/09/12' (2014).
[18] ibid 109.
[19] ibid.

Additionally, in 2005, as required, Pacific Rim made its draft EIS available to the public in order to solicit feedback. However, as the document was largely in English, over 1,000 pages long, and interested parties were prohibited from making copies in order to read it on their own, the ability of locals to comment was fairly limited.[20] In 2006, the company submitted its final EIS, allegedly believing that they had included all relevant documentation and that their licence would be granted immanently.[21]

Throughout 2006, against the background of the legal questions related to land ownership, Pacific Rim continued exploration activities as well as pursuing their environmental permit, which included addressing concerns raised in public consultations.[22]

Between December 2006 and 2008, MARN and other government agencies ceased official communications with the company. During this time, MINEC hired an outside expert, Dr Manuel Vidal-Pulgar, to assess the appropriateness of metallic mining for El Salvador. In his report, Vidal-Pulgar concluded that '"the Ministry of Environment is not equipped to effectively assume a strong environmental policy regarding mining activity" . . . due to lack of experience and expertise on the subject, lack of sufficient personnel, and an insufficient budget'.[23] This is relatively unsurprising, given that mining was a relatively new industrial activity for El Salvador and the Ministry of Environment itself was only nine years old. Vidal-Pulgar further noted that Salvadorans exhibited distrust of the Ministry of Environment's capabilities to adequately assess the potential impacts of mining activity and expressed concern regarding water use and contamination, deforestation, and the ministry's inexperience.[24] Furthermore, he found that the country lacked a 'comprehensive vision' for mining development, a water policy to ensure universal access to water, and inadequate mechanisms for citizen participation in decision-making processes.[25] He concluded that if mining activity were to progress at this stage, it would result in growing social conflict. Instead, he suggested that a strategic environmental assessment be carried out to identify the potential environmental impacts mining would actually have in the country.[26]

As a result of this report, the Minister of Environment explained that the ministry would not authorize any project that posed an environmental risk and specifically mentioned the ministry's lack of capacity to regulate the mining industry. However, the Minister subsequently publicly reversed his position, stating that El Salvador did not legally prohibit mining.[27] In 2007, a new minister reiterated that

20 Interview with Saul Baños, FESPAD, 13 August 2014.

21 Thomas Shrake, 'Witness Statement of Thomas C. Shrake, ICSID Case No. ARB/09/12' (2010).

22 'Claimant Pac Rim Cayman LLC's Memorial on the Merits and Quantum' (n 17).

23 'The Republic of El Salvador's Counter-Memorial on the Merits, ICSID Case No. ARB/09/12' (2014) 95.

24 ibid.

25 ibid 95.

26 ibid.

27 'Claimant Pac Rim Cayman LLC's Memorial on the Merits and Quantum' (n 17).

the ministry would not grant permits for mining concessions until the study on the potential effects of mining had been completed.[28] Ultimately, this environmental assessment was not carried out by President Saca but by the subsequent administration in 2009.

During this period, local communities in Cabañas expressed concern regarding the potential mining activity in their region to Oxfam America.[29] This resulted in violent encounters, including the murders of some anti-mining activists, allegedly by pro-mining actors.[30] It was also during this period that the aforementioned opinion poll on mining in El Salvador was carried out by the Universidad Centroamericana, which showed that the majority of Salvadorans opposed mining activity in the country.

During 2007 and 2008, company representatives continued to meet unofficially with high-level bureaucrats, who assured them that the delays in granting their licence would be resolved.[31] During this period, public opposition to the project was mounting, with the Catholic Bishop's Conference of El Salvador making a statement against mining.[32] At this time, the company officially relocated its headquarters to Reno, Nevada. According to Luis Parada, one of El Salvador's lawyers on the case, in 2007, the company first threatened the government with arbitration, and shortly thereafter El Salvador engaged the legal services of the Washington firm Dewey & LeBouef LLP.[33]

In 2008, President Tony Saca held a press conference at which he stated his intention to revisit the legal framework of mining in the country (Notice of Arbitration). In its Notice of Arbitration, the company claims that, despite the delays in the process of granting a permit, it was not aware of a dispute with the government until Saca's 'de facto' ban on mining.[34] In December 2008, Pacific Rim officially filed its Notice of Intent to Arbitrate.[35]

[28] 'The Republic of El Salvador's Counter-Memorial on the Merits' (n 23).

[29] Thelma Mejia, 'Mineria-America Central: Nuevo Fiebre Del Oro', *TierraAmerica* (2007) <https://ecolamancha.wordpress.com/2007/11/26/nueva-fiebre-del-oro-en-america-central/> accesed 22 April 2022; 'The Republic of El Salvador's Counter-Memorial on the Merits' (n 23).

[30] 'The Republic of El Salvador's Counter-Memorial on the Merits' (n 23); Thomas M Power, 'Metals Mining and Sustainable Development in Central America. An Assessment of Benefits and Costs' (2009) Oxfam America <https://www.oxfamamerica.org/explore/research-publications/metals-mining-and-sustainable-development-in-central-america/> accessed 24 April 2022.

[31] Shrake (n 21).

[32] CEDES, 'La Explotación Minera En El Salvador—Cuidemos La Casa de Todos' (CEDES 2007) <https://caritas.sv/nuestro-trabajo/documentos/otros/65-cuidemos-la-casa-de-todos/file> accessed 22 April 2022.

[33] Interview with Luis Parada, 15 September 2014.

[34] According to Luis Parada, this claim is disingenuous, given the company's 2007 arbitration threat and the fact that he was approached to join their legal team at this time. Moreover, an insistence of ignorance of the dispute until 2008 was an attempt to allow the company to argue that its 2007 nationality change was not motivated by a desire for jurisdiction under CAFTA, which it did not have as a Canadian company: see Luis Alberto Parada, 'Witness Statement of Luis Alberto Parada, ICSID Case No. ARB/09/12' (2011).

[35] 'Notice to the Government of the Republic of El Salvador of Intent to Submit a Claim to Arbitration under Chapter 10 of the Central America–United States–Dominican Republic Free Trade Agreement'.

During the election campaign of 2009, FMLN candidate Mauricio Funes expressed his opposition to mining and, in a public event with the Mesa, confirmed that no new mining permits would be granted were he to win the election.[36] Subsequently, company representatives claim, they reached out to both President Saca and President-elect Funes to determine whether a negotiated solution could be reached.[37] However, a number of interviewees suggested that the company's only interest was in the granting of the mining concession; they would not accept a negotiated monetary settlement.[38]

El Salvador's de facto ban continued for several years, and, in 2012, the government officially suspended all administrative procedures related to mining.[39] As has been discussed elsewhere, government officials and those familiar with El Salvador's legal strategy in the arbitration suggested that the government felt unable to push an anti-mining legislative agenda while the case was ongoing as this might jeopardize both the country's defence in the case against Pacific Rim and provoke more investment claims from miners affected by a broad ban.[40] However, following El Salvador's successful defence in the arbitration, the FMLN-controlled legislature passed a legal ban on metallic mining in 2017.[41]

By 2013, Pacific Rim was facing severe financial difficulties and was purchased by the Canadian–Australian company OceanaGold Ltd for $10.2 million, allowing it to continue the arbitration process against El Salvador.

5.2.1 The Arbitration: *Pacific Rim Cayman v El Salvador*

Pacific Rim served El Salvador with a Notice of Arbitration in April, 2009, and the tribunal was constituted in September of that year. The arbitration proceedings came to a close in 2016. A summary of the investor's claims against El Salvador is presented in Table 5.1.

Saca's 2008 de facto ban on mining was at the heart of the investor's case against El Salvador as they claimed that until that time, they were not aware of any dispute with the state. Indeed, in the Claimant's Memorial on the Merits, Pac Rim's legal team writes that until 2008, the investor believed it would be granted an environmental permit; 'then, with the announcement of the *de facto* ban on metallic

[36] Interview with Rodolfo Calles, Mesa, 14 July 2014.
[37] Shrake (n 21).
[38] Interview with Saul Baños, 13 August 2014; interview with Luis Parada, 14 September 2014.
[39] Pedro Cabezas, 'Incoming Minister of the Environment Confirms Continuation of Mining Moratorium in El Salvador' (2014) <http://www.stopesmining.org/j25/index.php/salvadoran-mining-ban/301-incoming-minister-of-the-environment-confirms-continuation-of-mining-moratorium-in-el-salvador> accessed 23 February 2022.
[40] Williams (n 1) 32.
[41] ibid.

Table 5.1 Arguments

Alleged breach of CAFA/ domestic investment law	**Claimant's arguments**
10.3 National treatment; 10.4 Most favoured nation treatment; Art. 5 Equal protection and Art. 6 Non-discrimination	Respondent treated the claimant in an arbitrary manner; there was no indication that the EIA was inadequate on technical grounds; other industries that raise similar environmental concerns extended more favourable treatment
10.5 Minimum standard of treatment	Despite the fact that the claimant has complied with all legal requirements to be granted exploration and exploitation licences, the Respondent refuses to allow mining activity that is permitted by its own legislation.
CAFTA Art. 10.7 and Art. 8 Investment law expropriation and compensation	The Respondent's conduct has rendered the investment worthless, which therefore constitutes an indirect and direct expropriation.

mining in Mach 2008, the Executive Branch of the Salvadoran Government illegitimately swept aside the legal and regulatory regime upon which [the] Claimant had relied'.[42] The claimant argued that this ban on mining deprived the company of its assets and had no legal justification. Therefore, while the claimant went into great detail regarding the various administrative delays which they faced in their attempts to secure environmental and exploitation permits, these are not the measures they challenged. Rather, they discussed this lengthy administrative process in order to demonstrate that despite these delays, they were continually assured by various officials that the government supported the project and that all required licences would eventually be granted.[43] The claimants therefore attributed the delays, until Saca's 2008 announcement, neither to deficiencies in their own documentation submitted to the various ministries, legitimate environmental concerns, nor to political opposition to the project. Rather, they focused on a lack of bureaucratic capacity due to the recent arrival of the mining industry in El Salvador.

On the other hand, El Salvador's defence argued that there were deficiencies with the company's applications. First, the government contended that Pacific Rim never successfully completed the purchase of the concession site from local owners and was thus unable to provide proof of legal ownership of the entire site.[44] Moreover, instead of concentrating on meeting the requirements for the original concession site, including submitting a final feasibility study, the company

42 'Claimant Pac Rim Cayman LLC's Memorial on the Merits and Quantum' (n 17) 2.

43 ibid.

44 'The Republic of El Salvador's Preliminary Objections under Articles 10.20.4 and 10.20.5 of the Dominican Republic–Central America–United States Free Trade Agreement (CAFTA)' (n 16).

continued to expand its exploration activities on land that it did not own. The government alleged that the company was given opportunities to resubmit a feasibility study but did not do so and instead allowed its exploration licences for the land to which it had a title to expire in 2005. The government further argued that the company was unable to secure a 'social licence to operate', in large part by not adequately addressing the concerns of local communities, particularly regarding water usage. The defence claimed that these environmental concerns were shared by the MARN; in particular, the government found deficiencies or lack of information regarding the company's environmental management plan, proposed mitigation measures, cyanide transport, and a mine closure plan.[45] Moreover, these specific concerns arose as the MARN was coming to terms with its lack of capacity to adequately monitor and regulate mining activity.[46] Therefore, the defence argued, 'there was never, as the Claimant alleges, a "ban" (denoting a permanent prohibition) on metallic mining. Rather … El Salvador made the reasonable decision to suspend the review of applications for environmental permits related to metallic mining.'[47]

El Salvador contended that this policy shift was based on recognition of its lack of technical capacity to properly regulate the mining industry and that this position was supported by the precautionary principle enshrined in the Salvadoran Constitution.[48] Moreover, the *amicus curiae* brief submitted by the Center for International Environmental Law argues that 'the facts underlying the [company's] claim are deeply intertwined with the social and political change' related to democratization in El Salvador, which led to the emergence of 'the grassroots, peaceful opposition to Pac Rim's proposed mine'.[49] However, El Salvador denied that Pacific Rim was unduly affected by this policy shift, given that it did not meet the requirements to be granted the necessary permits.

The tribunal ultimately sided with El Salvador, dismissing the company's claims in their entirety, finding that Pac Rim had not completed a purchase of the land making up the concession, as required by the country's mining law. Notably, the tribunal fails to address the company's contentions of political motivations for the de facto ban in the award on the merits.[50]

[45] 'The Republic of El Salvador's Counter-Memorial on the Merits' (n 23).
[46] ibid.
[47] ibid 121.
[48] Lise Johnson, 'El Salvador Argues that Domestic Investment Law is not a Portal for Pacific Rim Mining Company to Reach International Law Protections' *IA Reporter* (9 January 2014).
[49] Marcos Orellana, 'Application for Permission to Proceed as Amici Curiae ICSID Case No. ARB/09/12' (2011) 1, 5.
[50] Award, ICSID Case No ARB/09/12.

5.3 The Role of Domestic Interests and Institutions in *Pacific Rim Cayman v El Salvador*

This section provides an analysis of the domestic interests that led to a reversal of El Salvador's official stance towards mining and the eventual decision to go to arbitration against Pacific Rim. The evidence here supports the arguments made in both Chapters 3 and 4 about the importance of state capacity and domestic actor preferences in contributing to the emergence of investor–state arbitration cases.

5.3.1 Domestic Interests: Small-Scale Agriculture, Water Use, and the Environment

Domestic groups relevant to this case existed at the local and national level and range from traditionally politically disadvantaged groups to some of the most influential actors in the country. Despite this heterogeneity, there was a high degree of coherence in the concerns that they shared. Arguably, this is what led to the successful mobilization of a widespread anti-mining movement in the country.

The groups with the most at stake in the conflict with Pacific Rim were the local communities which would have been directly affected by mining operations, and they spearheaded the opposition. The communities, located in the province of Cabañas, are mostly subsistence farmers, and thus rely heavily on local surface water for crops and livestock as well as for their own consumption. As mentioned earlier, El Salvador suffers from a lack of access to drinking water, with almost all surface water in the country severely contaminated, a particularly severe problem in rural areas.[51] Mining is a highly resource-intensive activity and uses significant amounts of water in its extraction processes, while contributing to the contamination of ground water through its use of chemicals such as cyanide and arsenic. According to Pacific Rim's own EIS, the project would use 240,000 gallons (908,499 litres) of water per day—the amount the average Salvadoran family uses over a twenty-year period.[52] Thus, the threat of water shortages and further contamination of drinking water for both humans and animals was a significant concern for local communities. Moreover, despite being rural, the area in which the mine was to be located is quite densely populated (194 persons/km^2), intensifying any adverse effects and increasing the possibility of displacement.[53]

[51] Andres McKinley, 'A Brief Contextual Analysis of the Legal Suit of Pacific Rim Mining Company against the Government of El Salvador' (2009) Oxfam America; Orellana (n 49).

[52] Leah Wilson, 'Resisting CAFTA and Metal Mining in El Salvador' (2010) <http://www.cispes.org/programs/anti-mining-and-cafta/resisting-cafta-and-metal-mining-in-el-salvador> accessed 23 February 2022.

[53] Orellana (n 49).

The potential benefits of the mining project apparently did not outweigh the drawbacks for the community. In a news article, the mayor of San Isidro, the municipality closest to the mine site, expressed doubt as to whether the jobs that would be created by the project would be accessible to local community members; '[t]hey talk of 600 jobs, but we ask ourselves how many people from this area will really be able to work with the technology that they bring .... Because if not, I doubt that 100 employees will be from this area.'[54] In fact, during the course of the arbitration, the company stated that 220 permanent jobs would be created.[55] However, in an interview, one of the leaders of the Mesa summed up the concerns of the local communities: 'Definitely it isn't the best solution to permit mining in the country—not environmentally, not politically, and even less economically. The companies take everything [out of the country], and leave problems, leave contamination.'[56] This sentiment was echoed by an official from MARN, who stated that, 'the Pacific Rim project obviously was going to generate revenue; however the environmental damages would not be covered by the project. Economically, it had utility for the communities in the area and for the country, but only in the short term.'[57]

5.3.2 Organization of the Anti-Mining Movement

The anti-mining movement was able to organize successfully at the local, national, and transnational level, and involve important domestic political institutions. The primary actor in the opposition to mining in El Salvador was the Mesa, which brought together numerous older community organizations under its banner, playing 'a critical brokerage role, linking across community, environmental, human rights, activist research and religious organisations'.[58] Although the communities were initially unsure of how to respond to the presence of the mining company, some groups made the decision to visit mining-affected communities in Honduras and Guatemala on a fact-finding mission.[59] Alarmed at what they saw, they began to organize seriously, and the Mesa was convened in 2005 (Interview with Rodolfo Calles, 14 July 2014).

They fairly quickly founded a movement in which

[54] Rodrigo Baires Quezada, 'Explotación Minera: Los Conflictos Del Oro' *El Faro* (2006) <http://archivo.elfaro.net/secciones/observatorio/20060619/observatorio1_20060619.asp> accessed 23 February 2022. This and other news articles have been translated from Spanish by the author.

[55] 'Claimant Pac Rim Cayman LLC's Memorial on the Merits and Quantum' (n 17).

[56] Interview with Rodolfo Calles, Mesa, 14 July 2014.

[57] Interview with MARN official, 6 August 2014.

[58] Spalding (n 8) 8.

[59] Both countries have considerably more experience with mining than El Salvador, hosting mines that are infamous for contributing to severe environmental contamination and human health problems, for example, the San Martin mine in Valle de Siria in Honduras, owned by GoldCorp, and the Marlin mine in Guatemala, owned by Glamis Gold.

> everyone is involved … in the first place the affected communities, in almost all places where there is mining, the people are aware of the problems. In some places, especially Chalatenango, the mayors are involved. The community development organizations and the Church are involved at the national level, research institutions and universities are against mining.[60]

The spread of information regarding the environmental and human costs of mining was an important strategy for the anti-mining movement, and the Mesa emphasized the threat mining posed to the national water supply, as well as the lack of widespread economic growth associated with mining activity. At the national level, the Universidad Centroamericana held a 'National Forum against Mining' in 2006 and in 2007 carried out the aforementioned public opinion poll, which indicated that a majority of the population of El Salvador was against mining activity in the country. A number of think tanks and research institutes were also involved in carrying out and disseminating studies on the impact of mining, and international NGOs such as Oxfam America have lobbied the government to adopt an anti-mining stance.[61] These NGOs also hired outside experts—hydrologists, economists, environmental scientists, and geologists from the United States and Switzerland—to produce reports and analyses of the company's EIS. These experts were highly critical of the company's environmental protection measures; for example, American hydrologist Robert Moran observed in his report that the standards proposed by Pacific Rim for acceptable levels of cyanide in mine run-off fell short of American and Canadian standards.[62]

Domestic governmental institutions supported the anti-mining movement, including the office of the Ombudsman for the Defense of Human Rights (PDDH for its initial in Spanish), an institution created during the post-war peace process. The Ombudswoman for the Defense of the Environment (an office within the PDDH), was involved with the work of the Mesa from 2005, and the PDDH's official position on the issue was against both mining in El Salvador and investment arbitration in general.[63] The support of the Catholic Church also contributed significantly to the movement's success. As Spalding notes, Catholicism is the country's dominant religion, and the institution enjoys high institutional trust scores among opinion poll respondents. Therefore, 'the call by Salvadoran bishops for greater environmental protection, in keeping with pronouncements from other church authorities in Central America and beyond, presented the mining industry with serious challenge'.[64]

60 Interview with Rodolfo Calles, 14 July 2014.
61 Spalding (n 8).
62 ibid.
63 Interview with anonymous official, PDDH, 23 July 2014.
64 Spalding (n 8) 21.

Finally, on the political level, the FMLN's strong support base in the provinces of Cabañas and Chalatenango—the regions affected by potential mining activity—incentivized the party to adopt an anti-mining line, and a number of FMLN deputies were directly involved in the activities of the Mesa. On the other hand, many ARENA deputies remain in favour of attracting mining to the country.[65]

According to Calles, the mining movement was successful despite the predisposition of the state to be friendly towards the industry; as he explains, 'there is a law that permits mining, there are mining companies that want to exploit minerals, all the economic conditions exist for mining to take place. However the [anti-mining] stance of the communities and pressure from the people do not allow for it.'[66]

5.4 State Interests and Policy Decisions

The Mesa and allied organizations were undoubtedly successful in placing mining on the national agenda. But how was the decision made to enact the de facto mining ban and proceed to arbitration with Pacific Rim? What made a state which had put significant efforts towards creating an investment that was climate friendly to outside investment take such anti-investor measures? Finally, what role did uncertainty or lack of awareness regarding the IIA play in the decision-making process? When government officials took these measures, did they anticipate that it would trigger an investor–state arbitration proceeding or were they unaware of the possible consequences of these policy decisions?

The Mesa's efforts to convince various important domestic institutions and the broader public that mining was not appropriate for El Salvador was well timed, given the shift in the nation's political mood. As discussed earlier, the traditionally right-leaning electorate was experiencing a shift to the left that coincided with the Mesa's efforts. This put significant pressure on ARENA in the lead-up to the elections in 2009, which likely contributed to Saca's efforts to 'publicly distance his administration from some traditional party positions . . . one area where this division can be seen is in his emerging position on the mining concessions which he began to question publicly in 2008'.[67]

Moreover, it is clear that Funes' adoption of an anti-mining position was directly related to the FMLN's traditional support base among the peasants of Cabañas and Chalatenango, where almost all mining activity in the country has been located. The role of electoral pressure in the decision to enact the de facto mining ban was

65 Interview with Edgardo Mira, 29 July 2014.
66 Interview with Rodolfo Calles, 14 July 2014.
67 Spalding (n 8) 29.

emphasized by a number of interviewees, who doubted the sincerity of Saca's anti-mining position. As Saul Baños, the lawyer for the Mesa argued:

> I believe that they saw it as a benefit to their image. Above all, knowing [Saca's] record, I can say that rather than good intentions, or an environmental concern, it was a political question. It's not the same as if he had done it at the beginning of his mandate. And moreover, if it had been a genuine interest, he could have promoted a law that banned mining.[68]

It thus seems that Saca made this announcement in the context of an election in which mining had become a key issue and his presidency was at stake, while others in his government and party held pro-mining and investment preferences.

While the political utility of an anti-mining position in the lead-up to the 2009 elections is clear, this does not negate the fact that the bureaucratic resistance to Pacific Rim's project began several years earlier. It is important to note that mining was relatively new to El Salvador and, as both news articles and interviewees suggested, the government never had a clear policy towards the industry. For example, when asked why the government had changed its stance towards mining, one interviewee stated 'I don't think the government changed its position, rather El Salvador never had a clear position on [mining] or the environment. It's a very controversial subject, and I think that the institutional [capacity] of the MARN was never very strong.'[69] The *amicus* brief submitted by the Center for International Environmental Law (CIEL) to the arbitration tribunal echoes this sentiment, arguing that the potential for IIAs to cause 'regulatory chill' is exacerbated in developing countries, where 'rapid legislative development and implementation is needed rather than obstacles to the application of new laws'.[70] In the early 2000s, as Pacific Rim was in the midst of applying for exploitation permits, no studies had been carried out regarding the viability of mining in the country, and even then, observers were criticizing the government for not having a clear position on mining.[71] It is possible that, prior to the opposition movement spearheaded by the Mesa, officials in El Salvador had never seriously considered the impact of mining on the country. When faced with the strong opposition to mining from the public, it had to develop a policy position in an ad hoc manner.

Indeed, as this lack of serious consideration of the possibilities of mining implies, extractive industries never played a significant role in El Salvador's economic development plan. As one government official explained, El Salvador identified a number of strategic sectors in which it endeavours to attract investment—textiles,

[68] Interview with Saul Baños, 13 August 2014.
[69] Interview with Marjorie Trigueros, 22 July 2014.
[70] Orellana (n 49) 13.
[71] Felix Pacas, 'Centroamérica Cierra Filas Contra La Minería' *Comunica en Linea* (2007).

confections, aeronautics, pharmaceuticals, electronics, and business services such as call centres. Mining has never been a priority for the government.[72] An official from PROESA, El Salvador's investment promotion agency, underlined this point: 'PROESA doesn't have a policy of promoting mining . . . it's necessary to respect the will of the country that doesn't want to attract investment in certain sectors.'[73] Therefore, the lack of reliance on mining (compared to other countries in Latin America such as Peru and Guatemala, which depend heavily on the sector and have not conceded to anti-mining movements) may have allowed El Salvador to be more receptive to anti-investor public pressure in this case. This observation is strengthened by the insistence of several interviewees from various government bodies that El Salvador has only had disputes with investors in 'difficult' strategic sectors such as mining and energy, not with companies in the areas El Salvador wishes to promote such as manufacturing.[74]

Finally, how did the 'strategic setting', in this case, a setting in which state policy options are constrained by the IIA, affect decision-making regarding Pacific Rim? Was this dispute ultimately caused by cost–benefit calculations of policymakers or a lack of awareness of their obligations under CAFTA and the national Investment Law?

There was no consensus among interviewees regarding policymakers' levels of awareness of IIAs and the possibility for investment arbitration before the government's dispute with Pacific Rim and other mining companies. The ARENA government had no known experience with investor–state disputes prior to 2009.[75] Moreover, a number of interviewees spoke negatively of the technical capacity of various government bodies. As one ex-government employee noted, 'I think that the dispute resolution mechanisms are not well known. The majority of public officials don't know them, nor are they aware of the content of the bilateral investment treaties we've signed.'[76] Luis Parada, a member of El Salvador's legal team, is of the opinion that prior to the Pacific Rim case, 'there were perhaps one or two officials in the [Ministry of Economy] who were aware of [the IIA] but they had no idea how it would work.'[77] However, others argued that there were processes in place to ensure that new policies were in compliance with IIA obligations and, 'in such a small country there is a great deal of central control, too much, and we have tried to sensitize government employees' to the obligations of investment treaties.[78]

However, regardless of the levels of awareness among public officials regarding the provisions of CAFTA and the Investment Law before the advent of the Pacific

[72] Interview with anonymous government official, 18 July 2014.
[73] Interview with anonymous official, PROESA, 7 August 2014.
[74] Interview with anonymous government official, 18 July 2014; interview with PROESA official, 7 August 2014.
[75] Interview with anonymous official, 12 August 2014.
[76] Interview with Marjorie Trigueros, 22 July 2014.
[77] Interview with Luis Parada, 15 September 2014.
[78] Interview with anonymous official, PROESA, 7 August 2014.

Rim arbitration, witness statements from both the prosecution and the defence make it clear that the threat of arbitration was communicated to President Saca's administration before the official Notice of Intent was sent. Moreover, the president made public statements claiming that he would rather pay fines than allow the granting of mining permits.[79] Therefore, it is clear that the government of El Salvador did make conscious cost–benefit calculations in the face of opposing public and investor pressure and chose to concede to the former.

5.5 Conclusion

There is significant evidence that the anti-mining preferences of broad interest groups played a clear role in shifting the preferences of the government towards the industry. From the end of the civil war in the early 1990s, El Salvador's conservative government had a very open policy towards investment and made efforts to attract mining projects. Moreover, it appears that many government actors were initially quite supportive of Pacific Rim's projects. However, faced with mounting public pressure against mining, in the lead-up to a contested election, the government reversed its position. Indeed, it is clear that political considerations did play a role in state actors' decisions regarding mining development in El Salvador, and the anti-mining movement should be given credit for drawing national attention to the issue. Even if the MARN and other government agencies had been debating the merits of mining for several years, the timing of Saca's announcement suggests that he was not swayed primarily by environmental concerns. As mentioned in Chapter 2, executives that are able to act unilaterally and face incentives (in this case, electoral pressure) to enact policy reversal vis-à-vis an investment seem quite likely to do so. This underscores the role of changing domestic preferences in contributing to investor–state disputes.

However, state capacity appears to have also played a role in this dispute. As both the claimant and the state mentioned repeatedly during the arbitration proceedings, mining was new to El Salvador. The claimant used this as an excuse for the many delays it faced in trying to obtain its environmental and exploitation licences, arguing that this lack of capacity slowed down the process but was not indicative of actual opposition to the project based on genuine environmental concerns on the part of policymakers. Therefore, the claimant argued, these delays were not an expression of a purposive policy decision but rather errors which prevented the government from adhering to its stated policy (and legal obligations) of allowing the investor's project to go ahead. The government did not deny that there was a lack of capacity, particularly within the MARN to properly regulate mining activity.

[79] Notice of Arbitration, *Pac Rim Cayman LLC v Republic of El Salvador* (n 15).

However, it argued that there was recognition of the deficiencies within the bureaucracy, particularly regarding assessing and monitoring the environmental impact of mining in the country. Thus, they partially attributed these delays in the claimant's attempts to obtain the required licences, as well as the eventual broad 'policy shift' that placed a moratorium on mining, to the government's judgement that it did not at the time have the institutional capacity to regulate mining. In this case, then, a lack of state capacity also contributed to the investor–state dispute in question. However, given the government's aforementioned open stance towards mining and the significant need for FDI in the country, it is likely that the public opposition played an important role in pointing out this lack of institutional capacity and the weaknesses in the country's regulatory policies related to mining. In the absence of public opposition to mining, the government may not have felt the need to address these issues in the face of increased investment in the extractive sector.

Finally, interviewees suggested that Salvadoran officials did not have much awareness of CAFTA and the potential for investment arbitration prior to this case, especially in the MARN. Therefore, they likely did not consider CAFTA obligations during the processes to assess the project and decide whether or not to grant Pacific Rim the necessary licences. However, as El Salvador's legal representative noted, the investor communicated to the executive at several points that it was considering investment arbitration. Indeed, Luis Parada claimed that arbitration was threatened as far back as 2007, and the investor stated that they reached out to both the outgoing President Saca and the incoming President Funes regarding the conflict. Indeed, President Saca himself announced that he would rather the government pay $90 million as a result of the arbitration than grant the investor the concession (Memorial on the Merits). Therefore, whether the potential benefits were political support or environmental protection (or likely, a bit of both) the government of El Salvador clearly decided that these outweighed the potential costs posed by arbitration.

However, despite the apparent victory of the anti-mining movement in altering the preferences of the Salvadoran government, mining remained a possibility for El Salvador until the arbitration proceedings came to a close, in El Salvador's favour. It was only then that the Congress passed legislation officially banning metallic mining in the country, an outcome attributed by observers to El Salvador's success in the arbitration with Pacific Rim.[80]

This brings us to the wider relevance of this case—it highlights the potential effect that investor–state dispute settlement (ISDS) can have on the development of policy in issue areas adjacent to foreign investment. Indeed, it is arguable that the arbitration case played a role in stalling decision-making regarding the status of

[80] Williams (n 1).

mining in the country. This was in part due to the fear that passing legislation officially banning mining would provoke further arbitration cases. Over twenty-five mining companies had concessions granted to them, and while the administrative processes regarding their permits were suspended, according to employees at Oxfam America, the fear of provoking these investors to make claims against the state impeded the government from promoting a law to officially ban mining.[81] This statement was echoed by Yanira Cortez, deputy attorney for the environment in the PDDH office in an interview with *The Guardian*: 'There are so many permits on standby right now, so there is fear that these companies will follow the lead of Pacific Rim.'[82]

One interviewee also suggested that the state had analysed the situation and decided that 'in this moment we can't pass a law [prohibiting mining] because it would be counter-productive in the case against Pac Rim'.[83] Similarly, Luis Parada, El Salvador's legal counsel stated:

> That there is no official position on mining is in part due to the arbitration. There are two bills currently before parliament, one is a moratorium and one is an outright ban that would prohibit metallic mining. The government has not taken action on either one, in part because they are waiting for the arbitration to be over.[84]

One reason for this may be that in the context of the arbitration, the defence's argument relied primarily on proving that Pacific Rim (a) did not meet the technical requirements for an environmental permit to be granted, or complete its feasibility study; (b) failed to adequately address the concerns of the local communities as well as outside experts; and (c) did not complete the purchase of the land required for their operations.[85] Moreover, El Salvador argued that numerous external experts advised the MARN to suspend mining activity due to the ministry's lack of technical capacity to ensure that it did not cause environmental damage and because constitutionally, the government is required to adopt a precautionary principle towards protecting the environment and human health.[86] However, the MARN's report on mining was only completed in 2012. Therefore, as mentioned above, the defence argued that:

> El Salvador's decisions regarding metallic mining in general and Pac Rim's environmental permit specifically did not have any impact on Pac Rim ... El Salvador's

[81] Interview with Oxfam America employee, 12 August 2014.
[82] Claire Provost, 'El Salvador Groups Accuse Pacific Rim of "Assault on Democratic Governance"' *The Guardian* (10 April 2014) <http://www.theguardian.com/global-development/2014/apr/10/el-salvador-pacific-rim-assault-democratic-governance> accessed 23 February 2022>.
[83] Interview with anonymous official, PDDH, 23 July 2014.
[84] Interview with Luis Parada, 15 September 2014.
[85] 'The Republic of El Salvador's Counter-Memorial on the Merits' (n 23).
[86] ibid.

policy decision did not affect any rights with regard to exploration licences because Pac Rim did not have a right to the exploration licenses for which it claims damages.[87]

Thus, in the context of the arbitration case, El Salvador attempted to highlight the technical aspects of its decision-making regarding Pacific Rim's application for an exploitation licence rather than the political contestation, which I have argued contributed first to President Saca's decision to announce a de facto ban on mining and then to President Funes' declaration that no mining would take place were he to be elected, and his subsequent continuation of this ban. Of course, this does not discount the legitimate concerns that the MARN had about its own technical capacity to monitor the mining industry or the faults in Pacific Rim's application materials; I do not argue that these considerations played no role in the state's decision-making. However, before the tribunal, the defence made a concerted effort to deny the claimant's position that the decision to withhold Pacific Rim's licence was a political one. If a law banning mining had been passed after the company had first threatened arbitration, this could undermine the state's argument that it based its decision on technical criteria.

This emphasis on the technical aspect of decision-making is likely due to the lack of value arbitral tribunals have historically placed on a state's political considerations—measures which are seen to be applied hastily due to political pressure are not considered legitimate under the IIA regime, and indeed the normative content of the IIAs and arbitral decisions privileges technical criteria over political considerations.[88]

Indeed, it is difficult to imagine how a country like El Salvador might enact a measure such as ban on mining, if any concessions had previously been granted, and not subsequently provoke investment arbitration. El Salvador certainly is not above reproach in the way it dealt with Pacific Rim, and it is not clear whether or not the key decision-makers held genuine reservations about the suitability of mining in El Salvador or were more concerned with maintaining political support. However, there were legitimate questions regarding the feasibility of mining in such a densely populated and water-insecure country. In an era when citizens, non-state actors, and international organizations are increasingly concerned with environmentally sound and sustainable development, there may be increased calls, especially in countries such as El Salvador that do not have a well-defined position on the industry and are not overly dependent on it, to rethink the promotion of investment in the extractive industry. Therefore, it may become politically as well as

[87] ibid 125.

[88] Nicole Yazbek, 'Bilateral Investment Treaties: The Foreclosure of Domestic Policy Space' (2010) 17 South African Journal of International Affairs 103; Todd Tucker, 'The Concept of the State in Investor–State Arbitration' in Shaheeza Lalani and Rodrigo Polanco Lazo (eds), *The Role of the State in Investor–State Arbitration* (Brill Nijhoff 2015).

environmentally desirable not to grant licences to extractive projects, regardless of whether they technically meet the legal requirements already in place. Of course, while the passing of anti-mining legislation is perhaps a more desirable approach, as it could avoid charges of breach of national or most favoured nation treatment provisions, legislative measures may still be challenged as expropriations. Thus, the *Pacific Rim v El Salvador* case demonstrates the ways in which ISDS may inhibit broader policy change.

6
Bilcon of Delaware Ltd v Canada

This chapter presents the investor–state dispute between Canada and Bilcon of Delaware Ltd, a construction company from New Jersey. The company proposed a quarrying project in Nova Scotia in order to supply itself with the raw material it needed for roads and other construction projects. The project was to comprise a quarry and marine terminal from which the material would be shipped to the United States. The potential investment generated significant opposition from nearby communities and civil society groups and underwent a very strict environmental assessment process by a panel of experts, who ultimately recommended that the government not approve the project. Following an official notice that the project would not be approved, the investor turned to arbitration under the North America Free Trade Agreement's (NAFTA's) Chapter 11. As will be discussed in greater detail, this case is quite clearly an example of the contribution of changing domestic preferences towards an investment to investor–state disputes rather than a dispute that arose out of a lack of state capacity to maintain an investment-friendly environment.

Beyond this, the case is significant in a number of ways. First, it underscores the element of increased uncertainty that investor–state dispute settlement (ISDS) brings to domestic policymaking as, at the federal level, officials were aware of the possibility of an investment claim brought under NAFTA but did not think it likely in this case. Additionally, it demonstrates the challenge that ISDS can pose to the raising of regulatory standards and the updating or evolution of domestic legal norms.[1]

6.1 IIAs and Investment in Canada and Nova Scotia

Although Canada has traditionally been a net importer of capital, with an economy based largely on natural resources, its stance on foreign investment has fluctuated over the years.[2] While, during the 1970s, the Foreign Investment Review Agency maintained fairly stringent barriers to investment, Canada's investment climate

[1] Lise Johnson and Lisa Sachs, 'Eyes Wide Shut on ISDS', *The Hill* (22 April 2015).

[2] Mark A Luz and Marc Miller, 'Globalization and Canadian Federalism: Implications of the NAFTA's Investment Rules' (2002) 47 McGill Law Journal 951.

The Political Economy of Investment Arbitration. Zoe Phillips Williams, Oxford University Press.
DOI: 10.1093/oso/9780198865940.003.0006

was liberalized during the 1980s with the Investment Canada Act (ICA).[3] In the late 1980s, Canada also began to assert its interests as a capital exporter, signing a number of bilateral investment treaties (BITs), known in Canada as foreign investment protection agreements (FIPAs).[4] Finally, Canada furthered its commitment to free trade and investment with the signing of the Canadian–US Free Trade Agreement in 1988 and NAFTA in 1994. Canada is in fact quite dependent on foreign direct investment (FDI), particularly from the United States—at the time of the dispute with Bilcon, 30 per cent of Canadian employment and 75 per cent of its manufacturing exports came from US FDI.[5]

This chapter focuses on a case that was triggered by a series of measures taken by both the federal government and the provincial government of Nova Scotia—a province with, at that time, less experience with foreign investment than other parts of the country. FDI in the Atlantic Provinces of Canada is quite low, although Nova Scotia hosts the largest amount of FDI in the region; during the time period relevant to this study, the average annual inflow to the province was US$1.6 billion, although this is due almost entirely to its off-shore oil production.[6] Beyond oil extraction, Nova Scotia has traditionally relied on fishing, agriculture, and mining. With the overall decline of the fishing industry in the region, Nova Scotia, along with other Atlantic provinces, suffered from higher rates of unemployment than other parts of the country. Therefore, in the early 2000s the provincial government, led by the Progressive Conservative party, promoted low business taxes and the attraction of FDI as a strategy to encourage economic growth and increase employment rates.[7] The areas which the province identified as key economic sectors included fishing and fish products; extractive industries such as forestry, mining, oil, and gas; agriculture; tourism and culture; communications; and life sciences.[8] In particular, Nova Scotia welcomed investment in the mining sector, as laid out in the Department of Natural Resources' 1996 report 'Minerals—A Policy for Nova Scotia', which commits to ensuring a competitive business climate and promoting the province's mineral potential.[9] As the claimants state in their Notice of Intent, it was in the context of this push for foreign investment that they initiated their investment in the province.[10]

[3] Laura Dawson, 'Potash and BlackBerries: Should Canada Treat All Foreign Direct Investment the Same?' (2012) MacDonald-Laurier Institute <https://www.macdonaldlaurier.ca/files/pdf/Should-Canada-Treat-All-FDI-The-Same-Commentary-June-2012.pdf> accessed 24 April 2022.

[4] Luz and Miller (n 2).

[5] Gilbert R Winham, 'Advice on the Application and Implications of the North American Free Trade Agreement (NAFTA) to the Proposed Whites Point Quarry and Marine Terminal Project' 1 <https://www.ceaa.gc.ca/archives/pre-2003/D67F0296-1/WP-1818.pdf> accessed 24 April 2022.

[6] APEC (Atlantic Provinces Economic Council), 'Attracting the Big Bucks: Foreign Investment in Atlantic Canada' (2005).

[7] NSED, 'Opportunities for Prosperity: A New Economic Growth Strategy for Nova Scotians' (Nova Scotia Economic Development 2000).

[8] APEC (n 6); NSED (n 7).

[9] DNR, 'Minerals—A Policy for Nova Scotia' (Department of Natural Resources 1996).

[10] 'Notice of Intent to Submit a Claim to Arbitration under Section B of Chapter 11 of the North American Free Trade Agreement, Bilcon of Delaware Ltd. v. Canada' (2008).

6.1.1 Canada and NAFTA

Negotiations for NAFTA followed the entering into force of the Canadian–US Free Trade Agreement (CUFTA) and Mexico's subsequent suggestion of a bilateral trade agreement with the United States.[11] Despite long-standing economic interdependence, Canada's efforts to lower trade barriers with the United States, first through CUFTA and subsequently with NAFTA, faced resistance both within the government and from the electorate due to a long-standing fear of American encroachment on Canadian sovereignty in general and specific concerns relating to the weakening of Canada's much more active welfare state.[12] According to Abbott, Canada therefore joined the NAFTA negotiations 'defensively', as the country had very little previous economic interest in Mexico but did not want to be left out of the United States' efforts to liberalize Latin American markets.[13]

NAFTA was a highly detailed trade agreement, comprised of twenty-two chapters, including Chapter 11 on investment, and was unique in that, at the time this dispute unfolded, it was the only ratified international agreement which regulated substantial investment flows between developed countries. NAFTA's ratification was followed by increased FDI flows between the three signatories, which many observers attribute to the agreement in general and Chapter 11 in particular.[14]

The rationale behind the inclusion of an investor–state arbitration clause in NAFTA was primarily the protection of US investors in Mexico, particularly given the country's history of expropriations in the petroleum industry.[15] However, as we saw in Chapter 2, the outcome of NAFTA Chapter 11, in terms of investor–state disputes, has been somewhat different; Canada has been a respondent in at least as many cases as Mexico, and the United States is not far behind. Indeed, according to one federal official with whom I spoke, 'when [Canada] entered into NAFTA, we didn't think we would get sued as much as we are'.[16] Beyond the number of cases, Abbott argues that the dispute settlement mechanism has 'been invoked by private investors in circumstances that were not contemplated by NAFTA negotiators'.[17] These likely include the challenges to long-standing Canadian institutions such as Canada Post and the Canadian Healthcare Act.

[11] Frederick M Abbott, 'NAFTA and the Legalization of World Politics: A Case Study' (2000) 54 International Organization 519.

[12] Stephanie R Golob, 'Beyond the Policy Frontier: Canada, Mexico, and the Ideological Origins of NAFTA' (2003) 55 World Politics 361.; R Johnson and R Mahon, 'NAFTA, the Redesign, and Rescaling of Canada's Welfare State' (2005) 76 Studies in Political Economy 7.

[13] Abbott (n 11).

[14] ibid.

[15] Jennifer A Heindl, 'Toward a History of NAFTA's Chapter Eleven' (2006) 24 Berkeley Journal of International Law 672.

[16] Interview with anonymous Federal official, 11 April 2014.

[17] Abbott (n 11) 522.

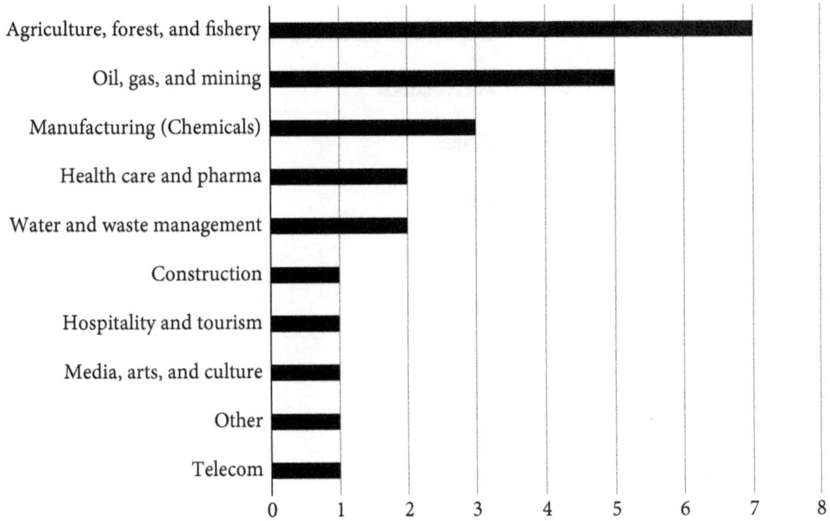

Figure 6.1 Canada as a respondent by industry

Canada was served with its first notice of intent in 1996 by a Mexican generic pharmaceuticals manufacturer, but arbitration never commenced.[18] The first case that progressed to arbitration, and which has subsequently become fairly infamous, is that of *Ethyl Corp*. *Canada*, in which an American chemicals manufacturer challenged Canada's ban of MMT, a gasoline additive. Faced with an arbitration case that appeared to be going in favour of the investor, Canada repealed the ban, issued an apology to the company, and settled out of arbitration for $13 million.[19] Thus, the *Ethyl* case was exemplary of the 'capitulatory' manner in which Canada resolved its early arbitration cases.[20] More recently, Canada has settled high-profile cases with Abitibi Bowater for the expropriation of timber and water rights and with Dow Agrosciences over a dispute involving another chemical ban. Canada has also lost significant cases, including one with Mobil Investments over the imposition of research and development requirements as well as the challenge by Bilcon Ltd discussed in this chapter. On the other hand, Canada has won a number of important cases, including challenges to its national postal service, lumber export policies, and the Canada Health Act. Most recently, the country was successful in defending itself against its first non-NAFTA claim, brought by an Egyptian telecom investor. The sectors in which Canada has faced disputes are displayed in Figure 6.1.

[18] Canadian Centre for Policy Alternatives, 'NAFTA Chapter 11 Investor–State Disputes' (CCPA 2010).
[19] ibid.
[20] Gus Van Harten, 'Reform of Investor–State Arbitration: A Perspective from Canada' (2011) <https://digitalcommons.osgoode.yorku.ca/all_papers/31/> accessed 24 April 2022.

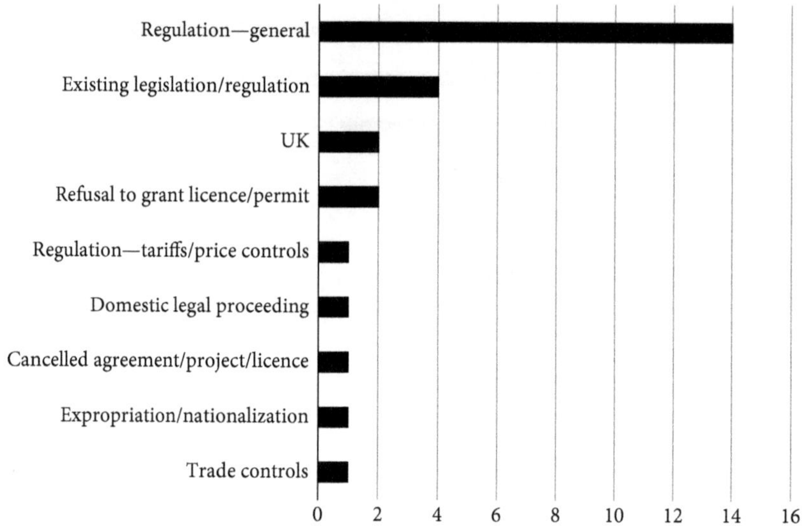

Figure 6.2 Measures taken by Canada

Many of the sectors in which Canada has experienced disputes mirror those that appear in the top ten sectors for arbitration cases overall. On the other hand, as can be seen in Figure 6.2, almost half of all cases in which Canada has been the respondent have been triggered by investors challenging a regulatory measure.

Canada's experience with NAFTA arbitration has generated significant criticism from civil society, particularly surrounding high-profile cases related to environmental protection measures such as the dispute with Lone Pine Resources, a gas exploration company challenging Quebec's provincial ban on fracking and the case discussed in this chapter.[21] Some observers have further expressed concern regarding the impact of NAFTA on Canadian federalism as it impedes the ability of provinces to regulate FDI, 'an area where provinces have traditionally exercised significant control. [The result] will likely be a concomitant expansion in federal power at the expense of the provinces.'.[22] Other observers take the position that 'Chapter 11 has not caused an "erosion of federalism", rather it has created circumstances in which governments may have to pay for federalism and for the maintenance of democratically instituted policies.'[23] As will be discussed, this statement is certainly applicable to the arbitration case between Bilcon and Canada, in which

[21] See, eg The Council of Canadians 'Lone Pine Resources Files Outrageous NAFTA Lawsuit Against Fracking Ban' (3 October 2013) <https://canadians.org/update/lone-pine-resources-files-outrageous-nafta-lawsuit-against-fracking-ban> accessed 23 February 2022.

[22] Luz and Miller (n 2) 976.

[23] Andres McKinley, 'A Brief Contextual Analysis of the Legal Suit of Pacific Rim Mining Company against the Government of El Salvador' Oxfam America (2009) 100.

the federal government was found to be in violation of NAFTA as a result of actions taken primarily by the provincial government of Nova Scotia.

6.2 The Dispute between Bilcon Ltd and Canada

The claimants, the Clayton family, own a cement company based in New Jersey and proposed to construct a 152-hectare quarry and marine terminal on Whites Point in Digby Neck, Nova Scotia, on the shore of the Bay of Fundy. The company was eager to find sources of aggregate outside the state of New Jersey, where, due to higher regulatory standards, opening new quarries was no longer feasible.[24] While aggregate is ideally consumed close to the source as transport costs are high, shipping the extracted aggregate from Nova Scotia to the US eastern seaboard was considered an acceptable alternative.[25] Initially, the investors claim they met with significant support from the provincial government, especially from Conservative provincial Minister of Fisheries and Agriculture, Gordon Balser, who was also the representative of the riding in which the quarry was to operate.[26]

In 2002, the company first filed an application with the Nova Scotia Department of Environment and Labour (NSEL) to operate a smaller 3.9 hectare quarry on the site ultimately designated for the larger project.[27] This smaller quarry was to be operated in order to gather data for the assessment of the extractive process on the environment as well as to stockpile aggregate for future operations.[28] The NSEL determined that as the initial blasting of the rock was itself likely to have detrimental environmental effects, the proponent required authorization from the federal Department of Fisheries and Oceans (DFO) to proceed. In turn, the DFO concluded that an environmental assessment for the larger site, of which this smaller quarry was ultimately a part, was required in order for any blasting activity to take place.[29]

The involvement of the federal DFO put the project under both provincial and federal jurisdiction, and thus the Canadian Environmental Assessment Act (CEAA) directed the environmental application process. In 2003, the DFO advised the claimants to engage the services of an environmental consultant who was familiar with the CEAA process, although the government alleges that they failed

[24] Noah Richler, 'Rock Bottom' [2007] *The Walrus* <http://www.thewalrus.ca/rock-bottom> accessed 23 February 2022.

[25] ibid.

[26] Award on Jurisdiction and Liability, *William Ralph Clayton, William Richard Clayton, Douglas Clayton, Daniel Clayton and Bilcon of Delaware Inc v Canada* (PCA) Case No 2009-04 (2009).

[27] The size of the quarry, at 3.9 hectares, was not accidental, as legally a quarry larger than 4 hectares would require approval from the Minister of Environment.

[28] Statement of Defence of the Government of Canada, *William Ralph Clayton, William Richard Clayton, Douglas Clayton, Daniel Clayton and Bilcon of Delaware Inc v Canada* (PCA) Case No 2009-04 (2009).

[29] ibid.

to do so for several years.[30] At this time, as will be discussed at greater length in subsequent sections, public concern over the project was growing, indicated by the dozens of letters from concerned citizens and environmental groups archived on the CEAA website. Various government agencies also expressed environmental concerns regarding the disruption to marine life habitat, although according to correspondence archived on the CEAA, other officials doubted that the project posed a significant threat.[31]

In 2004, the federal Minister of Environment and his provincial counterpart agreed that the company's proposed project would be assessed by a Joint Review Panel (JRP), which is undertaken when the minister is of the opinion that a project may generate 'significant adverse effects' about which there is public concern.[32] The JRP was comprised of three university professors: biologist Robert Fournier, planner Jill Grant, and geologist Gunter Muecke. The Panel was to review Bilcon's environmental impact statement (EIS) and solicit feedback from the public on what should be included in the statement. The Panel was then to make further recommendations on the EIS, allow the company to address its concerns, and make a final recommendation to the federal and provincial government based on its own expertise and public comments, regarding whether the project should be given government approval to move forward.

The Panel accepted over 600 submissions from the public on what should be included in the EIS and held public hearings in June of 2007. During the hearings, it received testimony from 78 citizens and a further 126 written submissions from local individuals and organizations. Based on this input, as well as consultations with federal ministries, such as Environment Canada and Health Canada, the JRP issued its recommendation in November of 2007 that the project posed a threat to the 'core values of the community' as well as 'existing and future environmental, social and cultural conditions'.[33] Shortly thereafter, the federal and provincial governments officially rejected the company's proposal. In 2008, the company announced its intent to arbitrate, and arbitration commenced in 2009.

6.2.1 The Arbitration: *Bilcon of Delaware Ltd v Canada*

The arbitral tribunal was constituted in April 2009 under United Nations Commission on International Trade Law (UNCITRAL) arbitration rules, was administered by the Permanent Court of Arbitration (PCA), and took place in

[30] Correspondence between Paul Buxton, Project Manager for Bilcon and the DFO, 14 April 2003.

[31] Award on Jurisdiction and Liability, William Ralph Clayton, William Richard Clayton, Douglas Clayton, Daniel Clayton and Bilcon of Delaware Inc v Canada (n 26).

[32] Canadian Environmental Assessment Agency, 'What Is an Environmental Assessment by Joint Review Panel?' (CEAA).

[33] Robert Fournier, Jill Grant, and Gunter Muecke, 'The Environmental Assessment of the Whites Point Quarry and Marine Terminal Project: Joint Review Panel Report' (2007).

Table 6.1 Arguments and rulings

Alleged breach of NAFTA	Claimant's arguments	Tribunal's ruling
1102 National Treatment	Respondent (in particular various ministries and the JRP) extended more favourable treatment to Canadian investors in like circumstances.	Tribunal finds a breach of 1102.
1103 Most Favoured Nation	Respondent extended more favourable treatment to non-Canadian investors with regard to the type and duration of environmental assessment.	Tribunal declines to find a breach of 1103 (investors claims are time barred).
1105 Minimum Standard of Treatment	Misapplication of domestic law; bias and political interference on the part of provincial politicians.	Tribunal finds a breach of 1105.

Toronto, Canada. The tribunal released its final Award in March of 2015. A summary of the investor's arguments and the tribunal's rulings is laid out in Table 6.1. According to the investors, their legitimate expectations, based on the welcome it initially received from provincial officials, as well as the province's policies regarding investment and mining, were frustrated unfairly and in violation of NAFTA articles 1102, 1103, and 1105 (see Table 6.1). The specific measures at the heart of the dispute relate directly to the environmental assessment imposed on the project.[34] First, the investors claimed that the decision of the provincial and federal governments to submit their project to the JRP was unwarranted, given the features of their proposed project. Moreover, they argued, other investors—both foreign and Canadian—in 'like circumstances' were not subjected to the demanding environmental review process.[35]

Additionally, the decision to assess the project by means of a JRP was, the claimants argued, not due to legitimate environmental concerns on the part of the government but to political bias against the project. In the provincial elections of 2003, Progressive Conservative MP Gordon Balser, who had been quite welcoming of the project, lost to local fisherman and Liberal candidate Harold Thériault, who, during the public hearings held by the JRP, claimed that he won the election based on his opposition to the project. Moreover, Robert Thibault, Minister of the DFO and federal MP for the riding (electoral district) in which the proposed quarry

[34] Statement of Claim, *Bilcon of Delaware Inc v Government of Canada* (PCA) Case No 2009-04 (2009).

[35] Award on Jurisdiction and Liability, *William Ralph Clayton, William Richard Clayton, Douglas Clayton, Daniel Clayton and Bilcon of Delaware, Inc v Canada* (n 26).

would be located, reversed his earlier support for the quarry in the face of public opposition, coming out strongly against it in the public hearings. The claimants argued that these public statements against the quarry were motivated solely by the electoral concerns of Mr Thibault.[36] They further argued that the delays they suffered after the project was put under the jurisdiction of the DFO were due to the minister's desire to extend the process as long as possible.[37] Therefore, the claimants argued that 'behind the scenes there was inappropriate political interference in the regulatory process'.[38]

The claimants also took issue with both the way in which the JRP carried out its public hearings and the criteria the Panel used to evaluate the project. Regarding the former, the claimants suggested that nationalistic and anti-American sentiments were allowed to dominate the public hearings.[39] Most important, according to the investors, was the basis on which the JRP ultimately rejected the project—namely, that it conflicted with 'core community values'. According to the claimants, this concept:

> is not among the environmental impacts that are lawful or proper scope of an environmental assessment process under the laws of federal Canada or Nova Scotia. The guidelines for the JRP refer to various social effects, like impact on values such as 'sense of place', but do not refer to the concept of 'community core values'.[40]

The claimant also argued that the JRP members were biased against the project and, in particular, did not consider possible mitigation efforts which could offset the environmental effects of the quarry. Finally, the claimants argued that in the wake of the JRP's recommendation, Nova Scotia's Minister of Environment refused to meet with them to hear their concerns or allow them any written input to contest the JRP's decision. Therefore, they argue, the Minister 'abdicated his responsibility to exercise his independent discretion, denied procedural fairness to Bilcon and failed to explain his decision'.[41]

The government of Canada refuted these claims. First, the government denied that the claimants were given special incentives or treatment to convince them to make their investment, and any meetings between the investors and government officials took place after the decision was made to invest.[42] Furthermore, they argued that given the ecologically sensitive nature of the site chosen by the investor, underscored by its status as a United Nations Educational, Scientific and Cultural

[36] Statement of Claim, *Bilcon of Delaware Inc v Government of Canada* (n 34).
[37] Award on Jurisdiction and Liability, *William Ralph Clayton, William Richard Clayton, Douglas Clayton, Daniel Clayton and Bilcon of Delaware Inc v Canada* (n 26).
[38] ibid 4.
[39] ibid.
[40] ibid 6.
[41] ibid 7.
[42] ibid.

Organization (UNESCO) Biosphere, the claimant should have expected a rigorous environmental assessment process.[43] Finally, Canada denied that the expressed environmental concerns were disingenuous and cited correspondence between ministries to that effect.

While Canada did not deny that Minister Thibault had an interest in the project, given it was to be located in his riding, the government rejected the claim that he had undue influence on the project's approval process.[44] Minister Thibault, in a sworn affidavit, stated that he had been aware from the outset of both the positive potential the quarry could bring to his riding and the growing concern among his constituents. He further stated that he did not interfere with the assessment of the quarry and did not contribute to, or desire, a delay in the process. In addition to Minister Thibault, a number of other government employees contributed sworn affidavits regarding the decision-making process surrounding the project and were subjected, as the arbiters note in their summary, 'to rigorous cross-examination' during the arbitration proceedings.[45] Overall, Canada claimed that all provincial and federal employees 'consulted with each other in a normal and lawful manner'.[46]

Canada also defended its decision to subject the investor to the rigorous JRP process. Given the project's size, including both a quarry and a marine terminal, the project would in the very least been subject to a comprehensive study, 'itself an extensive and rigorous kind of assessment'.[47] However, because of the public concern the proposed project had generated, the decision to use a JRP, which would allow significant input from the public, was considered reasonable. Moreover, the government contested that the projects cited by the claimant as being in like circumstances were not truly comparable, in large part due to varying levels of public concern surrounding them.[48] The government also contested the illegality of the 'core community values' criteria and further noted that, as per the guidelines of the review process, the claimant was given adequate notice by the JRP of the inclusion of this concept in its assessment criteria.[49]

Finally, Canada denied that the JRP was an entity for which Canada was responsible under international law and further stated that the claimants' argument that Canada breached NAFTA Article 1105 contravened international norms surrounding the 'minimum standard of treatment', which is generally seen to set a very high threshold and 'address matters where state behaviour

[43] ibid.

[44] Statement of Defence of the Government of Canada, *William Ralph Clayton, William Richard Clayton, Douglas Clayton, Daniel Clayton and Bilcon of Delaware Inc v Canada* (n 28).

[45] Award on Jurisdiction and Liability, *William Ralph Clayton, William Richard Clayton, Douglas Clayton, Daniel Clayton and Bilcon of Delaware Inc v Canada* (n 26) 9.

[46] ibid 8.

[47] ibid 9.

[48] Statement of Defence of the Government of Canada, *William Ralph Clayton, William Richard Clayton, Douglas Clayton, Daniel Clayton and Bilcon of Delaware Inc v Canada* (n 28).

[49] Award on Jurisdiction and Liability, *William Ralph Clayton, William Richard Clayton, Douglas Clayton, Daniel Clayton and Bilcon of Delaware Inc v Canada* (n 26).

is egregious'.[50] Therefore, a misapplication of domestic environmental law should not, Canada argued, be seen to breach this standard, especially when the findings of the JRP could have been fought by the claimant under domestic judicial processes.

As can be seen in Table 6.1, the majority of the arbitrators on the Bilcon tribunal ruled that Canada did breach NAFTA Articles 1102 (National Treatment) and 1105 (Minimum Standard of Treatment). The ruling of breach of Article 1105 hinged on the JRP's failure to take into account possible mitigation processes when conducting the environmental assessment, based on its belief that the project must not be carried out at all.[51] According to the tribunal, this violated CEAA guidelines and did not allow the final decision-makers—the governments of Canada and Nova Scotia—to access all the necessary information to fully assess the project. This was, the tribunal decided, a disappointment of the legitimate expectations of the investor—that the project 'would be assessed on the merits of its environmental soundness'—based on the initial welcome they had received from provincial officials.[52] The tribunal blamed this outcome on they what they called the JRP's 'unprecedented' core community values approach, which was 'inimical to the proponents having any real chance of success based on an assessment of their individual project on its merits in accordance with the laws in force at the time'.[53]

The tribunal further agreed that Canada had breached Article 1102, guaranteeing national treatment to foreign investors. The tribunal agreed with the claimant that the decision to refer the project to the JRP was unusual but ruled that these claims were time barred, given that the decision was taken over three years before the investors turned to arbitration.[54] Instead, the breach came from the treatment that the investors experienced as a result of the JRP's failure to take possible mitigation measures into consideration—something that domestic investors in like circumstances had not suffered.[55]

As mentioned earlier, these rulings were not made unanimously, as Donald McRae, the arbitrator appointed by Canada, dissented on the ruling of the breach of Article 1105. He argued that the core community values concept was meant to capture the 'human environment effects' of the project, which was well within the mandate of the JRP and which its final report makes clear.[56] He further did not agree with the majority that any possible misapplication of Canadian law by the JRP could amount to a violation of the international minimum standard of

[50] ibid 20.
[51] ibid.
[52] ibid 130.
[53] ibid.
[54] NAFTA limitations period of three years.
[55] Award on Jurisdiction and Liability, *William Ralph Clayton, William Richard Clayton, Douglas Clayton, Daniel Clayton and Bilcon of Delaware Inc v Canada* (n 26).
[56] *Bilcon of Delaware Inc v Government of Canada* (PCA) Case No 2009-04 (2015), Dissenting Opinion of Professor Donald McRae.

treatment.[57] Finally, McRae warned of a possible chilling effect for environmental assessment as a result of this ruling.[58]

6.3 The Role of Domestic Interests and Institutions in the *Bilcon v Canada* Case

This section provides a more in-depth look at the domestic interest groups implicated in the potential Whites Point Quarry project and the way in which these groups interacted with provincial and national institutions. It then discusses the decision-making process by policymakers and the extent to which Canada's investment-protection commitments under NAFTA were taken into account.

6.3.1 Domestic Interests: Environmental Groups, Fishermen, and Eco-Tourism Providers

As mentioned in the JRP's final report, the proposed quarry generated significant resistance in the communities around Digby Neck on both environmental and economic grounds. The interested parties came both from the local communities and from provincial and national environmental groups.

The Bay of Fundy is a UNESCO Biosphere reserve and home to the endangered North Atlantic right whale, Atlantic salmon, and leatherback turtles.[59] Concern regarding the sensitive environment was emphasized in the public commentary on the project by local citizens, government officials, and international environmental groups such as the World Wildlife Fund (WWF) and the Sierra Club. For example, the WWF noted in a letter to the CEAA that 'large-scale development, like that proposed for Whites Point, has the potential to destroy or degrade sensitive marine areas before we fully know what merits protection'.[60] The letter further noted that, as a member of the Right Whale Recovery Implementation Team, the WWF was concerned about the implications of the project. The Sierra Club of Canada similarly cited concerns regarding right whales, among other environmental issues such as threats to local biodiversity and greenhouse emissions, in its submission of comments on the draft guidelines of the EIS.[61] For its part, in 2005 the DFO

[57] ibid.

[58] ibid.

[59] Statement of Defence of the Government of Canada, *William Ralph Clayton, William Richard Clayton, Douglas Clayton, Daniel Clayton and Bilcon of Delaware Inc v Canada* (n 28).

[60] World Wildlife Fund, 'Comments on Proposed Review Panel for Digby Neck Quarry' (21 January 2005) email to CEAA (on file).

[61] Sierra Club of Canada, 'Comments on the Draft Guidelines for the Environmental Impact Statement of the Whites Point Quarry and Marine Terminal Project' submitted to the CEAA (January 2005) (on file).

submitted comments to the CEAA on the draft EIS guidelines, underlining its concern for local fish habitats in general and specific at-risk species such as the Atlantic salmon and right whale.[62]

The environmental concerns of the community were quite closely linked to concerns regarding the economic impact of the project. The primary economic activity in the area has traditionally been commercial fishing, particularly for scallops and lobsters.[63] The concerns that local fisherman had regarding the project were expressed in letters to the CEAA and input into the formulation of the EIS guidelines. For example, a local fishermen's association wrote to the DFO expressing its opposition to the project due to contamination of the bay from ballast water brought by the ships coming from New Jersey, where coastal waters have been contaminated with a lobster parasite.[64] As the letter explains,

> as a result of the proposed quarry operations vessels will transport cargo from the Digby Neck area . . . to the coastal waters of New Jersey. . . . When these vessels enter our Fundy waters they will dump their ballast in their wake prior to arriving in our port. It is well documented that ballast water transports foreign organisms that harm kelp, seaweed, clams, worms, fish, and various other sea life.[65]

Therefore, the association wrote, the quarry project would undermine future fishing operations' sustainability, and it concluded, 'we strongly oppose a development where the negative far outweighs the positive'.[66] A local fishery articulated a number of concerns regarding the impact of the quarry in a letter to the DFO, which included navigational problems caused by the large marine terminal for small fishing boats as well as increased traffic in the Bay. The letter exhorts the DFO to 'take an open approach to this project by considering these concerns, instead of letting large companies rule with big numbers'.[67] A second lobster fisherman's association wrote in with similar concerns.[68]

Additionally, the area had recently become a destination for eco-tourism activities such as whale watching, birding, kayaking, and canoeing. In a letter to the DFO very early on in the assessment of the project, the Partnership for the

[62] Fisheries and Oceans Canada, 'Re: Whites Point Quarry and Marine Terminal—Comments on the EIS Guidelines' email to CEAA (on file) (2005).

[63] Statement of Defence of the Government of Canada, *William Ralph Clayton, William Richard Clayton, Douglas Clayton, Daniel Clayton and Bilcon of Delaware Inc v Canada* (n 28).

[64] Fournier, Grant, and Muecke (n 33).

[65] West Nova Fishing Coalition, 'Opposition to "Vessel Transportation" Resulting from the Proposed Product to Be Mined on Digby Neck Nova Scotia' (January 2005) submitted to CEAA (on file).

[66] ibid.

[67] Walker Fisheries Ltd, 'Proposed Marine Terminal White's Cove' email to CEAA (17 March 2003) (on file).

[68] LFA District 34 Lobster Committee, 'Fishing Industry Concerns Regarding Habitat, Water Quality, Social and Economic Concerns Issues to be Incorporated into the Guideline Development for the Preparation of the Environmental Impact Statement to be Carried out by Bilcon of Nova Scotia Corporation' submitted to the CEAA (24 March 2003) (on file).

Sustainable Development of Digby Neck & Islands Society wrote that 'tourism operators in the Bay of Fundy area are presently working hard to promote such sports as salt water kayaking, canoeing and other small boat activities'.[69] In the event that a large marine terminal was built in the Cove, the letter explains, these small craft would be put in danger, being forced away from the shoreline and into the strong currents of the bay in order to navigate around the terminal. A local whale-watching tour organizer wrote to the CEAA, extensively detailing concerns both on the effect of the quarry on local whale and dolphin populations and on the tourism industry in the area.[70]

Therefore, while the quarry would bring jobs to the area, there were concerns that these economic benefits did not outweigh the costs. The company predicted that it would provide thirty-four permanent jobs to the community, but the area supported ten lobster fishing licences, which provided approximately thirty-five jobs.[71] Overall, the lobster industry contributed $300 million to the area, and $37 million came from tourism activities.[72] Thus, the potential harm to these key industries generated far more fear from the local communities than the opportunities provided by the quarry could allay. As one interviewee summarized:

> it's not every day that projects get that kind of reaction from the communities, and that was probably a product of the location and its magnitude, and it's a large project in a rural community that has some environmental sensitivities . . . a lot of concerns originated in the cross section of those issues.[73]

Over the course of the project assessment, hundreds of local residents wrote letters to the CEAA and other government bodies expressing their opposition to the project. Many of these letters spoke not just about the potential negative impact of the quarry on specific aspects of the environment or economic activities but also about concerns related to a broader view of what kind of development was appropriate for the area. For example, one resident wrote "let's . . . wholeheartedly embrace a new vision for Nova Scotia based on green industries, renewable energy, and high-tech enterprises'.[74] Others spoke of the importance of preserving the area as it was, where residents could 'listen to wild seals sunning themselves on the rocks, watch

[69] The Digby Neck Community Development Association, 'Comments on Draft Agreement Establishment of a Joint Review Panel for the Whites Point Quarry Project between the Minister of the Environment, Canada and the Minister of the Environment and Labour, Nova Scotia' email to CEAA (8 September 2003) (on file).

[70] Brier Island Whale and Seabird Cruises Ltd, 'Letter Submitted to the Joint Review Panel' submitted to the CEAA (18 January 2005) (on file).

[71] Richler (n 24).

[72] ibid.

[73] Interview with anonymous provincial official, 29 May 2014.

[74] Helen Whidden, 'White's Point Quarry Digby Neck Presentation to Review Panel June 23, 2007' (23 June 2007) submitted to the CEAA (on file).

the sun set, breathe clean air, enjoy the beauty and unspoiled landscape'.[75] Finally, a recurring theme was that the environment and local people would be suffering for the benefit of a foreign investor—as one letter writer expressed:

> this pristine, environmentally sensitive area is in danger of being sacrificed and shipped away by the boatload to another country for the paving of their roads! All this with precious little benefit for the people of Nova Scotia in general, and particularly for those whose lives would be disrupted by the advent of a mega-quarry.[76]

As will be discussed, these broader concerns, as well as specific worries regarding the local environment and established economic interests, were well articulated by the community and appear to have contributed to the criteria on which the project was judged.

6.3.2 The Organization of Domestic Interests

Opposition to the Whites Point quarry began in the local communities around Digby Neck, with concerned citizens coming together in a group called the Partnership for Sustainable Development of Digby Neck and Islands. Among the goals of the group were to 'preserve the pristine nature of Digby Neck and Islands and to promote sustainable development that enhances quality of life' and to 'stop the mega-quarry for Whites Cove, Little River, Digby Neck and to actively oppose other developments which are inconsistent with the above criteria'.[77] Ultimately, the group comprised 350 households (540 individual members) out of the approximately 800 households in and the Islands combined. This group organized fundraisers, raising $100,000 to hire experts to help them in their campaign to stop the quarry. The group also participated in the public consultations held by the investor, as well as the JRP process, and put up 'Stop the quarry' signs in the area. In 2002, the Municipality of Digby voted against the quarry, and 1,200 people signed a letter stating their opposition to the quarry, which was sent to the provincial parliament.[78] There was also political support at the local level; 'local MLAs [Members of the Legislative Assembly], federal MPs were coming out to speak against, local and municipal councils were mostly organized in opposition. There were relatively few speaking out in favour'.[79]

[75] Eva Holzwarth, 'Outline of Brief Presentation to the Review Panel' (7 June 2007) submitted to the CEAA (on file).

[76] Michaele Kustudic, 'Outline of Brief Presentation to the Review Panel' submitted to the CEAA (n.d.) (on file).

[77] Partnership for Sustainable Development of Digby Neck & Islands Society, 'Overview of the Society' email to the JRP submitted to CEAA (25 June 2007) (on file).

[78] Richler (n 24).

[79] Interview with JRP member, 30 May 2014.

Indeed, the local representatives at the both the federal and provincial level were involved in the fight against the quarry quite directly. Provincial representative Harold Theriault, previously a fisherman in the area, was particularly outspoken against the project, for example hosting a rally in 2006 outside of the provincial legislature in opposition to the quarry.[80] As the claimants noted in the arbitral proceedings, Theriault was adamantly against the quarry and credited his opposition to his electoral success over Gordon Balser, the Conservative MLA who had represented the riding when the project was initiated. Indeed, Theriault was elected by just 327 votes in 2003, suggesting that the issue of the quarry may have been a deciding factor.[81] Robert Thibault, the minister of the DFO as well as the federal representative for the Digby riding, was also an important actor in the decision-making process; during the arbitration proceedings, the claimants produced correspondence between Thibault and the Minister of Environment, in which the former recommended the JRP process for assessing the quarry.[82] Additionally, the claimants cited internal emails between DFO staff, one of which stated that the quarry 'is in our Minister's riding ... the announcement of a joint panel review is of the nature to take a lot of public pressure off the Minister's shoulders for the summer months'.[83] Thus, it does appear possible that the two elected officials for the area in which the quarry was to be located had an interest in the project, and the minister of the DFO may have exerted some influence on the assessment process, at the very least recommending the JRP.

The entire assessment process for the quarry guided what appears to be a great deal of public discontent and resistance to the project through official channels, and opportunities for public input existed at a number of stages throughout. For example, after preparing the guidelines for the EIS, the CEAA and the provincial Ministry of Environment provided the public with forty-five days to review the text and submit comments to the ministry, which were subsequently passed on to the JRP.[84] The JRP itself held hearings open to the public and was mandated to take the comments it received into account when issuing the EIS Guidelines that would be presented to the investor.[85] Numerous groups participated, providing testimony and written submissions, many of whom were mentioned in section 6.2.

As can be seen in its final report, the JRP required that the investor directly address public involvement, traditional community knowledge, and sustainable

80 CBC, 'Digby Quarry Opponents Step up Lobbying Efforts' *CBC News Nova Scotia* (4 August 2006).

81 Elections Nova Scotia, '21-Digby Anapolis' Province of Nova Scotia.

82 *Bilcon of Delaware Ltd. v. Government of Canada*, 'Memorial of the Investors' (PCA) Case No 2009-04.

83 ibid 34.

84 Government of Nova Scotia, 'Agreement Concerning the Establishment of a Joint Review Panel for the Whites Point Quarry and Marine Terminal Project between the Minister of the Environment, Canada and the Minister of Environment and Labour, Nova Scotia' <https://www.canlii.org/en/ns/laws/stat/sns-1994-95-c-1/latest/sns-1994-95-c-1.pdf> accessed 23 February 2022.

85 ibid.

development in its EIS. Moreover, it is clear that the JRP took community concerns seriously when writing its final report, as worries expressed by the community regarding ballast water, tourism, and fishing opportunities are echoed in the report. For example, the Panel wrote, 'the potential effects of the Project on the tourism industry are difficult to predict with any certainty, given the many factors involved, but the Panel acknowledges that those involved in the tourism industry believe that the Project is not consistent with articulated provincial and local policy'.[86] Less equivocal is its assessment of the quarry's potential impact on the local fishing industry as it concludes that 'the Project would likely have an adverse environmental effect on the socio-economic health and viability of some of the fishing communities of Digby Neck and Islands'.[87] As mentioned in the section 6.2, many community members expressed very strong concerns about the potential impact the quarry would have on their way of life and their preferred development trajectory for the area. It is perhaps this that the JRP refers to when it discusses the conflict between the proposed project and the 'community's core values'. Indeed, the Panel concluded that the greatest negative impact of the project concerned:

> community core values ... Individuals from Digby Neck and Islands identified these by stressing the importance of a strong sense of place, a living connecting with traditional lifestyles, harmony with the environment, combined with a strong sense of stewardship as a way of life.... The imposition of a major long-term industrial site would introduce a significant and irreversible change to Digby Neck and Islands, resulting in sufficiently important changes to that community's core values to warrant the Panel assessing them as a Significant Adverse Environmental Effect that cannot be mitigated.[88]

As was discussed earlier, it was this emphasis on core community values which formed the basis of the investor's claims and was the measure that the majority of the arbitral tribunal argued was a breach of the minimum standard of treatment requirement of NAFTA.

6.4 State Interests and Policy Decisions

How did provincial and federal policymakers make the decision to comply with the communities' demands regarding the quarry and reverse their earlier assurances to the proponent that the government welcomed their project? Moreover, to what extent were decision-makers aware that this policymaking process could trigger NAFTA arbitration?

86 Fournier, Grant, and Mueckle (n 33).
87 ibid 11.
88 ibid 14.

As described, the decision-making process itself is at the heart of the dispute—namely, why the project was subject to such stringent environmental assessment procedures and the terms of reference that the JRP used to make its final decision. The material archived by the CEAA gives some access to the decision-making process and the issues considered relevant by the various government departments involved.

The official consensus of the DFO was that the blasting activity of the quarry would endanger local fish stock, which made the DFO the 'responsible authority' for the assessment, thereby automatically requiring that the environmental assessment be carried out jointly by the federal and provincial governments. However, the choice to require the project to be evaluated by the JRP was more discretionary. The recommendation was made by Liberal MP and DFO Minister Robert Thibault, who wrote to the federal Minister of the Environment that:

> In light of the information provided by the proponent, DFO believes that the Whites Point Quarry and Marine Terminal, as proposed, are likely to cause environmental effects over a large area of both the marine and terrestrial environments.... I am of the opinion that an assessment by a review panel is the most appropriate level of assessment.[89]

As discussed in section 6.2, the archives of the CEAA show that the initial request to form a JRP came from the DFO, sent to the provincial Ministry of Environment, though the final decision was made by the federal and provincial environment ministers.

The other key issue raised by the claimant was the JRP's reliance on the concept of 'community core values' to assess the project, which the claimant argued was not a term that was included in Canadian or provincial policy. The basis for the terms of reference which the Panel was to use to assess the project can be found in provincial policy documents, and these suggest a possible foundation for the development of the core community values concept, although it is not explicitly identified. As one provincial civil servant noted, 'under our legislation, socio-economic impacts are considered part of environmental effects, and that is maybe a bit different than under different jurisdictions'.[90] Indeed, Nova Scotia's *A Proponent's Guide to Environmental Assessment* lays out an extensive definition of environmental impact, which includes both environmental and socio-cultural impacts. For example, the Guide defines environmental effect as 'any change ... including any effect on socio-economic conditions, on environmental health, physical and cultural heritage or on any structure, site or thing

[89] Robert G Thibault, 'Letter from Robert G. Thibault to David Anderson P.C. M.P., Minister of the Environment' submitted to the CEAA (26 June 2003) (on file).

[90] Interview with Nova Scotia provincial official, 29 May 2014.

including those of historical ... significance'.[91] The JRP Agreement which set the terms for their assessment (and to which the proponent was privy during the whole process) uses the same broad definition.[92] Thus the Panel was empowered, for example, to take the 'traditional knowledge' of the community into account when assessing the project. Following from this, the EIS Guidelines, which the JRP presented to the investor in 2005, included requirements that the investor 'identify the various perspectives and aspirations for the future with the region' and 'consider the relationship between the Project and the relevant community and regional social and economic development strategies, policies and plans'.[93] The Panel also asked that the investor consider 'the perceptions people have about their quality of life and their sense of place'.[94] Therefore, while political concerns were likely an important factor in the local MP's and MLA's opposition to the project, the JRP was explicitly required to consider these wide ranging concerns of the community. However, the term 'community core values' does not appear in these earlier documents. How the JRP arrived at the use of this term is an open question, although it seems possible, as Canada's arbitrator suggests in his dissent, that by 'core community values' the JRP simply meant to reference the human environmental effects that were clearly part of the Panel's mandate.[95] This was echoed by one of the members of the Panel, who explained that in their view, Nova Scotia's provincial legislation allowed for a broad interpretation: 'we were applying provincial legislation that includes social considerations. Federal [legislation] is limited to the physical environment, but the provincial legislation is more open. And that gave us much more latitude than would have been available in other provinces.'[96] The term 'core community values' is quite broad and does not appear in previous documents related to the specific case of the Whites Point quarry or in broader policy documents. However, it may be that the Panel was merely using a new term for what they understood to already be included in the provincial guide to environmental assessment.

How did the 'strategic setting', in this case, bound by Canada's NAFTA obligations, affect decision-making regarding the Bilcon quarry? Was this dispute ultimately caused by cost–benefit calculations of politicians and civil servants or by a lack of awareness or understanding of NAFTA?

Both the federal and provincial officials interviewed as part of this project claimed that there is generally a high level of awareness of NAFTA obligations at

[91] Nova Scotia Environment Policy Division Environmental Assessment Branch, 'A Proponent's Guide to Environmental Assessment' Government of Nova Scotia 36.

[92] Government of Nova Scotia (n 84).

[93] Environment Canada 'Environmental Impact Statement Guidelines for the Review of the Whites Point Quarry and Marine Terminal Project EAS #2002-395' (11 August 2006) Environment Canada.

[94] Fisheries and Oceans Canada (n 62) 36.

[95] *Bilcon of Delaware Inc v Government of Canada*, Dissenting Opinion of Professor Donald McRae (n 56).

[96] Interview with JRP member, 30 May 2014.

the federal level, and the Department of Foreign Affairs and International Trade (DFAIT)[97] regularly gives advice regarding obligations imposed by international economic agreements with the passage of new laws and regulations. As one federal official told me, 'as a result of our experience with NAFTA . . . we have gotten quite good at the federal level in taking account of our international investment obligations'. However, this same official admitted that 'at the provincial level, it's a work in progress'.[98] This sentiment was echoed by another official, who argued that there was greater awareness at the federal level: 'our expertise is there. It's growing in the provinces and territories but it wasn't on the radar for them earlier.'[99] A Nova Scotia official explained that, since the province has not been host to many foreign companies, 'we wouldn't be as familiar with potential NAFTA obligations. However, we do have folks that provide information and advice on that matter.'[100]

There is evidence that in this case, decisions were made with some degree of awareness of NAFTA provisions, although it appears that the consensus at the time was that it was unlikely that the investor would turn to arbitration. The archived material on the CEAA website includes emails sent between provincial departments and DFAIT regarding this issue. For example, in an undated email, a DFAIT employee writes that 'with regard to the North American Free Trade Agreement (NAFTA)—the current text in the EIS is generally fine'.[101] Moreover, a law professor from the nearby Dalhousie University was commissioned to prepare a report for the JRP on potential NAFTA obligations. This report concluded that 'on the basis of an analysis of both the rules and the case law, I do not believe any foreign investor associated with the project would have either opportunity or interest to invoke the provisions of NAFTA Chapter 11'.[102] Moreover, the public comments to the JRP show that even locally, the issue of NAFTA arose; as one member of the JRP told me, 'It was an issue that came up quite a bit during the assessment hearings. There were a lot of interveners talking about NAFTA, so I think that right from the beginning we were aware that it was a possible NAFTA challenge.'[103]

However, although they anticipated 'some kind of reaction' from the company, the NAFTA case 'came as a surprise to a lot of people'.[104] One provincial official noted:

> what surprised me personally was that if the company had a problem or issue about the process, they had under provincial law and Canadian law, the ability to

[97] At the time of writing, called Global Affairs Canada.
[98] Interview with Federal official, 2 June 2014.
[99] Interview with Federal official, 11 April 2014.
[100] Interview with Nova Scotia provincial official, 29 May 2014.
[101] Rachel McCormick 'Undated Email Sent to Nova Scotia Government from DFAIT Official' submitted to CEAA (on file).
[102] Winham (n 5) 15.
[103] Interview with JRP member, 31 May 2014.
[104] ibid.

> file for a review [in court]. I think that to us what was surprising was that this was the first avenue of complaint ... to go straight to NAFTA, that was surprising.[105]

However, a federal official expressed less surprise that even with attempts to ensure that the decision was compliant with NAFTA obligations, a dispute still arose: 'I would say that consultation is helpful in that our measures are consistent with international obligations, but it doesn't necessarily help us to avoid claims. Investors can bring claims if they want to.'[106] It is clear that NAFTA considerations were factored into the decision-making process regarding the Whites Point Quarry, regardless of the fact that some Canadian officials and outside experts predicted incorrectly that the investor would not turn to arbitration.

6.5 Conclusion

The dispute between Bilcon and Canada is a clear case of domestic non-state actors changing the preferences of state actors towards a specific investment project. Whether or not the investors in this case received special treatment or were offered incentives to invest in Nova Scotia by provincial officials, the province did have official policies in place to attract FDI and spur development in the mining industry. Moreover, that the investors were given the initial opportunity to go through the environmental assessment process implies that there were government officials who believed the project could be beneficial to the province. Indeed, George Balser, the provincial representative for the area when the initial investment was made, spoke about the benefits the project could bring in terms of employment.[107] However, as was discussed, local community members had concerns regarding the effect of the project on both the environment and existing economic activity in the area such as fishing and tourism. The quarry became an election issue in the 2003 provincial election, and an MP was elected to the riding who was sympathetic to the views of the quarry's opponents. This local resistance to the project may have also influenced the federal representative for the area Robert Thibault, who was the Minister of the DFO—indeed, as was discussed in section 6.3, it was Thibault who suggested the project be assessed by a JRP. Finally, the JRP took the concerns of local residents quite seriously and integrated them into its assessment of the project, it was empowered to do by the JRP agreement. Therefore, it appears that local interest group preferences were able to influence a number of stages of decision-making related to the Whites Point Quarry. In its defence, the government cites the high levels of local interest in the project as the reason it was considered appropriate to use

105 Interview with Nova Scotia provincial official, 29 May 2014.
106 Interview with Federal official, 2 June 2014.
107 'Bilcon of Delaware Ltd. v. Government of Canada, Memorial of the Investors' (n 80).

the JRP assessment process, while similar projects, including a nearby quarry, had been approved following a less stringent environmental assessment. Moreover, the JRP itself refers to the serious threat posed by the project to the 'core community values' as the reason that mitigation approaches were not thought to be sufficient. It is this decision, the failure to take into account the company's proposed mitigation measures, which the tribunal ruled was the most severe breach of Canada's NAFTA commitments. However, this can only be understood in the broader context of local opposition to the project and policymakers' and politicians' identification with these interests, for example, which led them to suggest the most stringent level of environmental assessment for the project. Following from this observation, it is possible to conclude that the support of citizens in the area provided some incentive for policymakers to change their preferences toward the quarry.

It is clear from the discussion in this chapter that these decisions were very much made 'in the shadow' of NAFTA obligations as both DFAIT and outsider experts were consulted regarding the possible breaches of NAFTA. This is unsurprising, given Canada's experience as a respondent in NAFTA claims, and policymakers I spoke to at the federal level explained that Canada's bureaucracy has developed some expertise in this area. While provincial policymakers were less familiar with NAFTA at the time, this cannot truly be considered a lack of capacity as federal-level expertise was relied upon in the decision-making. However, Canadian officials were nonetheless unable to predict that the investors in this case would choose to turn to arbitration rather than pursue any objections they had to the outcome of the environmental assessment process through domestic courts. Beyond the investor turning to arbitration, the final ruling of the arbitral tribunal was also difficult to predict and was quite remarkable for the expansive understanding of what constitutes a breach of international minimum standards of treatment (NAFTA Article 1105) as well as the domestic bodies that Canada is responsible for under international law—in this case, a panel of three university professors who issued a recommendation to the governments of Canada and Nova Scotia.

This underscores one aspect of the wider relevance of this case—namely, the uncertainty that ISDS introduces into policymaking for domestic actors. If even well-developed bureaucracies such as Canada's, which additionally has significant experience with NAFTA claims, cannot predict which policy measures may trigger an investor–state dispute, it is less likely that developing country policymakers or those whose countries have faced fewer disputes will be able to do so. While Canada can bear the costs of an arbitration proceeding and pay the final award if the tribunal rules against it, this type of uncertainty can be quite costly for poorer states.

This case also highlights the likelihood that investors will turn to ISDS if it is available to them. As discussed in previous chapters, ISDS was originally meant to protect foreign investors investing in weak or unstable states in which domestic courts could not be relied upon to fairly adjudicate disputes with the host state.

There are very few investment treaties which cover investment flows into developed states, and the assumption has generally been that extra protection for investors is not necessary in contexts in which the rule of law is stronger. As an overview of ISDS cases shows that most respondent states have been developing, middle-income countries, the initial rationale for ISDS seems justified. However, NAFTA is an important exception, as it covers FDI flowing from developed home states to developed host states. Although, as mentioned, Canadian officials assumed that if the investor decided to challenge the final ruling on the quarry they would do so through domestic courts, this proved not to be the case—instead, Bilcon turned immediately to international investment arbitration under NAFTA, arguing that Canada had breached international law. Therefore, the Bilcon case demonstrates that when given the opportunity, investors will use ISDS to challenge host state regulation both in developing and developed states—an important lesson in the face of the potential expansion of ISDS coverage through treaties such as the EU–Canada Comprehensive Economic and Trade Agreement (CETA).

Finally, the content of the measure challenged in this case speaks to the way in which ISDS may be used to limit the development of domestic legal norms.[108] While for the investors, the JRP's use of the concept 'core community values' and the general emphasis on the socio-economic impact of the project was an over-reach, to others it may be a welcome addition to the factors on which an industrial project can be judged. Beyond the merits of this specific term, however, this case highlights the ways in which ISDS can be used to challenge stricter regulations or the raising of certain standards—whether in protection of the environment or other public goods.[109] In Chapter 5, I discussed how this use of ISDS can pose a particular problem for middle-income, developing states. However, this case suggests that even developed countries with already high regulatory standards can be affected by ISDS.

[108] Johnson and Sachs (n 1).
[109] ibid.

7
AES Summit Generation v Hungary and Electrabel v Hungary

The case study presented in this chapter focuses on the disputes between Hungary and two foreign-owned electricity generators—AES Summit Generation and Electrabel. Both companies, along with a number of others, signed long-term power purchase agreements (PPAs) with the Hungarian government in the early 1990s. These agreements provided investors with a guaranteed profit on electricity sold to the state-owned distributor and were an important tool in the attraction of foreign investment into Hungary's newly privatized electricity sector after the end of communist rule. However, these agreements attracted criticism domestically as well as internationally. In Hungary, the PPAs were attacked by politicians for providing so-called 'luxury' or 'excess' profits for the foreign-owned generators. At the European Union (EU) level, the PPAs came to be considered illegal state aid and subject to an investigation by the European Commission (EC).[1] These various pressures led first to changes to the agreements and ultimately to their termination, which in turn provoked three known investment arbitration cases under the Energy Charter Treaty.[2]

Hungary prevailed in the two disputes discussed here, and, notably, both arbitral tribunals viewed as legitimate the state's political motivations for taking the contested measures; for example, the tribunal in the *AES Summit* case concluded that the government was 'motivated principally by widespread concerns relating to reducing . . . profits earned by generators and the burden on consumers' and that this was 'a perfectly valid and rational policy objective for a government to address luxury profits'.[3] The tribunal was less clear regarding the importance of the interests of the state-owned electricity company Magyar Villamos Müvek (MVM) in the policymaking process regarding the administrative pricing. However, the interests of MVM were central to both the reintroduction of the administrative pricing and the cancellation of the PPAs. Therefore, while on a rhetorical level the 'mass interests' of Hungarian energy consumers were an important determinant of this investor–state dispute, the interests of a very powerful state actor were also

[1] European Commission. 'Commission decision on State Aid awarded by Hungary through Power Purchase Agreements' (2008) The Commission of European Communities.
[2] Very little information about the third, *EDF v Hungary*, has been made public.
[3] Award, *AES Summit Generation Limited and AES–Tisza Erömü Kft v The Republic of Hungary*, ICSID Case No ARB/07/22.

The Political Economy of Investment Arbitration. Zoe Phillips Williams, Oxford University Press. © Zoe Phillips Williams 2022.
DOI: 10.1093/oso/9780198865940.003.0007

clearly taken into account in the decision-making process that eventually led to arbitration.

Of further interest is the impact of the EU accession process and EC investigation on the investor–state disputes discussed here. While the majority of the *AES* tribunal did not accept that concerns regarding legality under EU law drove Hungary to reintroduce administrative pricing, the tribunal for the *Electrabel* case did accept that these concerns motivated the government to take the measures in question. This outcome is notable for two reasons. On the one hand, the clash between commitments enshrined in investor–state contracts, and protected by international investment agreements (IIAs), and states' commitments under EU law suggests the potential for conflict between different international legal regimes.[4] Additionally, this case illustrates some of the reasons for which transition countries, in particular in Europe, may be more likely to be hit with investment claims. As will be discussed in section 7.1, the Hungarian government signed the PPAs during a period in which the need for foreign investment was acute, and though they were successful in attracting investment, they did not align with the preferences of all the stakeholders involved, in particular given some long-lasting reticence towards privatization of the electricity market. Furthermore, according to some interviewees, it was quite clear from early on that these agreements would need to be altered to comply with EU access requirements, which indeed appeared to play a role in change of preference towards the PPAs. Therefore, over the course of twenty-five years, Hungary, as a transition state, has experienced a very rapid evolution of policy regarding the free market and the market for energy in particular—first privatization and then liberalization of markets to comply with EU accession requirements. The interests of state and non-state actors have been affected, sometimes negatively, by these policy changes, and it is unsurprising that they have in turn pressurized the government for more favourable policies and outcomes. More generally, these policy changes are complex and different policy initiatives have at times had conflicting goals. Therefore, a lack of, or at least stretched, institutional capacity may also play a supporting role in causing these disputes; as discussed in Chapter 3, unclear rules may lead to non-compliance. Certainly, when expanding their argument to consider domestic (and transnational) factors, the policy instability that appears to have accompanied the learning processes associated with the turn to a free market economy, liberalization, and EU accession could be understood to contribute to a lack of clarity regarding Hungary's commitments under the ECT and thus have contributed to the disputes with investors. More generally, it is clear that some degree of policy instability is likely during the transition to a free market, and as was

[4] Indeed, legality of intra-EU bilateral investment treaties (BITs) and the Energy Charter Treaty has been an ongoing point of contention amongst investors, EU member states, and the European Community, with the Court of Justice of the European Union (CJEU) ruling in the 2018 *Achmea* decision that intra-EU BITs are in fact illegal under EU law.

discussed in earlier chapters, policy instability is in large part what determines political risk for investors. Therefore, the cases discussed in this chapter add further nuance to the interplay between political preferences and capacity and their role in causing investor–state disputes.

7.1 IIAs and Investment in Hungary

Following its first free elections in 1990, Hungary began the transition to a free market economy, which involved the privatization of firms in a number of 'strategic sectors', such as energy, telecommunications, and banking, much of which was accomplished through attracting foreign investment.[5] The desire to attract foreign direct investment (FDI) was not only ideological but also born of necessity: dated infrastructure and low levels of industrial capacity, debt servicing, and budget deficits all increased the pressure to attract outside investment, particularly from Western Europe.[6] Happily for the architects of privatization, Hungary has been one of the more successful post-communist European states in this regard, enjoying significant FDI inflows in the early years of privatization compared to its neighbours, in part due to reforms implemented before the transition period.[7] Between 1990 and 2005, FDI stock as a percentage of gross domestic product (GDP) rose from 1.6 per cent to almost 56 per cent.[8]

Hungary's efforts to open its economy and attract FDI were supported not only by domestic legal reforms but also by significant engagement on an international level. In 1991, Hungary signed the Europe Agreement with the EU, which outlined the first steps towards EU accession. This agreement contained commitments to significantly liberalize trade and ensure domestic compatibility with EU standards in areas such as taxation, state aid, and sectoral policies.[9] Additionally, during this period Hungary ratified many IIAs, signing the most BITs in the mid- to late 1990s, as well as the Energy Charter Treaty, which will be discussed at greater length in section 7.1.3. These agreements, which contained commitments to liberalize markets, placed significant pressure on the government—the Central and Eastern European states had far less time to come into compliance with EU policy and were

[5] OECD (Organisation for Economic Co-operation and Development), 'Regulatory Reform in Hungary. Enhancing Market Openness through Regulatory Reform' (OECD 2000).

[6] Kalman Kalotay and Gabor Hunya, 'Privatization and FDI in Central and Eastern Europe' (2000) 9 Transnational Corporations 39.

[7] OECD (n 5); Graham Hooley and others, 'Foreign Direct Investment in Hungary: Resource Acquisition and Domestic Competitive Advantage.' (1996) 27 Journal of International Business Studies 683.

[8] UNCTAD (United Nations Conference on Trade and Development), 'Country Fact Sheet: Hungary' (2006).

[9] OECD (n 5).

expected to be far more open to EU involvement, given the lower capacity of their domestic institutions, than Western European states had been.[10]

7.1.1 Investment in the Energy Sector

As mentioned earlier, the energy sector was largely privatized by the late 1990s. This involved the creation of a two-tier system, with the MVM retaining its coordinating and distributing role and remaining in state hands and the privatization of a number of electricity generators. By 1998, 50 per cent of the shares of the power generation companies were held by private parties.[11] These generators, sold primarily to Western European investors, were in varying states of disrepair, which contributed to the necessity of attracting investment via the long-term PPAs.[12] The legislation governing the electricity sector at this time, the 1995 Electricity Act, provided the regulatory structure for the newly privatized electricity market. The MVM remained a powerful player, acting as the single buyer for the power generated by the private plants.

As a number of interviewees noted, the government initially had difficulty attracting investment in the energy sector; investors were wary of investing in out-of-date facilities with no guaranteed returns, and regulators faced challenges determining the appropriate price for electricity—which at the time 'nobody really knew'.[13] Thus, under budgetary pressure to privatize, and following the advice of external consultants, the government offered investors the twenty-five-year PPAs.[14] The PPAs, signed between the MVM and the newly foreign-owned generators, placed on MVM the obligation to buy a fixed amount of electricity at a price determined by the Hungarian Energy Office (HEO), which would guarantee the investors a profit of between 8 and 10 per cent.[15] According to legislation adopted in 2000, the regulated prices were to remain in place until 31 December 2003, after which, in order to comply with EU requirements, the electricity prices were to be set by the generators.[16]

The interests of energy consumers were of importance to policymakers during the privatization period. During the communist era, energy prices were 'far from cost-covering' and significantly lower for households than industrial consumers.[17] In the mid-1990s, electricity prices rose by approximately 25 per cent, still less

[10] Jan Drahokoupil, *Globalization and the State in Central and Eastern Europe* (Routledge 2009).
[11] OECD (n 5).
[12] ibid.
[13] Interview with Energy Regulators Regional Association (ERRA) official, formerly an official of the Hungarian Energy Office, 14 April 2015.
[14] ibid.
[15] Interview with official at the Hungarian Competition Authority (HCA), 20 April 2015.
[16] ibid.
[17] OECD (n 5) 34.

than was pushed for by foreign investors.[18] According to commitments made to the International Monetary Fund (IMF) and the World Bank, electricity prices in Hungary were required to cover costs by 1996, and 1995 was the first year in which residential rates exceeded industrial rates.[19] However, a number of interviewees expressed the importance to the government of easing this transition for household consumers (also known as voters), and thus some effort was made to keep household prices low.[20] As will be discussed at greater length in section 7.2, this created a situation in which the MVM was buying electricity from the privatized generators at a fixed price under the PPAs and selling it to consumers at a price that would avoid too great a 'shock'. When administrative pricing ended in 2003, MVM began selling this electricity at a loss. This constituted the basis for the EC state aid investigation and incentivized the MVM to renegotiate the PPAs.

7.1.2 Hungary's Experience with Investor–State Dispute Settlement

Hungary signed and ratified its first IIA in 1987 with Sweden and has signed fifty-nine IIAs in total. Hungary experienced its first investor–state arbitration in 2001, a claim brought by AES Summit Generation, one of the investors discussed in this chapter. This dispute related to changes to AES Summit's PPA and was settled out of arbitration. Subsequently, as of 2017, Hungary has faced at least sixteen claims in the energy and telecom sectors, as well as a handful of other industries (see Figure 7.1). The most common measures triggering disputes in Hungary are the cancellation of agreements or projects and regulatory change.

As is common for Eastern European respondent states, the disputes faced by Hungary were brought by investors from Western Europe. Hungary is in fact one of the European transition states which has faced the greatest number of claims. At the time of the disputes discussed in this chapter, Hungary had faced three previous claims.

7.1.3 The Energy Charter Treaty

The claims discussed in this chapter were brought under the Energy Charter Treaty (ECT), a multilateral agreement with a wide geographical coverage, including most of Western and Eastern Europe, as well as Central Asian states. The treaty was ratified by the original signatories in 1994 and came into effect in 1998. The

[18] Interview with ERRA official, 14 April 2015.
[19] OECD (n 5).
[20] Interview with ERRA official, 14 April 2015; interview with Eva Voszka, 10 May 2015.

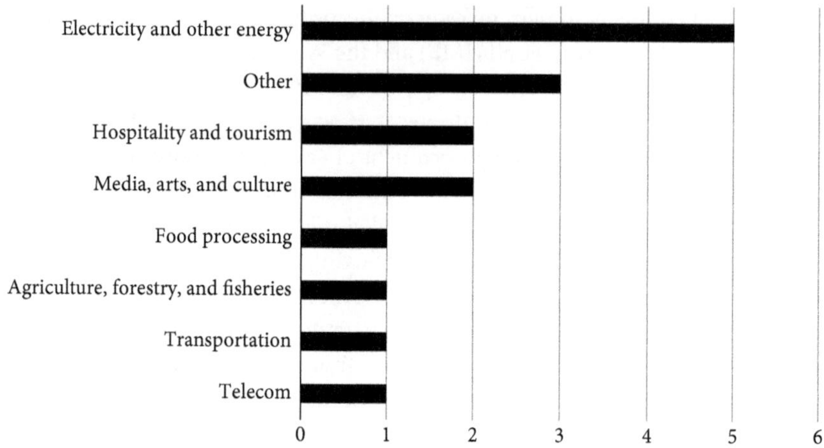

Figure 7.1 Hungary disputes by industry

ECT provides investment protection for firms investing in signatory countries and provides for investor–state disputes settlement using the International Centre for Settlement of Investment Disputes (ICSID) or United Nations Commission on International Trade Law (UNCITRAL) rules.

The ECT was initially proposed by the Dutch government to the Council of the European Communities in 1991, with the goal of creating a 'European energy community [and] a secure a market economy approach for the reconstruction and restructuring in the energy sector in the former communist countries'.[21] Thus, the treaty was meant to combine Western European interests in secure sources of energy with Eastern European interests in attracting investment. As it takes its cue on the liberalization of energy markets from EU directives on EU energy law, 'the ECT has served as a kind of "waiting room" for subsequent EU membership preparation for the accession countries in Eastern Europe'.[22]

As with many investment agreements, the investment chapter of the ECT purports to aim to increase investment by decreasing investor risk. The investment chapter of the ECT was modelled after the provisions in the North American Free Trade Agreement (NAFTA) and the US and UK model BITs.[23] Like these treaties, the ECT prohibits expropriation without prompt and immediate compensation and includes provisions guaranteeing most-favoured-nation (MFN) or national treatment and the controversial fair and equitable treatment (FET). The treaty requires that signatories create 'stable, equitable, favourable and transparent

[21] Jan Kleinheisterkamp, 'Investment Protection and EU Law: The Intra- and Extra-EU Dimension of the Energy Charter Treaty' [2012] Journal of International Economic Law 1, 2.

[22] Andrei Konoplyanik and Thomas Wälde, 'Energy Charter Treaty and Its Role in International Energy' (2006) 24 Journal of Energy & Natural Resources Law 523, 528.

[23] ibid.

conditions for investors' and provide 'constant protection and security' to investment. Additionally, the ECT requires signatories to respect all contractual agreements made with investors.

At the time of writing, the ECT has become a focal point of opposition to investor–state dispute settlement (ISDS), particularly in Europe, with EU member states threatening to withdraw from the treaty despite ongoing efforts at 'modernization' of the treaty. The concerns of these states relate primarily to the threat the treaty poses to efforts to combat climate change and, in particular, the transition to green energy sources.

7.2 The Disputes between Hungary and Electrabel and AES Summit Generation

Belgian company Electrabel SA and the British AES Summit Generation purchased majority shares in Hungarian electricity generation plants and signed long-term PPAs with the government in 1995 and 1996, respectively. AES Summit purchased a majority shareholding in the company Tiszai Eromu Reszvenytarsasag (which became AES–Tisza), which included a power station known as Tisza II and two other power stations. AES's investment was approximately US$130 million.[24] Electrabel bought majority shares of the Dunamenti power plant, acquiring it from a different investor in 2001.

As discussed in section 7.1, these agreements committed MVM to buying electricity at a fixed price from the generators. Between 1997 and 2003, the prices at which the electricity were sold were determined by the HEO and issued in price decrees that covered four-year cycles.[25]

In 2001, AES Summit Generation initiated an arbitration proceeding against Hungary, which has not been made public. The case was settled, and the investor signed a new PPA with the government. Also in 2001, the Hungarian parliament passed new legislation to partially liberalize the electricity market, which went into effect in 2003. From this date on, the generators that had signed PPAs with the MVM were able to negotiate a yearly agreement on electricity prices that the distributor would pay.[26] The liberalization of the market created so-called 'stranded costs' for the MVM; as customers were allowed to move from the public to the free market, the capacity which MVM was required to purchase from the generators exceeded demand and MVM was therefore paying for electricity from the PPAs

[24] Award, AES Summit Generation Limited and AES–Tisza Erömü Kft v The Republic of Hungary (n 3).

[25] Decision on Jurisdiction, Applicable Law and Liability, *Electrabel SA v Hungary*, ICSID Case No ARB/07/19).

[26] ibid.

that it was no longer able to sell.[27] MVM sent invitations to renegotiate the PPAs in 2003 but was not successful in reaching a new agreement with either AES Summit or Electrabel.

In 2004, Hungary acceded to the EU and was therefore required to have full market pricing for electricity by 2007. In 2005, the EC began an investigation into whether MVM's purchase requirements under these agreements constituted illegal state aid.[28] At the same time, a political debate arose in the Hungarian parliament regarding what were perceived by some political actors as unreasonably high profits of the electricity generators following the end of the administrative pricing regime in 2003.[29] In November 2005, the HEO sent a letter to the companies which had signed PPAs, in which it described the current rate of profit as 'unjustifiably high' and suggested a limit of 7 per cent profit.[30] Again, the government was unable to reach an agreement with the generators and, in 2006, reintroduced administrative pricing through the Price Decree.[31]

In 2007, the investor–state arbitration between AES Summit Generation and Hungary was registered at ICSID, with AES challenging the reintroduction of administrative pricing.

In 2008, the EC concluded its investigation, finding that the PPAs did constitute illegal state aid. Hungary did not contest this finding and, in 2008, passed legislation to terminate the PPAs. Electrabel subsequently turned to arbitration, also at ICSID, challenging both the price decrees and the PPA termination.

7.2.1 The Arbitration Cases

This section focuses mainly on the dispute between AES Summit Generation and Hungary, with some references to the Electrabel proceedings. As mentioned, the AES Summit claims focused solely on the reintroduction of administrative pricing, while Electrabel also challenged the termination of the PPAs. In both cases, Hungary defended the measures taken with reference to the requirements of EU accession, and the EC petitioned to present *amicus curiae* briefs in both cases. However, only the tribunal in the *Electrabel* case accepted that this had in fact influenced the policymaking process.

27 Hungarian Energy Office, 'Long-Term PPAs in Hungary', power-point presentation (2006) (on file).

28 European Commission 'AES Summit Generation Ltd. v. Republic of Hungary. Written Submission Pursuant to Art. 37 (2) of the ICSID Arbitration Rules' in *AES Summit Generation Limited and AES–Tisza Erömü Kft v The Republic of Hungary* ICSID Case No. ARB/07/22.

29 Award, *AES Summit Generation Limited and AES–Tisza Erömü Kft v The Republic of Hungary* ICSID Case No. ARB/07/22 (n 3).

30 ibid.

31 ibid.

Table 7.1 Summary of arbitration

Alleged breach of the ECT	Claimant's arguments	Tribunal's ruling
Fair and Equitable Treatment	FET includes honouring contractual obligations, which Hungary failed to do. This entails respecting legitimate expectations.	The tribunal declined jurisdiction over contractual claims; found no breach of the FET with regard to Hungary's treaty obligations.
Impairment of Investment by Arbitrary and Discriminatory Measures	Hungary's reintroduction of administrative pricing was arbitrary, non-transparent, and discriminatory and only aimed at four generators.	The tribunal found that the measure was not unreasonable in the face of concerns regarding the generator's profit rates.
National/Most Favoured Nation Treatment	Domestically owned power plants received more favourable treatment.	There was no breach of MFN/NT.
Constant Protection and Security	The 2006 Price Decree breached Hungary's obligation to provide legal security.	There was no breach of obligation to provide constant protection and security.
Expropriation	Hungary expropriated revenues which AES was guaranteed under the PPA.	There was no evidence of expropriation.

7.2.1.1 *AES Summit Generation v Hungary*

The ICSID tribunal for the arbitration between AES Summit Generation and Hungary was constituted on 21 November 2007. A summary of the investor's arguments is displayed in Table 7.1.

According to AES Summit, Hungary breached its obligations to the investor under the ECT by reintroducing administrative pricing in 2006, causing MVM to fail to fulfil its contractual obligations.[32] Additionally, by changing the agreement which it had reached with AES in 2001 (following the aforementioned arbitration case), Hungary failed to act in accordance with the investor's legitimate expectations and uphold its commitment under the ECT to provide a stable policy environment.[33] This policy measure was also taken in a non-transparent way as Hungary allegedly provided no explanation for how it arrived at the price levels enacted in the 2006 price decree.

[32] ibid.
[33] ibid.

AES Summit further argued that Hungary's decision to reintroduce administrative pricing was irrational and discriminatory. First, the claimant alleged, the government falsely portrayed this measure as a response to EC concerns regarding the potential illegal state aid represented by the PPAs. However, AES Summit argued that the profits it was making under the free-market pricing regime had no connection to the question of state aid. Additionally, the price decree of 2006 only affected four generators and was thus discriminatory. At the same time, domestically owned power plants were not subject to the same pricing decrees, and one, the state-owned Paks nuclear plant, was allowed to increase prices during this period. Therefore, the claimants argued that the return to administrative pricing was enacted primarily due to the political debate regarding the so-called 'luxury' or 'extra profits'.

Finally, there was significant debate on the applicable law governing the dispute and, in particular, how the ECT interacted with EU law. With regard to this debate, the claimants argued that due to the Vienna Convention's edict that a 'party may not invoke the provisions of its internal law as justification for its failure to perform a treaty', the potential breach of EU law could be used to defend Hungary's actions.[34]

In response to these allegations, Hungary argued that the investor could not have had any legitimate expectations that administrative pricing would not be reintroduced as the 2001 PPA signed by AES contained 'no representations by MVM or anyone else that the pricing regime would never change again in the future', and the PPA did not include a stabilization clause.[35] Additionally, Hungary denied that the new pricing scheme was decided upon in a non-transparent manner and noted that the claimants were invited to comment on the new scheme. However, they further argued that the ECT does not 'require states to comply with ideal notions of transparency, in which every single consideration in policy making is first publicly announced'.[36] Finally, in arguing that the decision to reinstate administrative pricing was not arbitrary, Hungary emphasized the fact that 'countries which are in the process of becoming members of the European Community are likely to have legislative changes'.[37]

In its defence, Hungary additionally emphasized the pressure it was under from the EC to terminate the PPAs, or to at least to 'minimize the effects of what the EC considered to be unlawful state aid'.[38] It underlined that the government had tried to renegotiate the PPAs with the generators and that AES had refused any renegotiation of the PPA. Therefore, 'when the authorities were unable to renegotiate the PPAs, they took the next step, which was the least drastic of the alternatives

[34] ibid.
[35] ibid 48.
[36] ibid 53.
[37] ibid 50.
[38] ibid.

available. They temporarily restored the system of price caps based on notions of reasonable return that had long been used in Hungary.'[39] Additionally, Hungary argued that it had legitimate concerns regarding the high profit levels of the generators at the expense of consumers.[40]

With regard to the claims of breach of MFN and NT, Hungary argued that the reason that the price decrees were only applied to four generators was that only these were identified as having overly high profits. The calculation of the reduction of profits was applied uniformly to all generators and therefore could not be considered discriminatory. Additionally, Hungary denied that it had expropriated the claimant's investments as they continued to make a profit under the administrative pricing.[41]

Finally, with regard to the tension between EU law and the ECT, Hungary argued, unsurprisingly, that the ECT must be 'read in light of one of its own objectives, which is to promote the European Union's key energy objectives, market liberalization and free completion', and therefore it cannot be read as divorced from EU competition law.[42] This argument underscores Hungary's claims that it acted in response to EC pressure to eliminate the state aid represented by the PPAs.

Overall, the tribunal ruled in Hungary's favour on all claims of breach of the ECT. First, the tribunal found that Hungary had made no claims guaranteeing that administrative pricing would never be reinstated, and thus the claimant could have no legitimate expectations to that effect. While the enacting of the price decrees did not perfectly meet the ideals of transparency, it did not amount to a breach of the ECT as the tribunal did not interpret the FET as requiring 'perfection' in state behaviour. Thus, 'the respondent's process of introducing the Price Decrees, while sub-optional [sic], did not fall outside the acceptable range of legislative and regulatory behaviour'.[43]

Of most interest is the tribunal's conclusion regarding the investor's claim of arbitrary and irrational policymaking. Like the claimant, the majority of the tribunal did not accept Hungary's argument that it reintroduced administrative pricing in response to pressure from the EC. This is due in part to the fact that, at the time the measure was taken, Hungary had not received the results of the EC's investigation into the potential state aid and therefore was under no obligation to act.[44] Additionally, the tribunal was not convinced that the price cap would truly address concerns regarding state aid. Instead, the tribunal concluded that Hungary

[39] ibid.

[40] Award, *AES Summit Generation Limited and AES–Tisza Erömü Kft v The Republic of Hungary* ICSID Case No. ARB/07/22 (n 3).

[41] ibid.

[42] ibid 33.

[43] ibid 69.

[44] Award, *AES Summit Generation Limited and AES–Tisza Erömü Kft v The Republic of Hungary* ICSID Case No. ARB/07/22 (n 3).

was motivated by the political debate surrounding the so-called 'luxury profits' of the generators. However, the tribunal found it nevertheless found that:

> it is a perfectly valid and rational policy objective for a government to address luxury profits. And while such price regimes may not be seen as desirable in certain quarters, this does not mean that such a policy is irrational.[45]

Hungary's nominee to the tribunal, Dr Brigitte Stern, dissented from the majority opinion regarding Hungary's motivations. She concluded that it was clear to Hungary at the time that the PPAs were in contradiction to EU policies. Indeed, she cited, amongst other evidence, notes from a meeting with the EC in 2004, where 'concerns were expressed by the Commission that the stranded costs . . . constitutes state aid to the generators, stating that "it must be ensured that none of the power plants reaches extra profits under the PPAs"'.[46]

7.2.1.2 *Electrabel v Hungary*

The facts of the *Electrabel* case are quite similar to those of AES Summit. However, in addition to challenging the price decrees, the Belgian investor also challenged the termination of the PPAs. The tribunal—which included Dr Stern as Hungary's nominee—came to similar conclusions regarding the motivations for the administrative pricing and also took more seriously the role of the EC's state aid findings on Hungary's decision-making.

Electrabel argued that the termination of the PPAs constituted a breach of the FET provision of the ECT, as it breached the investor's legitimate expectations, and that in particular the government did not take 'reasonable steps to protect Electrabel as an investor, by seeking an exemption from EU law in relation to the PPAs in Hungary's EU Accession treaty'.[47] Electrabel further claimed that its investment was expropriated as it was not adequately compensated by the government following the PPA termination.

The tribunal ruled that Hungary did not expropriate, directly or indirectly, Electrabel's investment. It further found that the termination of the PPAs did not breach the FET standard. In short, it found that Hungary was not responsible for the EC's decision regarding the PPAs, and that:

> where Hungary is required to act in compliance with a legally binding decision of an EU institution, recognized as such under the ECT, it cannot (by itself) entail international responsibility for Hungary. . . . The Tribunal considers that it would

[45] ibid 83.
[46] ibid 77.
[47] Decision on Jurisdiction, Applicable Law and Liability, *Electrabel SA v Hungary* (n 25).

> be absurd if Hungary could be liable under the ECT for doing precisely that which it was ordered to do.[48]

The tribunal differed from that of AES on the role of EC pressure in leading to the price decrees. Like AES, the tribunal found that the investor could have no reasonable expectations that administrative pricing would not be reintroduced. However, it found that this was particularly the case given the context of Hungary's accession to the EU and the necessity of liberalizing the domestic electricity market.[49]

Finally, like the AES tribunal, the Electrabel arbitrators accepted that Hungary had legitimate political motivations for enacting the price decrees. Indeed, as the arbitrators wrote in the final Award:

> There is no doubt that by late 2005 and early 2006, there was political and public controversy in Hungary over the perceived high level of profits. . . . However, politics is what democratic governments necessarily address; and it is not, *ipso facto*, evidence of irrational or arbitrary conduct for a government to take into account political or even populist controversies in a democracy.[50]

7.3 The Role of Domestic Interests in *Electrabel* and *AES Summit Generation v Hungary*

This section examines three potential factors which contributed to the shift in Hungary's preferences toward the PPAs. First, in the run up to a highly contested election, the opposition party employed the idea of the 'extra profits' of the foreign-owned generators in their campaign. They were able to do this successfully, a number of interviewees argued, given the long-standing ambivalence in the general population regarding privatization and foreign-owned companies as well as the fear of raising end-user prices of electricity. This led parliament to adopt legislation to reintroduce administrative pricing, the measure challenged by both AES Summit Generation and Electrabel. Second, and I argue, more importantly, following the partial liberalization of the electricity market in 2003, the MVM began to suffer losses under the PPAs. As will be discussed, even after privatization the MVM was seen an important player within the Hungarian state apparatus and was likely able to influence policy. The timing of the renegotiation of the PPAs in particular suggests MVM's influence. Finally, internal documents and interviewees suggest that Hungarian state actors were aware of a possible conflict between the

48 ibid VI–22.
49 ibid.
50 ibid VIIII–7.

PPAs and EU accession requirements, and it is likely that this also contributed to the termination of these agreements.

7.3.1 Political Parties and Energy Consumers

Political parties, ostensibly representing the mass interests of energy consumers, were able to influence the short-term policies of the government towards foreign-owned electricity generators by means of a political contestation—specifically through electoral pressure in the lead-up to the 2006 general elections.

As discussed, both arbitral tribunals acknowledged that the 'extra profits' of the foreign-owned electricity generators became the subject of an intense political debate. This is not surprising, given that energy and electricity have been election issues since the end of communist rule and that there had been a general unwillingness on the part of post-communist governments to expose consumers to dramatic price increases.[51] This fits into the more general pattern of political contestation in central Eastern European states; in these countries 'political contention has been closely … linked to the issue of social protection'.[52] Moreover, they note that in the post-communist era, there has been a steady alternation between left-wing and right-wing parties in power, and

> there has been no clear division of labour between the left and the right in the sense that the former has protected vulnerable social groups while the latter only the economy. Rather, all parties that hoped for mass popular support usually stressed the intrinsic relationships between economic and welfare protectionism …[53]

From the end of the communist rule to the mid-2000s, Hungary's political situation mirrored this description quite closely; from the mid-1990s on, elections were dominated by competition between the Socialist party and the conservative Fidesz, and until the general election in 2006, no incumbent had been granted a second term. Moreover, economic populism has dominated political competition, and Fidesz has focused on social protection.[54]

It was in this context that the right-wing Fidesz, then the opposition party, instigated the debate on the electricity generators' 'extra profits'. This debate emerged

[51] Interview with Peter Mihalyi, 15 May 2015.

[52] Dorothee Bohle and Bela Greskovits, 'Neoliberalism, Embedded Neoliberalism and Neocorporatism: Towards Transnational Capitalism in Eastern Europe' (2007) 30 Western European Politics 454.

[53] ibid.

[54] András Deak, 'Hungarian Dances—the Origins and the Future of Viktor Orbán's Revolution' (2013) 11 Lithuanian Annual Strategic Review 145.

in 2005 and took place both in parliament and in the press, with 'references in the press and elsewhere … made to generators' profits as 'extra', 'too high,' 'huge', and 'luxury'. The Hungarian public was described as 'defenceless' against rising prices and it was said that such 'luxury profits' must be 'knocked down'.[55] Following the advent of this debate, and in the lead-up to the election in April 2006, the Hungarian parliament passed the legislation to enact the price decrees (which set a cap on electricity prices) in March 2006.

According to a number of interviewees, the 'extra profits' discourse was a useful political tool in a highly contested electoral race; '[Fidesz] made harsh attacks on the government, and it was just one tool to [do so] … the "extra profits" served political purposes'.[56] Similarly, another interviewee explained that the idea of extra profits accruing to the generators was 'part of a political argument … I didn't see any detailed analysis of where this extra profit came from'.[57] However, the argument served the interests of both Fidesz and MVM; 'Fidesz and [party leader Viktor] Orbán invented this term extra profit, [which] was supported by the MVM leadership at the time … what Fidesz was saying [about the extra profits] was essentially correct and very much supported by the MVM'.[58] Indeed, given the ideological linkages between the upper-level management of the MVM and the Fidesz party suggested by Mihalyi (see later), it is not surprising that these actors would pursue common interests.[59]

However, the measures challenged by the investors were in fact taken by the Socialist government both before and after they won the election. Indeed, it appears that the incumbent government adopted the same discourse towards the generators at the time, perhaps in part because 'it was a way for the government to distinguish themselves from the governments of the mid-1990s who had sold everything'.[60] It was public pressure, according to another interviewee, that led the government to adopt these measures as it was 'perhaps the only possible way for this government not to lose face, when they had repeated the extra profit, they had to show something to the public'.[61] Indeed, concerns regarding keeping energy prices low for households (voters) appear to have spanned the political spectrum and had been a longstanding election issue. More broadly, the discourse of 'extra profits' resonated with a public that opinion polls indicate did not support

[55] Award, *AES Summit Generation Limited and AES–Tisza Erömü Kft v The Republic of Hungary* (n 3) 25.
[56] Interview with former HEO official, 28 April 2015.
[57] Interview with ERRA official, 14 April 2015.
[58] Interview with Peter Mihalyi, 15 May 2015.
[59] Indeed, since Fidesz has been in power since 2010, the government has taken a similar attitude towards a broader group of foreign investors, increasing state control of various industries including electricity and gas: Deak (n 54).
[60] Interview with Ministry of Economy official, 6 May 2015.
[61] Interview with former HEO official, 14 April 2015.

foreign ownership of large companies and was sceptical about capitalism in general.[62] Thus, an attack on the profits made by these firms 'absolutely resonated with voters'.[63]

However, in its defence, Hungary took pains to emphasize the technical rather than political reasons for why it reinstated administrative pricing, including as an attempt to meet EU requirements.[64] Specifically, Hungary argued that as the generators refused to renegotiate the PPAs, the short-term reintroduction of administrative pricing was the 'next best thing' to minimize the state aid to the generators. Furthermore, it is clear that the interests of the state-owned electricity company MVM played an important role in the overall treatment of the investors who had signed PPAs. In sections 7.3.2. and 7.3.3, I discuss the evidence that pressure from both the MVM and the EC led to the eventual cancellation of the PPAs.

7.3.2 MVM and Electricity Market Reform

This section discusses the shifting preferences of the state-owned electricity company toward the PPAs as, over time, some of these agreements became disadvantageous for the MVM. The interests of the MVM can be connected to both the measures challenged by the claimants discussed in this chapter—the ultimate cancellation of the PPAs and the interim reintroduction of administrative pricing.

After the Second World War, Hungary nationalized its electricity supply, and the Hungarian Electricity Board, the MVM, was formed in 1963.[65] The MVM was corporatized in 1991 after the fall of the communist regime and retained its central position in the Hungarian electricity supply system. At this time, the MVM was divided into two tiers, the first being responsible for the overall management and coordination of the electricity system and the second being further divided into fifteen energy generation and network companies, which became independent corporations that were nearly all privatized by 1997.[66]

The MVM was facing competing pressures at this stage. It was necessary to secure investment in the energy sector, which was, according to a former official in the HEO, 'not in a very good state'. In fact, during the first phase of privatization, the government was largely unsuccessful at attracting foreign investors, who 'sent back the signal that without ... a pricing regime, nobody will buy this'.[67] This problem was solved by the implementation of the PPAs, which were 'an absolutely

62 Deak (n 54).
63 Interview with Peter Mihalyi, 15 May 2015.
64 Interview with Balázs Felsmann, researcher at Regional Centre for Energy Policy (REKK), 8 May 2015.
65 OECD (n 5).
66 ibid.
67 Interview with former HEO official, 28 April 2015.

clear requirement for the investors'; while they committed the investors to upgrading the power generation infrastructure, they provided a guaranteed profit, and therefore no risk, to the investors.[68] At the same time, they allowed the government to maintain lower end user prices:

> Because the MVM was a state-owned company and could incur some losses, it was able to buy electricity at relatively high prices from the generators, and sell it at a lower price—the MVM was the actor that served this policy objective, the first one to make the deal attractive to investors, and on the other side guaranteed a low price for customers.[69]

During this period, the MVM was not a proponent of further liberalization.[70] Indeed, a number of interviewees suggested that the management of MVM continued to have a strong culture of centralized planning and saw itself as quite independent from the state. According to Peter Mihalyi, a former Deputy Government Commissioner for Privatization, many of the MVM bureaucrats had 'studied in the Soviet Union … they didn't have any background in the Anglo-Saxon economic way of thinking, and … also were fervent right-wing nationalists'.[71] Similarly, another interviewee described the MVM as having 'a very different attitude than any other private company' and recalled a meeting at which 'at one point, when I referred to the Hungarian government and the interests of the state, they said "We are the state." It was a different attitude'.[72]

The shifting interests of the MVM partially explain the timing of the cancellation of the PPAs. Given the aforementioned attitude of the MVM's managers, it is not surprising that the MVM initially tried to impede the process of further liberalization of the electricity market, including dragging its feet regarding the renegotiation of the PPAs. As more than one interviewee noted, it had been clear for some time within the Hungarian bureaucracy that, due to the impending EU accession, the PPAs would eventually have to be renegotiated or cancelled.[73] Indeed, a 2006 presentation from the HEO includes a reference to a 2002 piece of legislation containing the rules for the renegotiation of the PPAs and concludes that 'it would be necessary to renegotiate the PPAs … but this is not in the interest of the MVM'.[74] Indeed, during the late 1990s and early 2000s, 'the MVM was not incentivized to make this hard decision', and despite being pressurized by the government to renegotiate with the foreign-owned generators, they did not do so.[75]

68 Interview with ERRA official, 14 April 2015.
69 ibid.
70 ibid; interview with former HEO official, 28 April 2015; interview with Peter Mihalyi, 15 May 2015.
71 Interview with Peter Mihalyi, 15 May 2015.
72 Interview with ERRA official, 14 April 2015.
73 ibid; interview with Balázs Felsmann, researcher at REKK, 8 May 2015.
74 Hungarian Energy Office (n 27).
75 Interview with ERRA official, 14 April 2015.

EU accession required the end of the regulated pricing, and the market was significantly liberalized in 2003. This changed the situation of the MVM vis-à-vis PPAs; as mentioned, when customers were able to move to the free electricity market, MVM had an oversupply of electricity generated by companies covered by the PPAs. It was able to sell this excess supply to electricity traders but at a significantly lower price then what it had originally paid.[76] It was at this point, according Eva Vozska, a Hungarian researcher focused on state aid and competition policy, that the MVM understood that, in the long-term, the dual market would be worse for it than full liberalization.[77] This led to a shift in attitude of the MVM, both towards the pricing scheme and the PPAs more generally, and the demands of the impending EU accession, and the investigation into state aid in particular, allowed the MVM to put pressure on the generators; in this way, 'this EU investigation was very good for MVM, it was a tool so MVM could refer to this process and say "I have to do this, I don't want to but you see there is this investigation." '.[78] Tellingly, although the PPAs were officially cancelled in 2008, many agreements were subsequently renegotiated with the same generation companies on very similar terms. Those that were not —including with AES Summit and Electrabel—were those that had been the least profitable for MVM.[79]

As discussed earlier, the reintroduction of the administrative pricing, which introduced price caps, was due in large part to a political debate that emerged in the lead-up to the 2006 election. However, it was also clearly in the short-term interest of MVM as it was suffering significant losses since the end of the administrative pricing and the move to the dual market. In section 7.4, I will discuss the parallel EU pressure to renegotiate the PPAs.

7.4 State Interests and EU Accession

In its defence, Hungary argued that pressure from the EC investigation into whether the PPAs represented illegal state aid was behind the decisions to both temporarily reintroduce administrative pricing and ultimately cancel the agreements altogether.

There is evidence that policymakers were aware of the eventual necessity to terminate the PPAs, both from general policies regarding state aid related to EU accession and, more specifically, from meetings between European and Hungarian officials. In its *amicus* brief to the AES Summit tribunal, the EC noted that the issue arose prior to accession in 2004 as the Europe Agreement, signed between the

[76] ibid.
[77] Interview with Eva Voszka, Pezugykutato, 10 May 2015.
[78] Interview with ERRA official, 14 April 2015.
[79] ibid.

European Community and Hungary in 1993, 'contained rules on State aids very similar to those applicable under the EC treaty'.[80] The 2004 Act of Accession contains similar provisions prohibiting state aid.[81] In 2001, the EC adopted an official methodology for analysing state aid via stranded costs in the electricity sector and, based on this, in 2005, launched an official investigation into Hungary's PPAs.

Of course, the existence of official policies does not necessarily mean that Hungarian officials were aware of how these applied to the PPAs. However, the EC states that its concerns regarding the PPAs were communicated to Hungary at the outset of the investigation in 2005. Additionally, several interviewees noted that it had been clear for quite some time that the PPAs would conflict with EU accession requirements. As one interviewee claimed, 'because of the EU accession, years ago we had already started planning how to deal with the PPAs',[82] a process which began in the 2000s, at which time it was 'known that these agreements can be a problem and an obstacle to liberalization'.[83] In particular, the HEO seems to have been the most willing of government actors to renegotiate or cancel the PPAs; as its aforementioned presentation concluded in 2006, the PPAs did appear to constitute state aid, and thus 'it would be necessary to renegotiate or cease the PPAs'.[84]

Moreover, Hungarian officials communicated these concerns to the generators; as a former official of the HEO, explained:

> we believed that sooner or later the MVM would sell some of the assets and we would renegotiate some of these PPAs and after that, there would be a competitive market ... you can't join the European market when that contract exists, so we proposed several arguments, why it's useful to shorten or renegotiate the PPA. I personally invited AES for this discussion. They hired one of the best British advisers ... the answer was no, forget it, we signed an agreement, and we calculate our future profits from this formula.[85]

However, this official noted that the ultimate decision to renegotiate the PPAs did not lie with the HEO but with the government, and 'we could not convince the government to be brave enough to cancel the PPAs'. It appears, therefore, that while the MVM's interests were still served by the PPAs and the EC ruling on the state aid was still pending, the government was not motivated to cancel the PPAs outright. This was confirmed by a former State Secretary for energy, who explained that 'at the end, the Hungarian authorities were not ready to [terminate] these PPAs in

[80] 'AES Summit Generation Ltd. v. Republic of Hungary. Written Submission Pursuant to Art. 37 (2) of the ICSID Arbitration Rules' (n 28) 5.
[81] ibid.
[82] Interview with Balázs Felsmann, researcher at REKK, 8 May 2015.
[83] Interview with ERRA official, 14 April 2015.
[84] Hungarian Energy Office (n 27).
[85] Interview with former HEO official, 28 April 2015.

general and the EU had to take a resolution on that, and effectively the EU regulation stopped the potential usage of the PPAs'.[86]

Some of this reticence to renegotiate or terminate the contracts may have also been due to the resistance put up by the generators themselves to the idea. As was noted both by interviewees and in Hungary's defence before the arbitral tribunals, government officials had several times attempted to renegotiate the PPAs with these firms. However, according to one interviewee, 'it was clear that some of them accepted the renegotiation and from the beginning it was clear some of them would go to court, we didn't know what kind but it was clear that they would challenge the decision'.[87] Another interviewee expected that these conflicts would culminate in arbitration because 'sometimes you realize there is no room for [compromise], because here they wanted for an additional ten years all of the potential profits and we thought no you made enough profit compared to the privatization deals, we were so far from each other'.[88] This sentiment was echoed by one of Hungary's legal team, who noted that 'we were more or less aware of the possibility [of arbitration]. It didn't come as a complete surprise.'[89]

Therefore, it seems that policymakers, particularly in the HEO, were aware that EU accession would entail the eventual renegotiation or cancellation of the PPAs. However, these actors alone did not have the influence to force the issue, particularly when the MVM's interests were still served by the PPAs. However, changing market conditions, itself a result of the EU accession process, altered the MVM's view of the PPAs, and this coincided with more direct pressure, in the form of the state aid investigation, to cancel the agreements. As noted earlier, the Hungarian government defended the reintroduction of administrative pricing as a way to lessen the effect of the state aid in the face of its failure to renegotiate the contracts. As this measure was also taken in the midst of the political debate on 'extra profits', it is more difficult to tease out the most important causal factor in that policymaking decision. However, with regard to the cancellation of the PPAs, it appears that a happy convergence of the interests of the MVM and the government, due to its EU accession requirements, led to the cancellation of these agreements.

7.5 Conclusion

The conflicts between Electrabel and AES Summit Generation and Hungary, unlike the cases discussed in Chapters 5 and 6, were more obviously the result of the confluence of a number of factors. In the *Bilcon* and *Pacific Rim* cases, the

86 Interview with Balázs Felsmann, researcher at REKK, 8 May 2015.
87 Interview with former HEO official, 28 April 2015.
88 Interview with Balázs Felsmann, researcher at REKK, 8 May 2015.
89 Interview with member of Hungary's legal team in the *AES* and *Electrabel* cases, 16 April 2015.

governments took measures as a direct response to public pressure—in both cases, as a reaction to the threat of mining activity on local livelihoods and environment. In the disputes between Hungary and the foreign electricity generators discussed in this chapter, the link to mass interests is less direct, and the 'special interests' of the state-owned electricity generator, as well as external demands from the EC, appear to have had an influence on state decision-making regarding the PPAs.

However, the arbitral tribunals in both the *AES* and *Electrabel* cases highlighted the importance of mass interests in the governments' decision to reintroduce administrative pricing. While the claimants in both cases accused Hungary of taking this measure for purely political reasons, and thus representing it as 'irrational' policymaking, the arbitrators legitimized the idea that governments could in fact make political decisions regarding investments and that this was in itself not a breach of commitments under the ECT—an unusual finding for arbitral tribunals, that in particular stands in contrast to the conclusion of the tribunal in the *Bilcon* case.[90] A closer examination of the role of political interests complicates the picture slightly. While the debate over the generators' alleged 'extra profits' was indeed highly political, it does not seem to have emerged organically from the interests of the electorate so much as being manufactured by the opposition party in the run-up to a national election as a tool to criticize the incumbent government. However, it is clear that, as energy is a perennial election issue in Hungary and an apparent ambivalence of the population towards foreign ownership of large companies and the free market in general, this was fertile ground for the opposition party from which to generate public engagement in the issue.

At least as important as the public interest in the generators' extra profits, however, were the interests of the state-owned electricity company, the MVM. As the broader policy environment underwent significant changes between the late 1990s and early 2000s, MVM's interests with respect to the PPAs shifted. The PPAs served as a bulwark against further liberalization of the market, thus the conservative MVM was not incentivized to renegotiate or cancel them, despite some awareness of possible conflicts between the PPAs and EU accession requirements. However, as the market liberalization continued apace, the PPAs locked the MVM into a situation in which it was suffering significant losses via stranded costs. Thus, both the reintroduction of administrative pricing, which put a limit on the amount the MVM would pay to the foreign-owned generators, and the eventual early termination of the PPAs was clearly in the interests of the state-owned company. The degree to which it influenced Fidesz in its 'extra profit' discourse is difficult to ascertain, although ideological affinities between the party and upper management of the MVM suggest that this is certainly a possibility. Much clearer, however, are the links between the MVM's eventual shift in attitude towards the PPAs in general,

[90] Jonathan Bonnitcha and Zoe Phillips Williams, 'State Liability for "Politically" Motivated Conduct in the Investment Treaty Regime' (2019) 33 Leiden Journal of International Law 77.

and their termination (and subsequent renegotiation). This shift in preferences was due to changing market conditions and therefore ultimately cannot be separated from the effects of EU accession.

Therefore, the disputes between the electricity generators and Hungary cannot be seen as disconnected from the more general process of EU accession. Indirectly, the demands from the EU to liberalize the energy market changed the conditions under which MVM was operating and shifted its preferences toward the PPAs, which provided extra motivation for the government to push for their termination. More specifically, the EC investigation into the PPAs as illegal state aid put direct pressure on the government to terminate these agreements, and it did so conclusively following on from the EC's ruling in 2008.

Indeed, it seems that this is a clear case of admittedly very broad political and economic policy changes instigating a shift in state preferences towards the foreign investors, with the shifting interests of an important political actor—the MVM—leading the government to ultimately take the measures challenged by the investors. As discussed in section 7.1.2, the relevant policymakers were aware of the possibility of arbitration (and indeed had been taken to arbitration by AES Summit in 2001), and thus this case seems to be one where the 'preferences' argument clearly wins out over the 'capacity argument'.

However, in an indirect way, state capacity to manage the electricity sector plays a role, at least in the antecedents of the case. As discussed earlier in the chapter, due to the demands of the transition from the planned to the free market, Hungary was forced to offer the long-term PPAs to the investors in order to attract FDI. This placed MVM in a situation that would become disadvantageous as the electricity market was further liberalized. More generally, as a transition country, Hungarian administrators were faced with a difficult task 'not only ... of breaking up an incumbent monopoly power company but with adapting its whole economy to the rules of the market—and with the task of learning what this involved as the country went through the process'.[91] In this way, the disputes between Hungary and the electricity generators may fit into a broader pattern of disputes between investors and transition country governments and explain why these are so common. Indeed, transition countries are likely to experience issues related to the capacity of the state to manage newly privatized and liberalized markets and industries, as well as those related to the preferences of key actors—whether they be voters who have a distrust of the free market or industrial actors loathe to relinquish control of key sectors.

[91] OECD (n 5) 19.

8
Conclusion

Why do states end up defending themselves against arbitral claims brought by investors instead of rescinding the offending measures, retaining the investment, and avoiding potentially costly arbitration? On the one hand, investor–state arbitration may be the result of weak domestic institutions that fail to maintain the conditions required by an international investment agreement (IIA) and a lack of understanding of investment obligations on the part of state officials. On the other, these conflicts may develop when non-state or sub-state actors induce a shift in state preferences towards foreign direct investment (FDI), often in a specific sector or even individual projects. This could entail that the state prefers to uphold the measure in question and take its chance in arbitration. In both cases, the role of domestic institutions in causing or preventing investor–state disputes is central to the explanation, but the causal relationship is different.

What is the relevance of this approach to understanding investor–state arbitration? First, this investigation sheds light on the functioning of the international investment regime by highlighting the conflicts of interest which provoke arbitral claims. Moreover, as stated in the introduction, if we accept that investor–state dispute settlement (ISDS) has the potential to impose significant costs on states, it is important, when either justifying or criticising the regime, to have an understanding of why, and under what conditions, states incur these costs. Indeed, an additional goal of this project was to engage with some of the same questions raised by work on the impact of ISDS on domestic policy space, while avoiding the pitfalls of asking the regulatory chill question—in short, having to prove that the state did not take a measure out of fear of arbitration. However, like this book, at its heart the regulatory chill hypothesis is concerned with the content of the measures that may be thwarted by the threat of investment arbitration; if state actors are dissuaded from expropriating investments for private gain or harassing foreign investors, few observers would likely be concerned about regulatory chill. Similarly, if this project uncovered that the majority of the measures challenged in arbitration were unrelated to issues of broader public policy, there would be little ground for concern. However, these disputes often touch on issues of public rather than private interest because of both the industries in which they are concentrated and the types of measures which trigger them. Moreover, cases of investor–state arbitration have the potential to affect a wide array of stakeholders who, as can be seen in the proceeding chapters, are themselves at times advocating for the measures challenged by investors.

The Political Economy of Investment Arbitration. Zoe Phillips Williams, Oxford University Press. © Zoe Phillips Williams 2022.
DOI: 10.1093/oso/9780198865940.003.0008

Unsurprisingly, given the complexity of real-world policymaking, lack of capacity and political pressure from both broad and narrow interest groups both play a role in the emergence of investment arbitration cases. And, as was particularly highlighted by the chapters on El Salvador and Hungary, lack of state capacity early on in the life of the relevant investment project created conditions that later proved to be politically untenable, forcing the state to take measures which ultimately triggered the arbitration process.

8.1 Summary of Results

The investigation was conducted in three stages. First, almost 900 investor–state arbitration cases were coded on various dimensions. These included the income level of the respondent state, the industry of the investor, the domestic institution that took the disputed measure, and the type of measure taken. This allowed me to identify some broad patterns in investor–state disputes and contributed to the development of hypotheses that were tested statistically. The development of these hypotheses further depended on a reading of literature relevant to investor–state arbitration. Finally, in order to provide micro-level detail on some of the relationships uncovered in both large-N studies, I chose three case studies of investor–state disputes in Canada, El Salvador, and Hungary. The questions posed to these cases concerned the domestic interests behind the policies that were challenged by investors, how these interest groups managed to shift state preferences towards the investment, and the awareness of state decision-makers of the possibilities of investment arbitration.

As discussed in the introduction, while I do not use a comparative approach, each of these case studies represent, if not typical, important 'types' of cases for understanding the dynamics of the investment protection regime. For example, as a North American Free Trade Agreement (NAFTA) (now the United States–Mexico–Canada Agreement (USMCA)) signatory, Canada is one of the few developed states that has had significant experience as a host state to investment covered by an IIA. Therefore, Canada can serve as an example for other developed states that may, for several reasons, increasingly play host to FDI covered by investment agreements.[1] In many ways, El Salvador, as a middle-income democracy, is a typical case. Additionally, the dispute discussed in Chapter 5 is centred on extractive

[1] One reason this could increasingly be the case is that high-income countries sign trade and investment agreements, like the EU–Canada Comprehensive Economic and Trade Agreement (CETA), which contain ISDS provisions. Another reason may be that emerging market investors increasingly invest in these states and take advantage of the ISDS provisions in more traditional bilateral investment treaties (BITs). Finally, while at the time of writing the fate of the Energy Charter Treaty (ECT) in the European Union is hotly debated, countries like Spain and Italy have been respondents in dozens of ECT-based claims in recent years.

operations, which, as we have seen, is one of the industries most frequently involved in investor–state arbitration. Finally, the state measure which triggered the dispute—the refusal to grant (or revocation of, according to the claimants) a mining permit—is one of the types of measure most frequently challenged by investors. Therefore, this case provides more micro-level detail on many of the relationships expressed in the statistical analysis. Finally, the Hungarian case, in opposition to the two previous one, demonstrates the role that powerful domestic sub-state actors can have in fomenting a dispute with a foreign investor. However, beyond this, it underscores a number of capacity issues facing post-communist states in managing foreign investment, particularly in sectors such as electricity, which affect many domestic stakeholders.

The wide array of state policies and measures are challenged by investors via arbitration. This makes it near-impossible to develop a causal narrative to explain all cases of investor–state arbitration—for instance, it is difficult to explain an arbitration case that challenges unfulfilled contractual obligations in the same way as one that follows the imposition of new environmental regulations. However, what is common to many of these claims is a shift in policy related to an investment, which is therefore taken as the dependent variable in this study. This shift may be explained, as suggested earlier, by an *inadvertent* failure of the state to maintain the conditions expected by the investor or by a shift in preferences related to an investment, which leads to a *purposive* change of policy. Important to the latter is an awareness on the part of policymakers of the possibilities of arbitration—if the relevant state actors are not aware of the risk of arbitration, then the former explanation (based on the managerial approach to compliance) becomes more likely than the latter.

The case studies in particular demonstrate that issues of capacity and shifting political preferences are intertwined when it comes to state decision-making on investment projects. Nonetheless, I argue that that it is important to recognize the highly politically and socially embedded nature of investor–state arbitration cases.[2] The first suggestion that these legal claims are very much matters of domestic political contestation arises from the industries in which investor–state arbitration cases are concentrated. As can be seen in Chapter 2, almost 40 per cent of known investor–state disputes are related to investments in extractives (oil, gas, and mining) or energy generation. These industries directly affect a much wider range of stakeholders than, for example, manufacturing operations, and groups such as energy consumers or communities affected by extractive projects have mobilized to pressurize the state to take measures which trigger investment arbitration. Moreover, while overall the majority of measures in question are administrative, the single domestic institution that is most often involved in investor–state

[2] Nicolas Perrone, *Investment Treaties and the Legal Imagination: How Foreign Investors Play by Their Own Rules* (Oxford University Press 2021).

disputes is the legislature, clearly a body meant to respond to some extent to public pressure. However, this should not imply that administrative measures are taken in an environment free from external pressure. Indeed, as both the Canadian and El Salvadoran case studies demonstrate, there can be a clear link between voter or citizen pressure and administrative decisions, which in turn provoke an investor to turn to arbitration.

The results of the statistical analyses also suggest a role for political contestation in the emergence of investor–state arbitration cases. Specifically, the electoral democracy index was found to have a consistently positive, statistically significant relationship with the number of claims in a given country-year, suggesting that democracies can expect more claims, controlling for gross domestic product (GDP) and the amount of investment hosted. At the very least, this suggests that it is plausible that democratic contestation can lead states to take measures that trigger investment arbitration. Additionally, the positive relationship between the dependent variable and a governing nationalist party is suggestive of the political nature of these disputes, while the negative relationship between leftist governments and the number of claims is in line with the predictions in the literature.[3] Finally, the relationship between elections and investment claims also suggests a link between these disputes and domestic political demands. At the same time, the results of the statistical analysis presented in Chapter 3 suggest that we cannot discount capacity issues in contributing to the emergence of these disputes—financial crises and lack of bureaucratic capacity are both positively correlated with the incidence of investment claims.

The case studies further highlighted relationships between changing domestic preferences toward FDI (in general or with regard to specific investment projects) and the measures challenged in arbitration. This was the case in both the developed and developing country case studies. For example, *Bilcon v Canada* demonstrated that broad interest groups—in this case, local communities and local and national environmental groups—can affect state policy towards investors. The case of *Pacific Rim v El Salvador* was strikingly similar to the Canadian case in some key ways, despite the very different institutional setting. Similar domestic interest groups managed to shift state preferences towards the mining project, although in this case their efforts resulted in a de facto change of national policy rather than, in as in the Canadian case, a single decision to reject a project. Finally, the Hungarian case study focuses on the role of two different types of non-state actor pressure on shifting state preferences towards an investment. In this case, the powerful, narrower interests of the state-owned electricity company motivated the state's change in policy, although on a rhetorical level, the state-owned electricity company MVM and its allies in the Fidesz party leveraged mass interests (this time, energy

[3] Pablo M Pinto, *Partisan Investment in the Global Economy* (Cambridge University Press 2013).

consumers) to pressurize the government to reintroduce administrative pricing. However, the changing market conditions which were themselves the cause of MVM's change in preference towards the investor were the result of European Union (EU) accession requirements. Therefore, this final case study demonstrates how much broader shifts in policy—in this case Hungary's evolution towards a free-market economy—can also play a role in changing conditions for investors which they challenge via arbitration. In all cases, key decision-makers expressed an awareness of the possibility of ISDS, at the very least because they were threatened with arbitration by the investor in advance of the actual registering of the case, and therefore lack of awareness of IIAs can also not be seen as a sufficient explanation for investor–state disputes.

However, we also see the role that lack of capacity played in the arbitration cases examined in the case study chapters; in all three, a lack of capacity indirectly contributed to the eventual dispute. In Canada, policymakers were unable to predict that the investor would turn to arbitration following the decision to reject the project, despite consultation with in-house counsel at the federal level in the lead-up to the final decision on the quarry and significant experience with NAFTA claims. In El Salvador, the relationship was even less direct as an eventual recognition that the relevant ministries did not have the capacity to regulate the mining industry contributed to their decision-making regarding issuing new permits. Finally, in Hungary, the necessity of attracting investment in the 1990s and the weak bargaining position of the state vis-à-vis potential investors led to the formation of long-term agreements which at least some observers recognized early on would have to be terminated in order to comply with EU regulations. Therefore, in all these cases, some degree of bureaucratic weakness or lack of state capacity did contribute to the dispute but, at least in these cases, cannot be seen as the primary cause.

This may not be surprising when the chain of events which leads to arbitration is understood. As was discussed in Chapter 5 on El Salvador (and as work on regulatory chill hypothesis suggests), investors may unofficially threaten states with arbitration before officially registering the case at an arbitral forum. Additionally, most official arbitral processes include a 'cooling off' stage, during which the investor and state can negotiate and avoid arbitration. Therefore, states which may have inadvertently provoked an investor to turn to arbitration have ample opportunity to reverse the measures in question if their actual preferences towards the investment have not changed. It is therefore logical that states which do decide to follow through with the arbitration process are defending a policy objective, whether this is at the behest of narrow or broader interest groups.

The perhaps modest conclusion reached here is that, beyond the fact that the challenged measures represent shifts in preference towards (an) investment, rather than as inadvertent failures to comply with IIA obligations, the actors affected and the content of the measures suggest that these disputes are highly political and may represent instances in which the preferences of domestic and transnational actors are irreconcilable.

8.2 Theoretical Significance

Much of the mainstream international political economy (IPE) literature on domestic institutions and foreign investment, which tends to focus primarily on expropriation, comes to similar conclusions, in short that democracy level (and the attendant veto players) is positively correlated with respect for international agreements, property rights, and lower rates of expropriation. This work often credits audience (often electoral) costs with forcing governments to uphold commitments to investors—the underlying assumption being that democratic domestic audiences will be in favour with compliance with previous commitments made by the states and thus hold state actors accountable.

This project problematizes those conclusions, echoing the findings of sceptics such as Tomz,[4] who questions the assumption that democratic audiences will always be in favour of international treaty compliance. This in turn suggests that democratic domestic institutions will not always favour further globalization and liberalization when it comes to FDI.

The connection between democratic institutions and investor–state arbitration may be due in part to the dependent variable itself—the very wide array of measures challenged by investors in arbitration. It also echoes the conclusions of earlier work, such as that of Kobrin, who noted that political risk often results from the 'regular functioning of the political process'.[5] If this is the case, what does it mean that 'the regular functioning of the political process' is seen by foreign investors as detrimental to their interests and can be subsequently challenged by them in front of international tribunals? At the very least, it arguably has already led to significant pushback against the regime and calls for reform. As Simmons has noted, there is an increasing number of democratic states seeking to overturn arbitral rulings that have gone against them, which suggests that 'if the investment regime cannot accommodate the legitimate policy space of democratic governments . . . it may prove quite brittle indeed'.[6]

[4] Michael Tomz, 'Democratic Default: Domestic Audiences and Compliance with International Agreements', *Annual Meeting of the American Political Science Association* (2002).

[5] Stephen J Kobrin, 'Political Risk: A Review and Reconsideration' (1979) 10 Journal of International Business Studies 67, 84.

[6] Beth Simmons, 'Bargaining over BITs, Arbitrating Awards: The Regime for Protection and Promotion of International Investment' (2013) 66 World Politics 12, 28, 40.

8.3 Reform of the Investment Protection Regime

As discussed in the introduction, IIAs and the ISDS system have come under increasing criticism in recent years as the rate of new disputes has risen, developed states have found themselves as respondents in arbitration, and investors are increasingly seen to be challenging host country regulatory activities.[7] This has led to the assessment that the investment protection regime is undergoing a 'legitimacy crisis', a perception reinforced by the withdrawal of a number of states from the International Centre for Settlement of Industrial Disputes (ICSID) Convention (Bolivia, Ecuador,[8] and Venezuela); the withdrawal of states from their IIAs (Ecuador, Venezuela, South Africa, the Czech Republic, and Indonesia, as well as the European Community's (EC's) stance on intra-EU BITs); and the denouncement of ISDS by traditional home states such as Australia and Germany.[9] Most significantly, in 2019, EU member states reached an agreement to terminate intra-EU BITs. This in turn has triggered a number of states and international institutions to propose (and, in some cases, begin to implement) systemic reform. As laid out by UNCTAD, these paths to reform include clarifying and/or altering substantive provisions in IIAs, promoting alternative mechanisms of dispute settlement and conflict prevention, introducing an appeals process, and the creation of a standing investment court.[10] These options have been the subject, with varying levels of attention, to discussions in United Nations Commission on International Trade Law's (UNCITRAL's) ongoing Investor–State Dispute Settlement Reform process.[11]

Perhaps the easiest reform to implement would be the promotion of conflict avoidance and alternative dispute resolution mechanisms. These would include non-binding arbitration focused primarily on finding a solution to the conflict rather than determining the legality of a state measure.[12] These efforts could also be accompanied by the creation of domestic institutions which would screen government measures for their potential to trigger an investor–state dispute and implement 'investor care' conflict management systems which would monitor investor–state relationships for early warning signs of conflict. One such institution is Peru's Investor–State Dispute Management System. However, these

[7] Joachim Karl, 'Investor-state Dispute Settlement: A Government's Dilemma' (2013) 89 Columbia FDI Perspectives 1; UNCTAD (United Nations Conference on Trade and Development), 'Reform of Investor–State Dispute Settlement: In Search of a Roadmap' (UNCTAD 2013).

[8] Although as of writing, Ecuador has recently rejoined the ICSID Convention.

[9] Ricardo Melendez-Ortiz and others, 'Strengthening the Global Trade and Investment System for Sustainable Development' (2015) World Economic Forum, International Centre for Trade and Sustainable Development <http://e15initiative.org/wp-content/uploads/2015/09/E15_ICTSD_Strengthening_Global_Trade_Investment_System_21st_Century_Executive_Summary_1502.pdf> accessed 24 April 2022.

[10] UNCTAD (n 7).

[11] See <https://uncitral.un.org/en/working_groups/3/investor-state> accessed 24 February 2022.

[12] UNCTAD (n 7).

initiatives can only 'reduce the number of fully-fledged legal disputes' but do not tackle the greater questions of the legitimacy of the regime.[13] Moreover, they may in fact further entrench the investor protection norms, enshrined in IIAs, in domestic policymaking processes.[14]

Some states have already begun to reform their own IIAs, particularly by rewording provisions to ensure that these treaties do not infringe on their right to regulate, by clarifying the meaning of provisions, introducing exception clauses (related to industries or types of claims), and limiting access to ISDS. For example, the US 2012 Model BIT has clarified the meaning of indirect expropriation 'to exclude regulatory measures enacted in the exercise of the government's police powers'.[15] The 2021 Canadian Model Foreign Investment Protection Agreement (FIPA) makes similar changes.[16] However, 'international law has yet to identify in a comprehensive and definitive fashion precisely what regulations are considered "permissible" and "commonly accepted" as falling within the police or regulatory power of states, and thus, non-compensable'.[17] Therefore, the impact of changing or clarifying treaty provisions depends also on their interpretation by arbitral tribunals.

Given the latitude that tribunals have to interpret treaty provisions, many observers have instead (or in addition) called for the creation of an appellate court, which could review and correct erroneous arbitral decisions. According to UNCTAD, if 'constituted of permanent members, appointed by States from a pool of the most reputable jurists, an appeals facility has a potential to become an authoritative body capable of delivering consistent—and balanced—opinions, which would rectify some of the legitimacy concerns about the current ISDS regime'.[18] Schill echoes this sentiment, claiming that an appellate mechanism would increase the democratic legitimacy of the international investment regime, particularly if its judges are 'appointed by participating states in democratic processes, which are modeled, for instance, on how judges of other international courts are selected'.[19] However, he also notes that an appellate court could create further legitimacy problems as permanent institutions may be more likely to increase their jurisprudential powers

[13] ibid 5.

[14] Jonathan Bonnitcha and Zoe Phillips Williams, 'Investment Dispute Prevention and Management Agencies: Toward a More Informed Policy Discussion' (2022) International Institute for Sustainable Development <https://www.iisd.org/system/files/2021-10/investment-dispute-prevention-management-agencies-policy-discussion.pdf> accessed 24 April 2022.

[15] Thilini Perera and Dalma Demeter, 'A Balancing Act: Retaining Investor-State Dispute Settlement Provisions in Investment Agreements and Balancing Stakeholder Interests' (2013) 31 Australian Year Book of International Law 75.

[16] 'Canada Publishes 2021 Model Foreign Investment Promotion and Protection Agreement' (2021) 12 *Investment Treaty News Quarterly* <https://www.iisd.org/itn/en/2021/06/24/canada-publishes-2021-model-foreign-investment-promotion-and-protection-agreement/> accessed 24 April 2022.

[17] Perera and Demeter (n 15) 86.

[18] UNCTAD (n 7) 8.

[19] Schill (n 9) 8.

than the ad hoc system currently in place (a concern which relates to the creation of a standing court as well). Moreover, while the creation of appellate mechanism would be a positive step overall, it could also serve to increase the costs of arbitral proceedings, another criticism directed at ISDS.

Finally, the most radical reform to the investment protection regime would be the creation of a standing court, like the World Trade Organization (WTO), to settle investment disputes. This court would, like a potential appellate mechanism, consist of judges appointed or elected by states to sit on a permanent basis and potentially allow the participation of a third party as *amicus curiae*. Most obviously, this would decrease the perception of conflicts of interest inherent in the current system, in which many individual investment lawyers are appointed by parties to the dispute and often sit as both judges and lawyers. According to UNCTAD, the establishment of a court would 'go a long way to ensure the legitimacy and transparency of the system, facilitate consistency and curacy of decisions and ensure independence and impartiality of adjudicators'.[20] On the other hand, as UNCTAD notes, this would also be the most difficult reform to implement. However, there appears to be some momentum in this direction as, in the final months of 2015, the European Commission published its proposal for the creation of a standing court to be included in the now defunct Transatlantic Trade and Investment Partnership (TTIP) agreement negotiated with the United States. While TTIP negotiations failed, the commitment to establish a standing investment court has been enshrined in the CETA.

These pathways to reform echo the different assumptions made by the approaches to treaty compliance employed throughout this project. In particular, those reforms that attempt to decrease the incidence of investor–state disputes—such as an international advisory centre, promoted by some in the context of the ongoing UNCITRAL reform process,[21] as well as alternative dispute resolution and conflict avoidance mechanisms—align with the suggestions made by the managerial approach to increase compliance. For example, a mechanism to review state measures for potential conflict with IIAs could help states to avoid disputes arising from lack of bureaucratic capacity (although the poorest states probably do not have the 'in-house' expertise to monitor policymaking with an eye towards investment protection commitments).

However, as the case studies presented here demonstrate, the role of lack of capacity in investor–state disputes is more nuanced than a mere lack of understanding of the regime. In addition to an awareness of the provisions of IIAs, a better understanding of the preferences of potential stakeholders of an investment project, including non-state actors, could help avoid clashes between investors and sub-state and non-state actors. In particular, consultation with these stakeholders in the

[20] UNCTAD (n 7) 9.
[21] See <https://uncitral.un.org/en/multilateraladvisorycentre> accessed 24 February 2022.

pre-investment phase, especially for projects in the extractive industries, could significantly reduce conflict as both governments and investors become aware of potential opposition to a project.[22] This, in turn, could reduce the incidence of one of the measures which most often triggers investor–state disputes, which is the cancellation or revocation of licences and permits.

However, for consultation to be effective, governments must be willing, at the outset, to refuse an investment or ask an investor to modify plans in the face of domestic actor concerns, which may not be likely, particularly when the bargaining power between the two parties is unequal, as was the case, for example, in Hungary's efforts to attract FDI in the early 1990s. Moreover, while consultation and mediation may avoid fully fledged investor–state disputes in some cases, in others, such as in *Pac Rim v El Salvador*, the interests of the various stakeholders are irreconcilable. In this case, the solutions to treaty compliance which centre on increasing capacity will be of little use. Instead, reform of the international investment protection regime must focus on promoting both IIAs and ISDS which can better balance the interests of investors, states, and non-state actors.

[22] Moreover, the importance of consultation with affected communities is already widely recognized by numerous international organizations and standards such as Free, Prior and Informed Consent (FPIC), ILO Convention 169, and UNCTAD's new standards on investment and sustainable development.

Appendix

Chapter 3

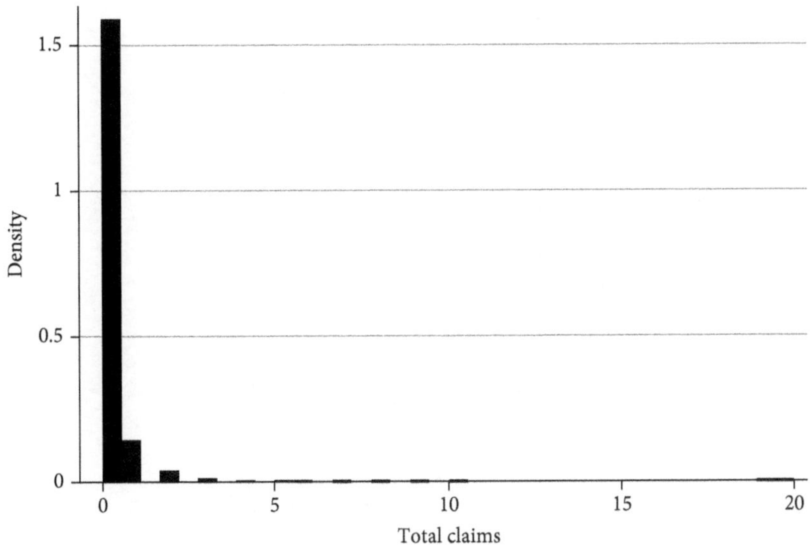

Figure 3.2 Distribution of DV

Table 3.2 Descriptive statistics

Variable	Obs	Mean	Std Dev	Min	Max
GDP per capita	3,978	8.861	1.228	6.068	11.959
GDP growth	3,978	0.03	0.164	−0.967	5.856
Financial crisis	4,371	0.083	0.276	0	1
Rule of law	4,119	0.536	0.314	0.021	0.998
Corruption	2,753	−0.113	1.024	−1.869	2.47
Governance effectiveness	2,747	−0.05	0.994	−2.446	2.437
Cumulative total claims	4,329	1.544	4.676	0	61

Table 3.3 Matrix of correlations

Variables	(1)	(2)	(3)	(4)	(5)	(6)	(7)
(1) GDP per capita	1.000						
(2) GDP growth	0.022	1.000					
(3) Financial crisis	0.100	−0.115	1.000				
(4) Rule of law (V-Dem)	0.576	−0.054	0.115	1.000			
(5) Control of corruption (WB)	0.705	−0.064	0.087	0.850	1.000		
(6) Governance effectiveness (WB)	0.764	−0.061	0.096	0.837	0.946	1.000	
(7) Cumulative total claims	0.151	−0.023	0.037	0.014	−0.059	0.007	1.000

Table 3.4 ZINB: State capacity

	(Model 1)	(Model 2)	(Model 3)	(Model 4)	(Model 5)	(Model 6)	(Model 7)
	total claims	total claims	total claims	total claims	total claims	total claims	total claims
Year	0.069***	0.069***	0.072***	0.068***	0.042**	0.044**	0.03**
	(0.016)	(0.017)	(0.013)	(0.016)	(0.02)	(0.02)	(0.014)
Treaties	0.027***	0.027***	0.026***	0.027***	0.026***	0.028***	0.016***
	(0.007)	(0.007)	(0.006)	(0.007)	(0.006)	(0.007)	(0.003)
FDI stock	0*	0*	0*	0*	0*	0*	0
	(0)	(0)	(0)	(0)	(0)	(0)	(0)
GDP per capita	0.0	–0.001	–0.007	0.024	0.209*	0.176	–0.011
	(0.112)	(0.112)	(0.113)	(0.112)	(0.123)	(0.131)	(0.075)
GDP growth		0.669					
		(0.741)					
Lag financial crisis			– 0.016				
			(0.301)				
Two-lag financial crisis			0.666***				
			(0.192)				
Rule of law index				–0.189			
				(0.334)			
Control of corruption					–0.461**		

(continued)

Table 3.4 Continued

	(Model 1)	(Model 2)	(Model 3)	(Model 4)	(Model 5)	(Model 6)	(Model 7)
	total claims	total claims	total claims	total claims	total claims	total claims	total claims
					(0.204)		
Govt effectiveness						−0.399**	
						(0.197)	
Lag cum claims							0.199***
							(0.023)
Lag cum claims 2							−.003***
							(0)
_cons	−140.206***	−141.319***	−147.569***	−138.338***	−87.642**	−92.239**	−62.777**
	(32.509)	(32.974)	(26.727)	(32.619)	(38.977)	(39.383)	(28.149)
inflate:top_ten_tr~y	−19.966***	−20.407***	−27.016***	−25.468***	−17.527***	−31.04***	−21.927***
	(0.535)	(0.533)	(0.477)	(0.544)	(0.586)	(0.561)	(0.526)
inflate:_cons	2.113***	2.107***	2.1***	2.096***	1.743***	1.861***	1.692***
	(0.305)	(0.306)	(0.305)	(0.307)	(0.356)	(0.327)	(0.312)
/lnalpha	0.72***	0.717***	0.666***	0.722***	0.669***	0.689***	0.198
	(0.226)	(0.227)	(0.189)	(0.226)	(0.199)	(0.205)	(0.172)
Observations	3051	3051	2980	3051	2249	2249	3051
r^2_p	.z	.z	.z	.z	.z	.z	.z

Note: Standard errors are in parentheses. ***$p < 0.01$; **$p < 0.05$; *$p < 0.1$.

Chapter 4

Table 4.1 Factor change in expected number of claims

	Factor change	*p* value	SD
Post-communist	1.32	0.289	0.397
Electoral democracy	3.11	0.025	0.262
Veto players	−0.49	0.162	0.313
Nationalist	2.06	0.032	0.294
Leftist	−0.5	0.07	0.262
Election	1.26	0.09	0.46
2-lag election	1.34	0.017	0.46
Resource rents	1.018	0.057	11.34

Table 4.2 Descriptive statistics

Variable	Obs	Mean	Std dev	Min	Max
GDP per capita	3978	13790.19	16634.835	432	156144
FDI stock	3350	85515.571	318715.28	0	6391293
Treaties in force	4332	19.426	23.829	0	155
Post-communist	4347	0.171	0.376	0	1
Electoral democracy index	4040	0.525	0.266	0.016	0.947
Veto players	3340	0.432	0.319	0	0.894
Nationalist	4117	0.535	0.276	0	1
Leftist	4117	0.224	0.277	0	1
Election	4347	0.275	0.447	0	1
Petroleum, coal, and natural gas	2494	699.228	2249.509	0	28552.68

Table 4.3 Matrix of correlations

Variables	(1)	(2)	(3)	(4)	(5)	(6)	(7)	(8)	(9)	(10)
(1) GDP per capita	1.000									
(2) FDI stock	0.392	1.000								
(3) Treaties in force	0.400	0.320	1.000							
(4) Post-communist	−0.111	−0.095	0.145	1.000						
(5) Electoral democracy	0.456	0.232	0.337	0.017	1.000					
(6) Veto players	0.4487	0.2307	0.3612	0.0608	0.7992	1.000				
(7) Nationalist	−0.092	0.052	−0.143	0.036	−0.234	−0.2390	1.000			
(8) Left	0.064	0.002	0.140	0.010	0.088	0.0248	−0.495	1.000		
(9) Election	0.018	0.034	0.010	0.086	0.092	0.0756	−0.014	−0.022	1.000	
(10) Resources % GDP	0.569	0.008	−0.048	−0.087	−0.142	−0.0755	0.035	−0.009	−0.029	1.000

Table 4.4 ZINB

	(1)	(2)	(3)	(4)	(5)	(6)	(7)	(8)
	total claims	total claims	total claims	total claims	total claims	total claims	total claims	total claims
Year	0.072***	0.073***	0.07***	0.072***	0.073***	0.072***	0.071***	0.075***
	(0.016)	(0.016)	(0.015)	(0.015)	(0.015)	(0.016)	(0.015)	(0.016)
Treaties	0.027***	0.028***	0.028***	0.028***	0.027***	0.027***	0.027***	0.028***
	(0.007)	(0.008)	(0.007)	(0.007)	(0.007)	(0.007)	(0.007)	(0.008)
FDI stock	0**	0**	0*	0**	0**	0**	0**	0**
	(0)	(0)	(0)	(0)	(0)	(0)	(0)	(0)
GDP per capita	0**	0**	0**	0**	0**	0**	0**	0**
	(0)	(0)	(0)	(0)	(0)	(0)	(0)	(0)
Post-communist	0.284	0.33	0.252	0.265	0.287	0.292	0.251	0.271
	(0.262)	(0.237)	(0.252)	(0.259)	(0.255)	(0.26)	(0.26)	(0.257)
Elect. democracy	1.177**	1.729**	1.296**	1.199**	1.163**	1.182**	1.13**	1.519**
	(0.512)	(0.694)	(0.529)	(0.502)	(0.498)	(0.513)	(0.491)	(0.614)
Veto players		–0.701						
		(0.501)						
Nationalist			0.729**					
			(0.355)					
Leftist				–0.676*				
				(0.397)				
Election					0.258*			
					(0.14)			

(continued)

Table 4.4 Continued

	(1)	(2)	(3)	(4)	(5)	(6)	(7)	(8)
	total claims	total claims	total claims	total claims	total claims	total claims	total claims	total claims
Lag election						−0.059		
						(0.095)		
LL election							0.284**	
							(0.13)	
Resources rents								0.017*
								(0.009)
_cons	−147.794***	−148.707***	−144.526***	−146.086***	−149.188***	−147.477***	−144.282***	−153.172***
	(31.336)	(31.114)	(30.528)	(30.986)	(30.268)	(31.451)	(30.924)	(32.536)
inflate:top_ten_tr~y	−33.421***	−38.792***	−35.339***	−34.605***	−33.21***	−32.857***	−31.527***	−33.024***
	(0.665)	(0.683)	(0.625)	(0.643)	(0.649)	(0.664)	(0.648)	(0.719)
inflate:_cons	2.088***	2.051***	2.05***	2.056***	2.078***	2.088***	2.075***	2.076***
	(0.373)	(0.373)	(0.367)	(0.366)	(0.373)	(0.373)	(0.372)	(0.377)
/lnalpha	0.704***	0.693***	0.646***	0.678***	0.688***	0.704***	0.671***	0.687***
	(0.199)	(0.182)	(0.183)	(0.198)	(0.186)	(0.199)	(0.189)	(0.193)
Observations	2900	2797	2879	2879	2900	2900	2829	2847
r2_p	.z	.z	.z	.z	.z	.z	.z	.z

Note: Standard errors are in parentheses. $^{***}p < 0.01$; $^{**}p < 0.05$; $^{*}p < 0.1$.

Table 4.5 ZINB: NAFTA

	(1)
	total claims
Yeard	0.078***
	(0.016)
Treaties	0.035***
	(0.006)
FDI stock	0**
	(0)
GDP per capita	0***
	(0)
NAFTA	2.423***
	(0.227)
Electoral democracy	0.996*
	(0.582)
_cons	−158.868***
	(31.271)
inflate:top_ten_tr~y	−17.093***
	(0.517)
inflate:_cons	1.938***
	(0.341)
/lnalpha	0.571**
	(0.231)
Observations	2852
r2_p	.z

Note: Standard errors are in parentheses. ***$p < 0.01$; **$p < 0.05$; *$p < 0.1$.

Chapters 5–7

Case	Interview #	Interviewee	Date
Canada	1	Anonymous federal official	11 April 2014
	2	Anonymous provincial official	29 May 2014
	3	Interview with JRP member (by phone)	30 May 2014
	4	Anonymous federal official (by phone)	2 June 2014
	5	Howard Mann, former NAFTA negotiator and defence lawyer for Canada, current legal counsel at IISD	5 April 2014
	6	Robert Taylor (background only)	6 April 2014
El Salvador	7	Anonymous official, PROESA	7 August 2014
	8	Marjorie Trigueros, FUSADES	22 July 2014
	9	Edgardo Mira, CEICOM	9 July 2014
	10	Luis Parada, Foley Hoag (by phone)	15 September 2014
	11	Rodolfo Calles, Mesa	14 July 2014
	12	Saul Baños, Mesa	13 August 2014
	13	Anonymous official, MARN	6 August 2014
	14	Anonymous official PDDH	23 July 2014
	15	Anonymous official	8 July 2014
	16	Anonymous official	12 August 2014
	17	Anonymous Oxfam employee	12 August 2014
	18	Anonymous (background only)	
	19	Anonymous (background only)	
Hungary	20	Anonymous official, ERRA	15 April 2015
	21	Anonymous	17 April 2015
	22	Eva Voszka, Pezugykutato	10 May 2015
	23	Peter Mihalyi	15 May 2015
	24	Anonymous	11 April 2015
	25	Anonymous	5 May 2015
	26	Felsmann Balasz	10 May 2015
	27	Anonymous	9 April 2015

Works Cited

Abbott FM, 'NAFTA and the Legalization of World Politics : A Case Study' (2000) 54 International Organization 519.

Aisbett E, 'Bilateral Investment Treaties and Foreign Direct Investment: Correlation versus Causation' (2007) CUDARE Working Papers 1032.

Aisbett E and Bonnitcha J, 'Compensation under Investment Treaties—as if Host State Interests Mattered' (2018) UNSW Law Research Series 18 <http://www5.austlii.edu.au/au/journals/UNSWLRS/2018/80.pdf> accessed 20 April 2022.

Aisbett E and Poulsen L, 'When the Claim Hits : Bilateral Investment Treaties and Bounded Rational Learning' (2013) 65 World Politics 1.

Albornoz F, Galiani S, and Heymann D, 'Foreign Investment and Expropriation under Oligarchy and Democracy' (2012) 24 Economics & Politics 24.

Allee T and Peinhardt C, 'Contingent Credibility: The Reputational Effects of Investment Treaty Disputes on Foreign Direct Investment' (2011) 65 International Organization 401.

Anderson JE, *Public Policy Making: An Introduction* (Houghton Mifflin 2003).

APEC (Atlantic Provinces Economic Council), 'Attracting the Big Bucks: Foreign Investment in Atlantic Canada' (APEC 2005).

Award, *AES Summit Generation Limited and AES-Tisza Erömü Kft v The Republic of Hungary*, ICSID Case No ARB/07/22.

Award, ICSID Case No ARB/09/12.

Award on Jurisdiction and Liability, *William Ralph Clayton, William Richard Clayton, Douglas Clayton, Daniel Clayton and Bilcon of Delaware Inc v Canada* (PCA) Case No 2009-04.

Azpuru D, 'The Salience of Ideology: Fifteen Years of Presidential Elections in El Salvador' (2010) 52 Latin American Politics and Society 103.

Bauerle Danzman S, 'Contracting with Whom? The Differential Effects of Investment Treaties on FDI' (2016) 42 International Interactions 452.

Bernasconi-Osterwalder N and others, 'Investment Treaties and Why They Matter to Sustainable Development: Questions and Answers' (2012) International Institute for Sustainable Development.

Bernasconi-Osterwalder N, Brewin S, and Maina N, 'Protecting against Investor—State Claims Amidst COVID-19: A Call to Action for Governments' (2020) International Institute for Sustainable Development <https://www.iisd.org/articles/policy-analysis/protecting-against-investor-state-claims-amidst-covid-19-call-action> accessed 9 April 2022

'*Bilcon of Delaware Ltd. v. Government of Canada*, Memorial of the Investors'.

Bilcon of Delaware Inc v Government of Canada (2009), Statement of Claim.

Bilcon of Delaware Inc v Government of Canada, PCA Case No 2009-04 (2015), Dissenting Opinion of Professor Donald McRae.

Birn A-E, Shipton L, and Schrecker T, 'Canadian Mining and Ill Health in Latin America: A Call to Action' [2018] Canadian Journal of Public Health 18.

Bohanes J and Vidal-Leon C, 'The ACWL's Contribution to Enhancing Legal Capacity of Developing Countries' in Joost Pauwelyn and Mengyi Wang (eds), *Building Legal Capacity*

for a More Inclusive Globalization: Barriers to and Best Practices for Integrating Developing Countries into Global Economic Regulation (The Graduate Institute, Geneva 2019).
Bohle D and Greskovits B, 'Neoliberalism, Embedded Neoliberalism and Neocorporatism: Towards Transnational Capitalism in Eastern Europe' (2007) 30 Western European Politics 443.
Bonnitcha J, 'Investment Treaties and Transition from Authoritarian Rule' (2014) 15 The Journal of World Investment & Trade 965.
Bonnitcha J, Poulsen L, and Waibel M, *The Political Economy of the Investment Treaty Regime* (Oxford University Press 2017).
Bonnitcha J and Williams ZP, 'State Liability for " Politically" Motivated Conduct in the Investment Treaty Regime' (2019) 33 Leiden Journal of International Law 77.
Brier Island Whale and Seabird Cruises Ltd, 'Letter Submitted to the Joint Review Panel' (18 January 2005) submitted to the CEAA (on File).
Bril-Mascarenhas T and Post AE, 'Policy Traps: Consumer Subsidies in Post-Crisis Argentina' (2015) 50 Studies in Comparative International Development 98.
Britton-Purdy J and others, 'Building a Law-and-Political-Economy Framework: Beyond the Twentieth-Century Synthesis' (2020) 129 Yale Law Journal 1600.
Busse M and Hefeker C, 'Political Risk, Institutions and Foreign Direct Investment' (2005) 23 European Journal of Political Economy 397.
Cabezas P, 'Incoming Minister of the Environment Confirms Continuation of Mining Moratorium in El Salvador' (2014) <http://www.stopesmining.org/j25/index.php/salvadoran-mining-ban/301-incoming-minister-of-the-environment-confirms-continuation-of-mining-moratorium-in-el-salvador> accessed 26 February 2022.
Caddel J and Jensen NM, 'Which Host Country Government Actors Are Most Involved in Disputes with Foreign Investors?' (2014) 120 Columbia FDI Perspectives 2.
'Canada Publishes 2021 Model Foreign Investment Promotion and Protection Agreement' *Investment Treaty News Quarterly* 12 (2021).
Cao X and Ward H, 'Winning Coalition Size, State Capacity, and Time Horizons: An Application of Modified Selectorate Theory to Environmental Public Goods Provision' (2015) 59 International Studies Quarterly 264.
CBC, 'Digby Quarry Opponents Step up Lobbying Efforts' *CBC News Nova Scotia* (4 August 2006).
Canadian Centre for Policy Alternatives, 'NAFTA Chapter 11 Investor–State Disputes' (CCPA 2010).
CEAA (Canadian Environmental Assessment Agency), 'What Is an Environmental Assessment by Joint Review Panel?' (CEAA).
CEDES (Conferencia Episcopal de El Salvador), 'La Explotación Minera En El Salvador—Cuidemos La Casa de Todos' (CEDES 2007).
Chaudoin S, 'Audience Features and the Strategic Timing of Trade Disputes' (2014) 68 International Organization 877.
Chayes A and Chayes A, 'On Compliance' (1993) 47 International Organization 175.
Chayes A and Chayes AH, *The New Sovereignty. Compliance with International Regulatory Agreements* (Harvard University Press 1995).
'Claimant Pac Rim Cayman LLC's Memorial on the Merits and Quantum, ICSID Case No ARB/09/12' (2014).
Cole WM, 'Mind the Gap: State Capacity and the Implementation of Human Rights Treaties' (2015) 69 International Organization 405.
Commission of the European Communities 'AES Summit Generation Ltd. v. Republic of Hungary, Written Submission Pursuant to Art. 37 (2) of the ICSID Arbitration Rules'.

Coppedge M and others, 'V-DEM 10 Codebook—March 2020' (2020) <https://www.v-dem.net/dsarchive.html> accessed 26 February 2022.

Côté C, 'The Chilling Effect of Globalization: A Look at the Impact of International Investment Agreements on National Regulatory Autonomy in the Areas of Health, Safety and the Environment' (PhD thesis, London School of Economics and Political Science 2014) <http://etheses.lse.ac.uk/897/> accessed 9 April 2022.

Cotula L, 'Democracy and International Investment Law' (2017) 30 Leiden Journal of International Law 351.

Davis C, *Why Adjudicate? Enforcing Trade Rules in the WTO* (Princeton University Press 2013).

Davis R and Franks D, 'Costs of Company–Community Conflict in the Extractive Sector' (2014) Shift Project, Corporate Responsibility Initiative, Harvard Kennedy School.

Dawson L, 'Potash and BlackBerries: Should Canada Treat All Foreign Direct Investment the Same?' (2012) MacDonald-Laurier Institute <https://www.macdonaldlaurier.ca/files/pdf/Should-Canada-Treat-All-FDI-The-Same-Commentary-June-2012.pdf> accessed 24 April 2022.

Deak A, 'Hungarian Dances—the Origins and the Future of Viktor Orbán's Revolution' (2013) 11 Lithuanian Annual Strategic Review 145.

Decision on Jurisdiction, Applicable Law and Liability, *Electrabel SA v Hungary*, ICSID Case No ARB/07/19.

DNR (Department of Natural Resources), 'Minerals—A Policy for Nova Scotia' (DNR 1996).

Downs GW, Rocke DM, and Barsoom PN, 'Is the Good News about Compliance Good News about Cooperation?' (1996) 50 International Organization 379.

Drahokoupil J, *Globalization and the State in Central and Eastern Europe* (Routledge 2009).

Durán JC, 'Estudio Sobre Conocimientos y Percepciones Hacia La Mineria' (2007) 63 Estudios Centroamericanos 59.

Echandi R, Nimac I, and Chun D, 'Retention and Expansion of Foreign Direct Investment: Political Risk and Policy Responses' (2019) <http://documents1.worldbank.org/curated/en/387801576142339003/pdf/Political-Risk-and-Policy-Responses.pdf> accessed 26 February 2022.

Eden L, 'Bringing the Firm Back In: Multinationals in International Political Economy' (1991) 20 Millennium—Journal of International Studies 197.

Elections Nova Scotia, '21-Digby Anapolis' Province of Nova Scotia.

Elkins Z, Guzman AT, and Simmons BA, 'Competing for Capital: The Diffusion of Bilateral Investment Treaties, 1960–2000' (2006) 60 International Organization 811 <http://www.journals.cambridge.org/abstract_S0020818306060279> accessed 26 February 2022.

Environment Canada 'Environmental Impact Statement Guidelines for the Review of the Whites Point Quarry and Marine Terminal Project' Project EAS #2002-395' (11 August 2006) Environment Canada.

Fatás A and Mihov I, 'Policy Volatility, Institutions, and Economic Growth' (2013) 95 Review of Economics and Statistics 362.

Fearon JD, 'Domestic Politics, Foreign Policy, and Theories of International Relations' (1998) 1 Annual Review of Political Science 289 <http://www.annualreviews.org/doi/abs/10.1146/annurev.polisci.1.1.289> accessed 26 February 2022.

Fisheries and Oceans Canada, 'Re: Whites Point Quarry and Marine Terminal—Comments on the EIS Guidelines', email submitted to CEAA (2005) (on file).

Fournier R, Grant J, and Muecke G, 'The Environmental Assessment of the Whites Point Quarry and Marine Terminal Project: Joint Review Panel Report' (2007).

Freeman NW, 'Domestic Institutions, Capacity Limitations, and Compliance Costs: Host Country Determinants of Investment Treaty Arbitrations, 1987–2007' (2013) 39 International Interactions 54 <http://www.tandfonline.com/doi/abs/10.1080/03050629.2013.751296> accessed 26 February 2022.

Frieden J and Martin L, 'International Political Economy: Global and Domestic Interactions' in Ira Katznelson and Helen V Milner (eds), *Political Science: The State of the Discipline* (WW Norton 2003).

Gaubatz KT, 'Democratic States and Commitment in International Relations' (1996) 50 International Organization 109.

Gaukrodger D and Gordon K, 'OECD Working Papers on International Improving the System of Investor-State Dispute Settlement' (OECD 2012).

Golob SR, 'Beyond the Policy Frontier: Canada, Mexico, and the Ideological Origins of NAFTA' (2003) 55 World Politics 361.

Government of Nova Scotia, 'Agreement Concerning the Establishment of a Joint Review Panel for the Whites Point Quarry and Marine Terminal Project between the Minister of the Environment, Canada and the Minister of Environment and Labour, Nova Scotia' <https://www.canlii.org/en/ns/laws/stat/sns-1994-95-c-1/latest/sns-1994-95-c-1.pdf> accessed 26 February 2022.

Graham BAT, Johnston NP, and Kingsley AF, 'How Sovereigns Steal: Political Constraints and the Choice Between Transfer and Expropriation Rents' (2012) *International Political Economy Society Annual Meeting.*

Guzman AT, 'Why LDCs Sign Treaties That Hurt Them : Explaining the Popularity of Bilateral Investment Treaties' (1997) 38 Virginia Journal of International Law 639..

Hafner-Burton E, Steinert-Threlkeld Z, and Victor D, 'Predictability v Flexibility: Transparency of Investor–State Arbitration' (2016) 68 World Politics 413.

Haslam PA and Tanimoune NA, 'The Determinants of Social Conflict in the Latin American Mining Sector: New Evidence with Quantitative Data' (2016) 78 World Development 401.

Heindl JA, 'Toward a History of NAFTA' s Chapter Eleven' (2006) 24 Berkeley Journal of International Law 672.

Henisz, Witold J, and Zelner BA, 'Political Risk Management: A Strategic Perspective' (2002) A Working Paper of the Reginald H. Jones Center.

Henisz WJ, 'POLCON_2005 Codebook' (POLCON 2005).

Henisz WJ and Mansfield ED, 'Votes and Vetoes: The Political Determinants of Commercial Openness' (2006) 50 International Studies Quarterly 189.

Holzwarth E, 'Outline of Brief Presentation to the Review Panel' submitted to the CEAA (7 June 2007) (on file).

Hooley G and others, 'Foreign Direct Investment in Hungary: Resource Acquisition and Domestic Competitive Advantage' (1996) 27 Journal of International Business Studies 683.

Hungarian Energy Office (HEO), 'Long-Term PPAs in Hungary', powerpoint presentation (2006) (on file).

Jakobsen J, 'Does Democracy Moderate the Obsolescing Bargain Mechanism ?' (2006) 15 Transnational Corporations 67.

Jakobsen J and Jakobsen TG, 'Economic Nationalism and FDI: The Impact of Public Opinion on Foreign Direct Investment in Emerging Markets, 1990–2005' (2011) 6 Society and Business Review 61.

Jensen NM, 'Democratic Governance and Multinational Corporations: Political Regimes and Inflows of Foreign Direct Investment' (2003) 57 International Organization 587.

Jensen NM, *Nation-States and the Multinational Corporation: A Political Economy of Foreign Direct Investment* (Princeton University Press 2008).

Jensen NM, Johnston NP, and Lee C, 'Crisis and Contract Breach: The Domestic and International Determinants of Expropriation' (2020) 15 Review of International Organizations 869.

Johnson L, 'El Salvador Argues That Domestic Investment Law is Not a Portal for Pacific Rim Mining Company to Reach International Law Protections' *IA Reporter* (9 January 2014).

Johnson L and Sachs L, 'Eyes Wide Shut on ISDS' *The Hill*, 22 April (2015) <http://thehill.com/blogs/congress-blog/foreign-policy/239560-eyes-wide-shut-on-isds> accessed 26 February 2022.

Johnson R and Mahon R, 'NAFTA, the Redesign, and Rescaling of Canada's Welfare State' (2005) 76 Studies in Political Economy 7.

Joubin-Bret A, 'Establishing an International Advisory Center on Investment Disputes' in Joost Pauwelyn and Mengyi Wang (eds), *Building Legal Capacity for a More Inclusive Globalization: Barriers to and Best Practices for Integrating Developing Countries into Global Economic Regulation* (The Graduate Institute, Geneva 2019).

Kalicki J and Medeiros S, 'Fair, Equitable and Ambiguous: What Is Fair and Equitable Treatment in International Investment Law?' (2007) 22 ICSID Review 24.

Kalotay K and Hunya G, 'Privatization and FDI in Central and Eastern Europe' (2000) 9 Transnational Corporations 39.

Karl J, 'Investor-state Dispute Settlement: A Government's Dilemma' (2013) 89 Columbia FDI Perspectives 1.

Kaufmann D and Kraay A, 'Worldwide Governance Indicators' (2022) <http://info.worldbank.org/governance/wgi/> accessed 9 April 2022.

Keijzer N, Kraetke F, and van Seters J, 'Meeting in the Middle? Challenges and Opportunities for EU Cooperation with Middle-Income Countries' (2013) 140 European Center for Development Policy Management Discussion Paper.

Kerner A, 'Why Should I Believe You? The Costs and Consequences of Bilateral Investment Treaties' (2009) 53 International Studies Quarterly 73.

Kingsbury B and Schill S, 'Investor–State Arbitration as Governance: Fair and Equitable Treatment, Proportionality and the Emerging Global Administrative Law' (2011) 2 Transnational Dispute Management 9.

Kleinheisterkamp J, 'Investment Protection and EU Law: The Intra- and Extra-EU Dimension of the Energy Charter Treaty' (2012) Journal of International Economic Law 1.

Knutsen C, 'Democracy, Dictatorship and Protection of Property Rights' (2011) 47 Journal of Development Studies 164.

Kobrin S, 'Expropriation as an Attempt to Control Foreign Firms in LDCs: Trends from 1960 to 1979' (1984) 28 International Studies Quarterly 329.

Kobrin SJ, 'Political Risk: A Review and Reconsideration' (1979) 10 Journal of International Business Studies 67.

Kobrin SJ and Krasner S, *Managing Political Risk Assessment: Strategic Response to Environmental Change* (University of California Press 1982).

Konoplyanik A and Wälde T, 'Energy Charter Treaty and Its Role in International Energy' (2006) 24 Journal of Energy and Natural Resources Law 523.

Krajewski M, 'The Impact of International Investment Agreements on Energy Regulation' in Christoph Herrmann and Jörg Philipp Terhechte (eds), *European Yearbook of International Economic Law (EYIEL)* vol 3 (Springer-Verlag 2012).

Krajewski M, 'Investment Law and Public Services' (2013) 5 <SSRN:https://ssrn.com/abstract=2038514> accessed 24 April 2022.

Kustudic M, 'Outline of Brief Presentation to the Review Panel' submitted to the CEAA (n.d.) (on file).
LFA District 34 Lobster Committee, 'Fishing Industry Concerns Regarding Habitat, Water Quality, Social and Economic Concerns Issues to Be Incorporated into the Guideline Development for the Preparation of the Environmental Impact Statement to Be Carried out by Bilcon of Nova Scotia Corporate' submitted to the CEAA (24 March 2003) (on file).
Li Q, 'Democracy, Autocracy, and Expropriation of Foreign Direct Investment' *International Studies Association Annual Meeting* (2005).
Long JS and Freese J, 'Predicted Probabilities for Count Models' (2001) 1 The Stata Journal 51..
Luz MA and Miller M, 'Globalization and Canadian Federalism: Implications of the NAFTA's Investment Rules' (2002) 47 McGill Law Journal 951..
Mann H, 'The Final Decision in Methanex v. United States: Some New Wine in Some New Bottles' (2005) International Institute for Sustainable Development <https://www.iisd.org/system/files/publications/commentary_methanex.pdf> accessed 6 April 2022.
Mann H, 'Issues in International Investment Law and the Regulatory State : Can Exceptions Clauses Create a Safe Haven for Governments ?' (2007) Issues in International Investment Law: Background Papers for the Developing Country Investment Negotiators' Forum, International Institute for Sustainable Development.
Mansfield ED, Milner HV, and Rosendorff BP, 'Why Democracies Cooperate More: Electoral Control and International Trade Agreements' (2002) 56 International Organization 477 <http://journals.cambridge.org/abstract_S002081830244177X> accessed 26 February 2022.
Mayeda G, 'Playing Fair: The Meaning of Fair and Equitable Treatment in Bilateral Investment Treaties' (2007) 41 Journal of World Trade 273 <http://papers.ssrn.com/sol3/papers.cfm?abstract_id=1427307> accessed 26 February 2022.
McKinley A, 'A Brief Contextual Analysis of the Legal Suit of Pacific Rim Mining Company against the Government of El Salvador' (2009) Oxfam America.
Mejia T, 'Mineria-America Central: Nuevo Fiebre Del Oro' *TierraAmerica* (2007) <https://ecolamancha.wordpress.com/2007/11/26/nueva-fiebre-del-oro-en-america-central/> accessed 22 April 2022.
Melendez-Ortiz R and others, 'Strengthening the Global Trade and Investment System for Sustainable Development' (2015) World Economic Forum, International Centre for Trade and Sustainable Development <http://e15initiative.org/wp-content/uploads/2015/09/E15_ICTSD_Strengthening_Global_Trade_Investment_System_21st_Century_Executive_Summary_1502.pdf> accessed 24 April 2022.
MINEC (Ministry of Economy) 'The Republic of El Salvador's Preliminary Objections under Articles 10.20.4 and 10.20.5 of the Dominican Republic–Central America–United States Free Trade Agreement (CAFTA), ICSID Case No. ARB/09/12' (2010).
Montt S, *State Liability in Investment Treaty Arbitration* (Hart Publishing 2009).
Moosa IA, *Foreign Direct Investment. Theory, Evidence and Practice* (Palgrave 2002).
Moravcsik A, 'Taking Preferences Seriously: A Liberal Theory of International Politics' (1997) 51 International Organization 513.
Moravcsik A, 'Liberal Theories of International Law' in Jeffrey L Dunoff and Mark A Pollack (eds), *Interdisciplinary Perspectives on International Law and International Relations* (Cambridge University Press 2012).
Muchlinski PT, 'A Case of Czech Beer: Competition and in the Transitional Economies Competitiveness' (1996) 59 The Modern Law Review 658.

North DC and Weingast BR, 'Constitutions and Commitment: The Evolution of Institutions Governing Public Choice in Seventeenth-Century England' (1989) XLIX Journal of Economic History 803.

Notice of Arbitration, *Pac Rim Cayman LLC v Republic of El Salvador*.

'Notice of Intent to Submit a Claim to Arbitration under Section B of Chapter 11 of the North American Free Trade Agreement, Bilcon of Delaware Ltd. v. Canada' (2008).

'Notice to the Government of the Republic of El Salvador of Intent To Submit a Claim to Arbitration under Chapter 10 of the Central America–United States–Dominican Republic Free Trade Agreement'.

Nova Scotia Environment Policy Division Environmental Assessment Branch, 'A Proponent's Guide to Environmental Assessment' Government of Nova Scotia.

NSED (Nova Scotia Economic Development), 'Opportunities for Prosperity: A New Economic Growth Strategy for Nova Scotians' (NSED 2000).

OECD (Organisation for Economic Co-operation and Development), 'Regulatory Reform in Hungary. Enhancing Market Openness through Regulatory Reform' (2000) OECD <https://doi.org/10.1787/9789264181908-en>.

Orellana M, 'Application for Permission to Proceed as Amici Curiae ICSID Case No. ARB/09/12' (2011) 1.

Pacas F, 'Centroamérica Cierra Filas Contra La Minería' *Comunica en Linea* (2007).

Pandya SS, 'Democratization and Foreign Direct Investment Liberalization, 1970–2000' (2014) 58 International Studies Quarterly 475.

Pandya SS, 'Political Economy of Foreign Direct Investment: Globalized Production in the Twenty-First Century' (2016) 19 Annual Review of Political Science 455.

Parada LA, 'Witness Statement of Luis Alberto Parada, ICSID Case No. ARB/09/12' (2011).

Partnership for Sustainable Development of Digby Neck & Islands Society, 'Overview of the Society' email to the JRP submitted to CEAA (25 June 2007) (on file).

Pelc KJ, 'What Explains the Low Success Rate of Investor–State Disputes?' (2017) 71 International Organization 559.

Perera T and Demeter D, 'A Balancing Act: Retaining Investor–State Dispute Settlement Provisions in Investment Agreements and Balancing Stakeholder Interests' (2013) 31 Australian Year Book of International Law 75.

Perrone N, *Investment Treaties and the Legal Imagination: How Foreign Investors Play by Their Own Rules* (Oxford University Press 2021).

Pinto PM, *Partisan Investment in the Global Economy* (Cambridge University Press 2013).

Post AE, *Foreign and Domestic Investment in Argentina* (Cambridge University Press 2014).

Poulsen L, *Bounded Rationality and Economic Diplomacy. The Politics of Investment Treaties in Developing Countries* (Cambridge University Press 2015).

Power TM, 'Metals Mining and Sustainable Development in Central America. An Assessment of Benefits and Costs' (2009) Oxfam America <https://www.oxfamamerica.org/explore/research-publications/metals-mining-and-sustainable-development-in-central-america/> accessed 24 April 2022.

Provost C, 'El Salvador Groups Accuse Pacific Rim of "Assault on Democratic Governance"' *The Guardian* (10 April 2014) <http://www.theguardian.com/global-development/2014/apr/10/el-salvador-pacific-rim-assault-democratic-governance> accessed 26 February 2022.

Quezada RB, 'Explotación Minera: Los Conflictos Del Oro' *El Faro* (2006) <http://archivo.elfaro.net/secciones/observatorio/20060619/observatorio1_20060619.asp> accessed 26 February 2022.

Richler N, 'Rock Bottom' [2007] *The Walrus* <http://www.thewalrus.ca/rock-bottom> accessed 26 February 2022.
Rickard SJ, 'A Non-Tariff Protectionist Bias in Majoritarian Politics: Government Subsidies and Electoral Institutions' (2012) 56 International Studies Quarterly 777.
Rodrik D, 'Policy Uncertainty and Private Investment in Developing Countries' (1991) 36 Journal of Development Economics 229.
Salacuse J, 'Explanations for the Increased Recourse to Treaty-Based Investment Dispute Settlement: Resolving the Struggle of Life against Form?' in Karl P Sauvant (ed), *Appeals Mechanism in International Investment Dispute* (Oxford University Press 2008).
Sattorova M, *The Impact of Investment Treaty Law on Host States* (Hart Publishing 2018).
Schill SW, 'Crafting the International Economic Order: The Public Function of Investment Treaty Arbitration and Its Significance for the Role of the Arbitrator' (2010) 23 Leiden Journal of International Law 401 <http://www.journals.cambridge.org/abstract_S0922156510000117> accessed 26 February 2022.
Schoenman R, 'What Happens When the Party Is Over ? The Impact of New Right Parties in Government on FDI Regulation' 1.
Schultz T and Dupont C, 'Investment Arbitration: Promoting the Rule of Law or Over-Empowering Investors? A Quantitative Empirical Study' (2014) 25 European Journal of International Law 1.
Shrake T, 'Witness Statement of Thomas C. Shrake, ICSID Case No. ARB/09/12' (2010).
Sierra Club of Canada, 'Comments on the Draft Guidelines for the Environmental Impact Statement of the Whites Point Quarry and Marine Terminal Project', submitted to the CEAA (on file).
Simmons B, 'Compliance With International Agreements' (1998) 1 Annual Review of Political Science 75 <http://www.annualreviews.org/doi/abs/10.1146/annurev.polisci.1.1.75> accessed 26 February 2022.
Simmons B, 'Treaty Compliance and Violation' (2010) 13 Annual Review of Political Science 273.
Simmons B, 'Bargaining over BITs, Arbitrating Awards: The Regime for Protection and Promotion of International Investment' (2013) 66 World Politics 12 <http://www.journals.cambridge.org/abstract_S0043887113000312> accessed 26 February 2022.
Slobodian Q, *The Globalists: The End of Empire and the Birth of Neoliberalism* (Harvard University Press 2018).
Spalding RJ, 'Transnational Activism and National Action: El Salvador's Anti-Mining Movement' Paper presented at workshop on the Domestic Effects of Transnational Activism, 11–12 April 20112.
St John T, *The Rise of Investor–State Arbitration: Politics, Law and Unintended Consequences* (Oxford University Press 2018).
Statement of Defence of the Government of Canada, *William Ralph Clayton, William Richard Clayton, Douglas Clayton, Daniel Clayton and Bilcon of Delaware Inc v Canada*, (PCA) Case No. 2009-04.
Sweet AS, Chung MY, and Saltzman A, 'Arbitral Lawmaking and State Power: An Empirical Analysis of Investor–State Arbitration' [2017] Journal of International Dispute Settlement 1 <https://academic.oup.com/jids/article-lookup/doi/10.1093/jnlids/idx009> acessed 26 February 2022.
Tallberg J, 'Paths to Compliance : Enforcement, Management, and the European Union' (2002) 56 International Organization 609.
The Digby Neck Community Development Association, 'Comments on Draft Agreement Establishment of a Joint Review Panel for the Whites Point Quarry Project between the

Minister of the Environment, Canada and the Minister of the Environment and Labour, Nova Scotia' email submitted to CEAA (8 September 2003) (on file).

'The Republic of El Salvador's Counter-Memorial on the Merits, ICSID Case No. ARB/09/12' (2014).

Thibault R, 'Letter from Robert G. Thibault to David Anderson P.C. M.P., Minister of the Environment' submitted to the CEAA (on file).

Tienhaara K, *The Expropriation of Environmental Governance: Protecting Foreign Investors at the Expense of Public Policy* (Cambridge University Press 2009).

Tobin JL and Rose-Ackerman S, 'When BITs Have Some Bite: The Political-Economic Environment for Bilateral Investment Treaties' (2011) 6 The Review of International Organizations 1.

Tomz M, 'Democratic Default : Domestic Audiences and Compliance with International Agreements' *Annual Meeting of the American Political Science Association* (American Political Science Association 2002).

Tsebelis G, 'Veto Players and Institutional Analysis' (2000) 13 Governance 441.

Tucker T, 'The Concept of the State in Investor–State Arbitration' in Shaheeza Lalani and Rodrigo Polanco Lazo (eds), *The Role of the State in Investor-State Arbitration* (Brill Nijhoff 2015).

UNCITRAL (United Nations Commission on International Trade Law) Secretariat, 'Possible Reform of Investor–State Dispute Settlement(ISDS) Note by the Secretariat A/CN.9/WG.III/WP.142' <https://undocs.org/en/A/CN.9/WG.III/WP.142> accessed 26 February 2022.

UNCTAD (United Nations Conference on Trade and Development), 'Investment Policy Hub' <http://investmentpolicyhub.unctad.org/ISDS/FilterByCountry> accessed 26 February 2022.

UNCTAD, 'Country Fact Sheet: Hungary' (2006) UNCTAD 2006.

UNCTAD, 'Bilateral Investment Treaties 1995–2006: Trends in Investment Rulemaking' (2007) UNCTAD.

UNCTAD, 'Reform of Investor–State Dispute Settlement: In Search of a Roadmap' (2013) UNCTAD.

McCormick R, 'Undated Email Sent to Nova Scotia Government from DFAIT Official' submitted to CEAA (on file).

Van Harten G, *Investment Treaty Arbitration and Public Law* (Oxford University Press 2007).

Van Harten G, 'Reform of Investor–State Arbitration: A Perspective from Canada' (2011) <https://digitalcommons.osgoode.yorku.ca/all_papers/31/> accessed 24 April 2022.

Van Harten G, *Sovereign Choices, Sovereign Constraints: Judicial Restraint in Investment Treaty Arbitration* (Oxford University Press 2013).

Vanduzer JA, 'Can International Investment Agreements Be Instruments for Sustainable Development? Systemic Capacity Challenges for Sustainable Development' in Joost Pauwelyn and Mengyi Wang (eds), *Building Legal Capacity for a More Inclusive Globalization: Barriers to and Best Practices for Integrating Developing Countries into Global Economic Regulation* (The Graduate Institute, Geneva 2019).

Vernon R, *Sovereignty at Bay: The Multinational Spread of US Enterprises* (Routledge 1971).

Walker Fisheries Ltd, 'Proposed Marine Terminal White's Cove' email submitted to CEAA (17 March 2003) (on file).

Wellhausen RL, *The Shield of Nationality: When Governments Break Contracts with Foreign Firms* (Cambridge University Press 2015).

West Nova Fishing Coalition, 'Opposition to "Vessel Transportation" Resulting from the Proposed Product to Be Mined on Digby Neck Nova Scotia' submitted to CEAA (January 2005) (on file).

Weymouth S, 'Political Institutions and Property Rights: Veto Players and Foreign Exchange Commitments in 127 Countries' (2010) 44 Comparative Political Studies 211 <http://cps.sagepub.com/cgi/doi/10.1177/0010414010382629> accessed 26 February 2022.

Whidden H, 'White's Point Quarry Digby Neck Presentation to Review Panel' 23 June (2007).

Williams ZP, 'Investor–State Arbitration in Domestic Mining Conflicts' (2016) 16 Global Environmental Politics 32.

Wilson L, 'Resisting CAFTA and Metal Mining in El Salvador' (2010) <http://www.cispes.org/programs/anti-mining-and-cafta/resisting-cafta-and-metal-mining-in-el-salvador> accessed 26 February 2022.

Winham GR, 'Advice on the Application and Implications of the North American Free Trade Agreement (NAFTA) to the Proposed Whites Point Quarry and Marine Terminal Project' 1 <https://www.ceaa.gc.ca/archives/pre-2003/D67F0296-1/WP-1818.pdf> accessed 24 April 2022.

Wood E, *Insurgent Collective Action and Civil War in El Salvador* (Cambridge University Press 2003).

World Bank, 'Doing Business in 2006' in *Doing Business* (World Bank 2006).

World Bank, 'Doing Business in 2007' in *Doing Business* (World Bank 2007).

World Wildlife Fund, 'Comments on Proposed Review Panel for Digby Neck Quarry' email to CEAA (21 January 2005) (on file).

Yazbek N, 'Bilateral Investment Treaties: The Foreclosure of Domestic Policy Space' (2010) 17 South African Journal of International Affairs 103

Zegarra LF, Rodríguez M, and Acevedo C, 'Competitiveness and Growth in Latin America. Country Case: El Salvador' (2007) Inter-American Development Bank <https://kipdf.com/country-case-el-salvador_5adeb9fc7f8b9af55f8b4604.html> accessed 9 May 2022.

Index

For the benefit of digital users, indexed terms that span two pages (e.g., 52–53) may, on occasion, appear on only one of those pages.

Tables and figures are indicated by *t* and *f* following the page number